# The National Security Papers
# 21 Oct 2000 to 13 Jan 2004

## (From the Attack on the USS Cole
## to the Creation of the Department of Homeland Security)

## By

## Robert Fenton Gary, among others

The National Security Papers 21 Oct 2000 to 13 Jan 2004 tells the story of the attorneys, legislators, and public officials who cobbled together solutions to major threats facing the USA during the period from the bombing of the USS Cole till the establishment of the Department of Homeland Security.

Anyone interested in history, the Navy, aviation, or nuclear power will find things in this book that contain elements of surprise and interest.

The story is told entirely by exchanges of letters, and the various writers and recipients are listed in the Index. There are a few formal presentations also included to fill in the technical details of the proposed solutions.

Any Agency in the National Security effort should have this book in its library.

Any University granting Doctoral Degrees in U.S. history, or National Security work should make this book available to its students.

Many Americans will find this book of value from the perspective of public interest advocacy, and how it works, as an exchange of information among many people, over an extended period of time.

Environmentalists who have concerns about radio-nuclides in spent fuel storage pools, will benefit from what they read here.

People at today's Department of Homeland Security who take an interest in the foundation of their Agency and its origins in teamwork done by multiple parties can benefit from reading these letters and presentations.

This book is never going to be on the best seller list. It's more of a perennial that will always be valued by professionals and members of the general public who take an interest in this nation's security.

This book is dedicated, in gratitude and respect, to the members of Congress, and the Executive Branch, who, during a critical period, stepped into the breach, went the extra mile, and kept this country secure.

# Table of Contents

Part A

**The USS Cole Attack and
Proximity Control Systems
for Navy Warships in Foreign Harbors**

**(21 Oct 2000 - 14 Sep 2001)**

M. Hourican to Rep Morella, 20 Dec 2000, 22

R. Gary to Sen John Warner, 16 Jan 2001, 23-25

R. Gary to Lt. Chapman, 23 Jan 2001, 26-28

R. Gary to Capt. R. Lippert, 29 Jan 2001, 29

R. Gary to M. Moseley, 13 Feb 2001, 30

RAdm. J.M. Zortman to R. Gary, 26 Feb 2001, 31

R. Gary to RAdm. J.M. Zortman, 1 Mar 2001, 32-35

R. Gary to Rep Morella, 5 Mar 2001, 36-37

R. Gary to Secty Rumsfeld, 7 Mar 2001, 38-40

R. Gary to CNO ADM Vern Clark, 19 Mar 2001, 41

R. Gary to Cdr P.J. Neher, 19 Mar 2001, 42-43

R. Gary to VP Cheney, 19 Mar 2001, 44-46

R. Gary to Chmn Burton, 29 Mar 2001, 47-50

Cdr P.J. Neher to R. Gary, 31 Mar 2001, 51

R. Gary presentation delivered in person at Navy Pentagon 31 Mar 2001 52-69

R. Gary to VADM Tim Keating, 18 Apr 2001, 70

RAdm Joseph J. Krol to R. Gary, 1 May 2001, 71

Sen Mikulski to R. Gary, 3 May 2001, 72

CNO ADM Vern Clark to Rep Morella, 8 May 2001, 73

Eric Edelman (Office of VP) to R. Gary, 26 Jul 2001, 74

R. Gary to Rep Morella, 12 Sep 2001, 75-77

# Part B

## The 9/11 Attack and Cockpit Access Controls for Commercial Airlines in USA

## (17 Sep 2001 - 16 Jul 2002)

R. Gary to Covington & Burling, 10 Oct 2001, 124-125

R. Gary to Administrator Garvey, 12 Oct 2001, 126

R. Gary to Rep Morella, 12 Oct 2001, 127

R. Gary to Lee Kreindler, Esq., 15 Oct 2001, 128-129

R. Gary to Jay Blackman, 16 Oct 2001, 130

**FAA** Document Management System docket log indicating a filing date of 17 Oct 2001 for emergency petition, under 14 CFR 25, by R. Gary concerning Airworthiness Standards (installation of security bars to block unauthorized cockpit access), 131-132

R. Gary to Forest Rawl, 22 Oct 2001, 133-134

R. Gary to John McGraw, 13 Nov 2001, 136

R. Gary to Sen Lugar, 20 Nov 2001, 137

Office of VP Cheney to R. Gary, 27 Nov 2001, 138

Kenneth W. Peppard to R. Gary, 14 Dec 2001, 139

R. Gary to Michael Jackson, 16 Jul 2002, 140-142

# Part C

**Preventing Airborne Attacks on Nuclear Power Plants in USA**

**(5 Aug 2002 - 13 Jan 2004)**

R. Gary to Condoleeza Rice, 31 June 2003, 180-181

R. Gary to Rep Chris Van Hollen, Re Heatwole, 3 July 2003, 182-183

R. Gary to Rep Chris Van Hollen, Re Ideas List, 3 July 2003, 184-187

R. Gary to Sen Mikulski, 14 July 2003, 188-190

Administrator ADM J.M.Loy to R. Gary, 22 Jul 2003, 191-192

Sen Mikulski to R. Gary, 23 Jul 2003, 193

R. Gary to Administrator ADM J.M Loy, 24 Jul 2003, 194-195

Office of Sen Chris Van Hollen to R. Gary, 6 Aug 2003, 196

R. Gary to Under Secretary Asa Hutchinson, 11 Aug 2003, 197-200

Sen Chris Van Hollen to R. Gary, 15 Aug 2003, 201

Sen Chris Van Hollen to Secty Tom Ridge, 15 Aug 2003

Asst Administrator Lee S. Longmire to R. Gary, 3 Sep 2003, 203-204

R. Gary to President G.W. Bush, 11 Sep 2003, 205

R. Gary to Asst Administrator Lee S. Longmire, 11 Sep 2003, 206-207

R. Gary to Chairman Richard A. Meserve, 16 Sep 2003, 208

# Part A

# The USS Cole Attack and Proximity Control Systems for Navy Warships in Foreign Harbors

# (21 Oct 2000 - 14 Sep 2001)

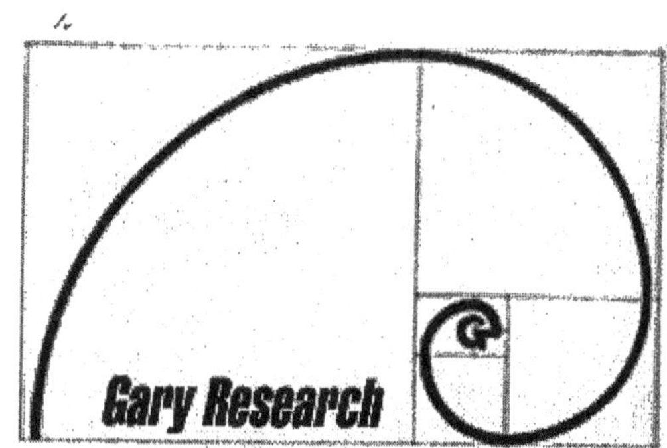


Robert Gary, M.B.A., J.D.
Principal Investigator

2211 Washington Ave., (#301), Silver Spring, MD 20910-2620        Tele: (301) 587-7147

Rep. Connie Morella                                    October 21, 2000
U.S. House of Representatives
Washington DC 20515

Dear Connie,

I'm writing you because, as one of your loyal constituents, I
know about your interest in technology and science, and I have a
solution that could prevent future attacks like that made on the
USS Cole. As a Navy veteran that occurrence is of great concern
to me, and I have put myself to working thinking of a method to
prevent such a thing from happening again.

The system I envision would be based on transponders about the
size of a pack of cigarettes worn around the neck of the lead man
in each small boat approaching a U.S. Navy vessel in a hazardous
foreign port of call. The squawk code on these transponders would
be installed a few hours before the ship made port by a black box
in the possession of a military attaché or other U.S. force
officer stationed locally -- but he would not know the nine digit
code. His black box would receive the code directly from the
ship's Captain, and install it directly in the transponders,
which could then be distributed to the lead men of all small
boats authorized to approach the U.S. Navy vessel. The code would
be Valid for a day, or a few days, and then would erase itself,
unless reset. Thus a lost transponder would be of no value to any
foe.

The procedure would be that Combat Information Center, located
directly below the bridge would radar and interrogate any
approaching surface vessel. If the code didn't squawk back right
the deck crew would be instantly notified to use lights,
megaphones, flashbangs, and warning shots to repel the
approaching small boat. If the small boat continued to approach
it would be sunk or disabled (with the intent to minimize loss of
life if possible). The mess could then be sorted out by
diplomatic and police forces as required. In high hazard ports of
call this procedure would be in effect 24 hours a day for the
entire time the ship was in or near the port.

The technology described here is all Off-the-Shelf. Nothing new needs to be invented. What is unique about this plan is that it is very cheap, very quick and easy to deploy, very reliable if the transponders are distributed to people that are trustworthy enough so that they deserve to be authorized to approach a U.S. Navy vessel in a small boat. A prototype could be fully tested within 12 months, and a modest demonstration project sent to the field within 24 months. A decision to go ahead with this plan would not involved enough contractor money to create the sort of snags that we see in air traffic control technology, where 15 Billion has been spent by the FAA over a period of 15 years, with no new system coming from this protracted and expensive effort.

My plan would cost about a million dollars to get a systems integrator to develop a prototype. The secure code receiver and mobile transponder programming black box would be the main cost. The little wearable mobile transponders about the size of cigarette packets, are really just cellphone technology. If the transponder sends out a scrambled digital code of nine digits, it can operate on a 9 volt battery. The beltway contractors who could easily handle such a project are known to you, and to everyone, and so I won't mention any of them by name.

Since the security loop is completely closed, and the originator of the nine digit code sends it ashore at the very last moment, and is the Captain of the ship coming into port, a lot of anxiety and shipboard morale problems will be averted by this elegant and simple system. The black box that is the code receiver ashore needs to be kept in a secure location, and the persons to whom the mini-transponders are given to wear need to be completely vetted. Without these features, my system would not be reliable. We would be better off building more Oilers and doing more refuelling at sea. This plan does contemplate the possibility of firing flashbangs and warning shots and possibly even sinking small boats in foreign harbors. The State Department might take a dim view of that, since it's not diplomatically correct, and may actually lose us some potential foreign "friends". Every security system that works has the potential to do some harm to somebody under some circumstances. The system that I have described would take some getting used to by a lot of people. But it's better than any alternative I can think of. It would also work for embassies, mobile teams of travelling dignitaries, aircraft on the ground, and ground-based military encampments.

Perhaps you will put this idea forward through official channels that are available to you. Whatever you decide to do, you have my vote in November, because of your past efforts on my behalf, and because your Congressional service is appreciated by me.

Very Truly Yours,


Robert Gary, Esquire

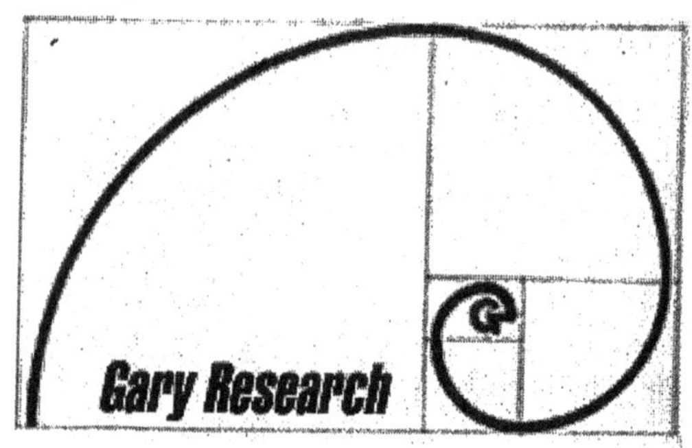

Robert Gary, M.B.A., J.D.
Principal Investigator

**Gary Research**

2211 Washington Ave., (#301), Silver Spring, MD 20910-2620          Tele: (301) 587-7147

Hon. Bill Cohen                                        October 27, 2000
Secretary of Defense
The Pentagon
Washington, DC 20301

Dear Secretary Cohen,

Since you and Senator Lugar are the two people most aware of security threats to the U.S., please allow me to share a few thoughts with you about the USS Cole.

Proximity defense in a harbor requires that approaching small boats be able to transpond a nine digit security code. This code should be transmitted ashore about 2 hours before a vessel like the USS Cole enters an unfriendly harbor, and it should be known only to the Captain. The receiver should be a black box controlled by the military liaison at the embassy, or some other pre-positioned military officer ashore. The black box programs a dozen micro-transponders about the size of cigarette packs which can be worn around the necks of the lead men in the approaching tenders. Since the nine digit code is created on a just-in-time basis, and the mini-transponders are handed out to persons of known reliability at the last moment before they approach the U.S. ship, your Combat Information Center shipboard can rely on the returns from the transponders to indicate that the tender is not a terrorist.

If the return sqwauk from the transponder isn't right, the deck crew should fire flashbang grenades at the approaching small boat immediately. If it fails to stop, live fire across the bow is warranted. If it still approaches, it should be disabled without loss of life if that is possible. If that cannot be done, it should be sunk.

This approach would have saved the USS Cole. It's not very diplomatic. It does require CIC to be up and running during the whole port visit. It might require some embarrassing cleanups and explanations. And we might even lose some "friends" because of it. But real-time proximity control will prevent the loss of U.S. Sailors and Marines, which, as a Navy vet, is important to me.

One other point, on a more general note. The erroneous conclusion drawn by many politicians in the wake of the USS Cole incident is that the United States really needs a ballistic missile defense system -- perhaps the one being considered for deployment to Alaska. This conclusion is simply not logical. Asymmetric warfare is not addressed by this conclusion. If something is going to be concluded from the incident on the USS Cole it would be more along these lines.

A W-88 type warhead is brought into the U.S. via the Panama Canal and Mexico, and taken by truck to Green Bay Wisconsin where it is built into a small powerboat. This powerboat, just like the one that approached the USS Cole, makes its way down lake Michigan and into the waterways of downtown Chicago, about 50 yards from the base the Sears Tower, where it is detonated by persons seeking Paradise. The yield is about 20 megatons, and takes out a five mile radius and kills 3 million Americans in less than 60 seconds. You, Senator Lugar, and I all know that this is a possibility. If one were to draw some logical conclusion from the incident on the USS Cole it would have something to do with small powerboats and asymmetrical warfare, and not with ballistic missile defense systems. We always seem to want to revisit old technologies and to fight the last war. We don't need Star Wars at this point, we need anti-terrorist capability, which probably has something to do with mobile and transportable nukes and the means to deliver them the way the shaped charge was delivered to the USS Cole.

The proximity defense system that I have outlined would take 24 months and $2 million to put into demonstration. I think this is very quick and very cheap by Washington standards. It does not require a huge upgrading in our intelligence capability, except the vetting of the lead men entrusted with the mini-transponders. That we need to be able to do with 100% reliability. If we can't do it, the next best thing is refuelling at sea. We could build and deploy more Oilers, and just stay out of ultra-hazardous ports of call.

My own efforts in this matter would be contributed for free, at your discretion and invitation, if you wish. I have served aboard Navy ships, and have some knowledge of design and of security. As a person offering free advice, I make no claim to be a professional, but if after hearing 100 other suggestions, mine appears to be the most sensible, I hope you will feel free to call on me, and permit me present it in greater detail.


Very Truly Yours,


Robert Gary

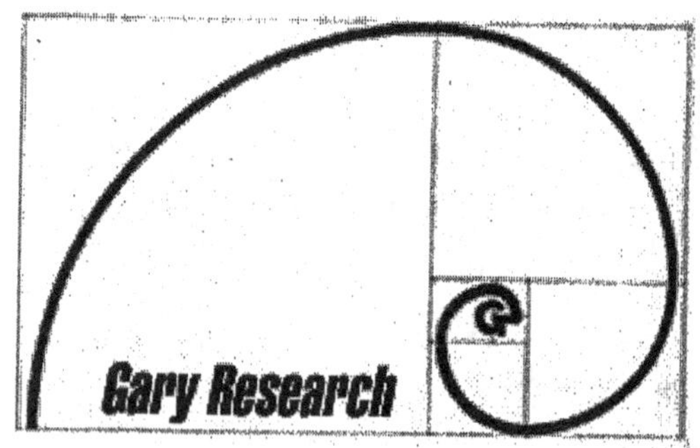



Robert Gary, M.B.A., J.D.
Principal Investigator

2211 Washington Ave., (#301), Silver Spring, MD 20910-2620          Tele: (301) 587-7147

Senator Richard Lugar                    October 28, 2000
U.S. Senate
Washington D.C. 20510

Dear Senator Lugar,

I would like you to consider a few points concerning the USS Cole, and more generally the national security, because I know you are one of perhaps half a dozen people in the U.S. that truly understands what we are up against as a nation seeking security for its citizens.

First, concerning the USS Cole, it is suggested that if, in the future, U.S. Navy ships deem it advisable to enter ultra-hazardous ports in countries known to harbor numerous terrorist organizations, some sort of proximity control system would be an improvement that might be helpful. I have in mind the following system. As a U.S. Navy Captain approaches the high risk port, when he's about two hours out, he makes up and transmits a scrambled nine digit code that is picked up by a black box on the hands of the military liaison or other U.S. officer ashore at the port. The black box then programs a dozen mini-transponders about the size of cigarette packs which can be worn around the necks of the lead men on tenders and other small boats authorized to approach the Navy ship. I assume that a dozen trustworthy and fully vetted people can be found and identified by the officer ashore. If this is not the case, we have no business being in that port at all, for any reason. The ship's Combat Information Center and surface radar needs to be up and running during the entire port visit. Any approaching vessel is sqwauked, and if it doesn't sqwauk back right the deck crew immediately fires long range flashbang grenades to warn it off. If it doesn't stop, it is disabled, with minimum loss of life. If it cannot be disabled it is sunk. This proximity control concept could also be used for parked aircraft, land encampments, and parties of dignitaries that need to be protected. It would cost about $2 million to put into demonstration, since no new technology is involved, everything is off the shelf and fully available right now. It takes one systems integrator to put it together, and a few months of shakedowns to make sure it works.

Another point, on a different subject, but also concerning the USS Cole. It was an error, in my opinion, to permit Yemen to shield the suspects from FBI interrogators. Having served as an international lawyer for the Navy in the Philippines, I can imagine that Yemen offered some sort of arguments that relied for their force on the idea of the national sovereignty of Yemen. The attack on the USS Cole was an act of war against the United States, and any nation which obstructs in any way our access to suspects in that act of war, is harboring and protecting enemies of the United States engaged in combat against the United States. It was a grave error to withdraw the FBI interrogators for this reason. It sets a precedent for all the Moslem nations, who now know that they can use their sovereignty to shield fugitives from American justice and war criminals. Pakistan and Afghanistan and Syria, Iran, and Iraq are going to play cat and mouse with us for a long time based on what we did in this case. Their asymmetric non-uniformed warriors will strike, and then retreat to safe havens. What we should have done is to physically control the perimeter of the building where the suspects are being held, and then slowly, by negotiations and by force if necessary capture the suspects and interrogate them. This would have permitted our larger investigation to proceed, and it would have made it much more difficult for the mastermind to maintain plausible denyability.

On another point concerning the issue of U.S. mishandling of the sovereignty concept, our actions with regard to the Panama Canal have created a zone of vulnerability for the USA against asymmetric warriors, whether Chinese or Moslem. The ships passing through that canal cannot be watched from all angles 24 hrs a day. It would be a very easy thing to unload a 400 lb steamer trunk to a small boat in the course of a routine transit. Such a trunk is just large enough to hold a W-88, which we know the Chinese have the legacy codes for, and which yields in the area of 20 megatons. The U.S. -- Mexico border is a sieve. Every day druglords bring across dozens of tons of drugs, in commercial trucks, fully protected by NAFTA, and by our strong desire to make nice will all other nations, no matter what the impact on our security. Imagine a truck drives across the border with the steamer trunk under a load of iron tiebars. It goes to Green Bay Wisconsin where a safehouse is waiting. The steamer trunk is now built into the hull of a small boat, sort of like the one that approached the USS Cole. The small boat is piloted by a couple of paradise seekers into the waterways of downtown Chicago, on the day after Labor Day in say 2003. Three million Americans would be dead in 60 seconds.

Under these conditions our national security establishment can think of nothing better to do than revert back wistfully to the Star Wars days of two decades ago. They want a ballistic missile defense system, when, after 15 years and $15 Billion spent they can't build a reliable air traffic control radar system for commercial airports. They want to hit a bullet with a bullet 50 miles up at Mach 4, and they say that what happened to the USS

Cole makes their agenda imperative. They are not being logical.
Big contracts, no doubt, have a logic all their own. Washington
being as it is, no action by the government can be counted on to
have any intrinsic merit in terms of being logical in a security
sense.

The U.S. must take serious steps to prepare itself for asymmetric
warfare, including mass casualty attacks using nuclear, chemical,
and biological weapons. The current Administration has been an
abysmal failure in the area of security, starting with filegate,
and proceeding through all sorts of debacles and errors of
judgment. If we continue on this path, as you and Secretary Cohen
know better than any of us, it's not a matter of "if" something
terrible happens, it's just a matter of when, and where. The
Nuclear Emergency Search Team needs to be beefed up a
hundredfold. If this means cutting the size of the Army, to
create the budgetary space, then so be it. Laws and treaties that
impede an integrated and effective program of national security
need to be removed, amended or renegotiated. The story needs to
be presented to the American People in candid and calm terms, but
in terms that create the political space to allocate resources,
and to control certain behavior, including restricting some
liberty of some citizens to do some things. Adequate security and
complete liberty may once have been fully compatible, but times
change, and adaptive nations, change as the times require for
their survival. Life, after all, is also one of the rights that
our Constitution protects.

I realize that this is a bad time to write a complicated letter
with lots of technical and legal points, right when an election
is taking place. My idea is that you are an unusual Senator, and
that you have a passionate interest in these subjects, and that
the staff member who glances over this letter will realize its
importance and bring it to your personal attention. I am not
seeking, nor will I accept any compensation for my efforts in
this area, but should you wish to meet with me, and hear my
proposals in greater detail, I am located in Silver Spring
Maryland, a 15 minute Metro ride from the Capitol, and would be
ready meet with you at your convenience. I am an attorney with 23
years of experience, mostly in the areas of federal law, and
nuclear safety. I'm a retired Navy JAG Officer. I have followed
your career and public statements on national security with very
close attention, and that's why I'm writing to you as the sole
member of the Senate to receive these ideas. Feel free to share
them with anyone else that seems an appropriate recipient -- I
have sent them to Rep Connie Morella and to Secretary Bill Cohen.


                    Very Truly Yours,


                    Robert Gary

CONSTANCE A. MORELLA
8TH DISTRICT, MARYLAND

COMMITTEE ON SCIENCE
SUBCOMMITTEE ON BASIC RESEARCH
CHAIR,
SUBCOMMITTEE ON TECHNOLOGY

COMMITTEE ON
GOVERNMENT REFORM
SUBCOMMITTEE ON CIVIL SERVICE
VICE CHAIR,
SUBCOMMITTEE ON THE DISTRICT OF COLUMBIA

## Congress of the United States
### House of Representatives

2228 RAYBURN HOUSE OFFICE BUILDING
WASHINGTON, DC 20515
(202) 225–5341
FAX: (202) 225–1389

www.house.gov/morella

51 MONROE STREET
SUITE 507
ROCKVILLE, MD 20850
(301) 424–3501
FAX: (301) 424–5992

November 7, 2000

The Honorable Richard Danzig
Secretary of the Navy
The Pentagon
Washington, D.C.  20350

Dear Secretary Danzig:

Robert Gary, a constituent of mine, recently sent me the enclosed letter which describes a proximity control system for use by Navy ships in unfriendly ports of call.  Based on my work as Chair of the House Science and Technology Subcommittee and review of this letter, it appears to have a great deal of merit.

The situation in Yemen and the tragic events involving the USS Cole has a number of my constituents who have contacted me, asking what might have been done differently, or what can be done differently in the future.  The enclosed letter presents what appears to be a very cheap, very quick and very reliable response utilizing a proximity control system.

Additionally, Mr. Gary, a retired Navy JAG, is willing to work without pay on this matter, and to meet with you, or your staff at your convenience.  Your reaction and response to his proposal would be greatly appreciated.  I am aware that thorough investigations are underway; however, this system seems to have immediate application which could  prevent a repeat of the USS Cole tragedy in the event that the current investigations are still underway.

Thank you and I look forward to hearing from you.

Sincerely,

Constance A. Morella
Member of Congress

CAM/lb
encl.

**DEPARTMENT OF THE NAVY**
OFFICE OF THE CHIEF OF NAVAL OPERATIONS
WASHINGTON, DC 20350-2000

IN REPLY REFER TO

5530
Ser N09N3/0U535950
16 November 2000

Mr. Robert Gary
Gary Research
2211 Washington Avenue (#301)
Silver Spring, MD 20910-2620

Dear Mr. Gary,

Thank you for your thoughtful letter addressed to Mr. Cohen of 27 October 2000.

I agree with your proposal to bolster the protection of naval vessels in "unfriendly harbors" by better controlling and tracking tenders and other small support boats. A number of commercial off-the-shelf products are available to provide such a transponder capability. A low-cost product that we are seriously investigating is an RF system that is currently used to control ground traffic at airports.

Additionally, the Navy intends to more aggressively pursue the basic physical security concept of *Defense in Depth*. Military forces depend upon a layered defense to prevent attack. Our ships and submarines will work harder to establish a method of standoff as a last resort to prevent unwanted boat traffic from approaching while pierside, at anchorage, and "in transit." This standoff will include a zone of interest, an influence zone, and finally an operations zone. Entry into these zones by unknown craft will trigger responses determined by realistic rules of engagement.

I also share your concern about asymmetric warfare and the possible use of weapons of mass destruction directed at population centers in the United States. This is a tough problem with no easy solution.

As a result of the USS COLE tragedy, the Navy is conducting a review of antiterrorism tactics, techniques, and procedures, in addition to insertion of technology to better safeguard our young men and women in uniform. As you indicated in your letter, your service in the Navy, which included time aboard ship, provides you unique insights. I personally welcome your continued involvement and ideas related to Navy's force protection efforts.

My point of contact for waterfront and shipboard security is Mr. Leopold L. Targosz, Jr., Head, Security Technology Integration Division, at (202) 433-9138.

D. R. CAVILEER
Assistant for Law Enforcement
and Physical Security

Mr. Robert Gary
Gary Research
2211 Washington Avenue (#301)
Silver Spring, MD 20910-2620

20 November 2000

Douglas R. Cavileer
Asst for Law Enforcement and Physical Security
Office of the Chief of Naval Operations
Department of the Navy
Washington, DC 20350-2000

Ref: 5530
Ser N09N3/0U535950
16 November 2000

Dear Mr. Cavileer,

I am pleased to receive your excellent letter of November 16, 2000 and I look forward to working with you directly face to face, on a volunteer basis, to develop a timely transponder-based technology that can be tested and deployed within a few months to protect Navy ships in high risk harbors.

One thought that comes to mind is the idea of "small, cheap, quick and simple". My transponder system could be tested by the Sarnoff Navy Lab using YPs right there in Annapolis harbor starting in May 2001, after the equipment has been selected and tested in the lab. Shakedowns could be completed by July 2001, and the SOP Manual for this system could be written in the meantime. Deployment to at least 3 ships could be accomplished by September 2001. Training could be completed by October 2001, at which point the transponder-based proximity control system would be fully operational on a 3 ship demonstration basis. After that, I think the Navy will like the system well enough to broaden its application.

Here are some of the strong points. Since the Captain of the port-visiting ship makes up the code on a last minute, on a completely random basis, he has the lives of his own shipmates in his own hands, which is precisely as it should be. No one else is privy to the code, since no one else needs to know it. This procedure would be excellent for shipboard morale.

Another strong point is that our officer ashore has 100% responsibility for distributing the code-loaded transponders to fully vetted totally reliable people. This is a person to person physical transfer, with the transponder strapped on the chest of the trusted tender chief boatman. It meets the SEAL standard of simplicity and avoids over reliance on the technical side of the system. Direct face to face contact is the basis of trust. If we can't identify friendly boatmen in foreign ports then we certainly have no business taking a Navy ship into those ports. I would have no problem with polygraphs, truth serum, and full background investigations of any foreign national that the

Navy reposes trust in at the level of giving that foreign national a coded proximity control transponder. Part of that trust is that the chief boatman will know his crew and be able to control what happens on his boat. It should be SOP that transponder wearers be the only armed people aboard their craft, and that they be trained to use their weapons if need be. Such craft should also be inspected at least once by an American military person ashore at a time just before they become active as tender boats to a Navy Ship. So my system is not 100% technical, or 100% technology-reliant. It is a sensible system that uses simple technology to leverage an already excellent set of security arrangements into real-time responsiveness on deck.

On another topic, the phrase "realistic rules of engagement" is really at the crux of the problem. That is the first line of defense for a Navy ship in a hazardous harbor. In the case of the USS Cole, I hold the U.S. Department of State largely responsible for what occurred. Navy (CNO, SECNAV and SECDEF) needs to take a far more proactive approach to working with the U.S. State Department so that we are never again maneuvered and negotiated into a position where the rules of engagement are so peaceful and gentle as to be dysfunctional -- a deck crew that is not locked and loaded and not authorized to fire unless fired upon -- a deck crew that has no non-lethal ordnance, it has live ammo or nothing as its possible choices. I was on a ship that resupplied at Oman in 1980 around the time of the Iran Hostage crisis, and as an International Lawyer, I was the only JAG to go ashore to observe the Vertrep process. You are right, I've been out there. I was also a Navy Recruiter JAG, and I can affirm that naval personnel don't sign on to be sitting ducks.

Navy should tell State what the rules of engagement are going to be. Navy ships are not "The Love Boat", nor are they diplomatic pawns to be manipulated and used on some sort of global chessboard designed to spend money on and curry diplomatic favor with "nations" like Yemen. Going there was a collosal error, and it wasn't all or mainly the Navy's fault. But if we had to go there, Navy should say whether firing non-lethal flashbang grenades in the harbor to send a message to approaching but unidentified small craft is "realistic rules of engagement" or not. Navy can, should, and will make it stick at the White House. That's the least that can be done to keep faith with servicemembers sent into harm's way. It's far better to explain the realities of this world to our diplomatic friends than to attempt to explain the inexplicable to grieving parents at Arlington National Cemetary. You agree, I know, and that's why I look forward to working with you to make a difference on this vital matter.

Sincerely,


cc: L.L. Targosz                          Robert Gary

Lisa Boepple                                      20 November 2000
Chief of Staff and Legislative Director
to Rep Connie Morella
2228 Rayburn Building
Washington, DC 20515

Re: <u>**Progress Report on USS Cole Proximity Control System**</u>

Dear Rep Morella,

Your letter to Secretary Cohen on my behalf regarding the USS Cole sort of worked. An assistant to the CNO wrote me back suggesting that any further correspondence be directed to his assistant. As you can see from Mr. Cavileer's letter the Navy's idea of improving their proximity control system is *"Defense in Depth"* which involves creating imaginary zones in the water around a Navy ship -- basically a 1950's idea, now brought forward and offered as their wonderful new solution. One may observe that no part of any of my ideas are included in this, and specifically, there's no just-in-time coded transponder, no flashbang grenades, no real time readiness on deck. I realize this is going to take 200 members of the House and about 30 Senators all saying the same thing to the Navy -- listen to what Robert Gary is telling you. Another way to accomplish the same result would be to get Secretary Cohen, or his successor before the Science and Technology Subcommittee and let me write the questions that he or she gets to answer. That way there would be a sort of conversation, back and forth, and maybe a negotiation could proceed that would result in real action from the Navy. I say a coded transponder-based proximity control system could be on three Navy ships by the Fall of 2001. They are asking bigger and bigger questions, looking into more and more history. In the end, they will produce a 10 foot tall stack of reports. If I could get into Secretary Danzig's office for 15 minutes we would have an actual system in place in less than a year. Please keep the initiative moving forward by whatever informal channels are available to you, and you can count on me to be there if the Navy ever decides to proceed.

Sincerely,


Robert Gary, Esq.

**Robert Gary (#301)**
**2211 Washington Ave**
**Silver Spring, MD 20910-2620**
**(301) 587-7147**

Hon William Cohen                          20 November 2000
Secretary of Defense
The Pentagon
Washington DC 20310

Ref: 5530
     Ser N09N3/OU535950
     16 November 2000

Dear Mr. Secretary,

A copy of the referenced letter is enclosed to keep you informed about the status of my negotiations with the Navy to create a transponder based proximity control system so that the kind of terrorist incident that occurred to the USS Cole can be thwarted in the future. I would like to have this system up and running on three Navy ships by the Fall of 2001. There's some headwind on this due to the Navy's desire to write a very comprehensive series of reports which will, no doubt, be very inclusive, but won't prevent a repetition of the bombing incident in the short term. My idea is to prevent the repetition first, and then write the reports as fully as possible when time permits. My system could be put into the design phase next month. Preliminary sea trials could begin in the Spring of 2001. A demonstration project involving three ships could be up and running by next Fall. My services are free, I work as a volunteer. I have no interest of any kind in any company that might benefit from any government contract with any agency or Department.

I realize that the Navy will do the right thing in a timely manner when there's about 30 Senators and 200 members of the House that are actively requesting it. Accordingly, I am proceeding to canvass the key Senators and Congresspersons who will have enough influence with their colleagues in the next Congress to get a broad consensus that the Navy would do well to implement my suggestions without delay -- just do it right away, and let the demonstration project prove itself. I want your active support. You can urge SECNAV and CNO to be truly responsive on this proposal, not just at the talking stage, but also at the doing stage, and to make that stage sooner rather than later -- not after all the reports are written, but even before.

                              Sincerely,


                              Robert Gary

Robert Gary (#301)
2211 Washington Ave.
Silver Spring, MD 20910

20 November 2000

Senator Richard Lugar
U.S. Senate
Washington DC 20510

Dear Senator Lugar,

Enclosed is the response received from CNO's office about my proposed transponder based proximity control system for situations like the USS Cole.

Based on a careful reading of this letter I feel it will take 30 Senators and 200 Members of the House to actively cause the navy to implement the system I propose. My own Representative happens to be on the Science and Technology Subcommittee in the House, which is quite helpful given the high tech nature of my proposal.

You are probably the single person on Capitol Hill with the greatest awareness of anti-terrorism safeguards, and so I'm hoping you will take an interest in this matter. Given a reasonable opportunity -- i.e. 15 minutes in the Secretary of the Navy's office for a face to face meeting -- I strongly feel that I could have a demonstration project up and running on three Navy ships by the Fall of 2001.

The Navy has proceeded to broaden the security issue more and more since the USS Cole terrorist strike, and to look into deeper and deeper historical issues. Several years from now, probably by the end of the next Administration, there will, no doubt, be a formidable 10 foot high stack of reports. I could have actual hardware up and running in 12 months, given 15 minutes of SECNAV's time. Could you arrange it?

Sincerely,


Robert Gary

(301) 587-7147

Robert.Gary@prodigy.net

Encl: Ltr from CNO's Asst Mr. Cavileer of 16 Nov 2000
      Robert Gary's answering letter of 20 Nov 2000

**CONSTANCE A. MORELLA**
8TH DISTRICT, MARYLAND

COMMITTEE ON SCIENCE
SUBCOMMITTEE ON BASIC RESEARCH
CHAIR,
SUBCOMMITTEE ON TECHNOLOGY

COMMITTEE ON
GOVERNMENT REFORM
SUBCOMMITTEE ON CIVIL SERVICE
VICE CHAIR,
SUBCOMMITTEE ON THE DISTRICT OF COLUMBIA

**Congress of the United States**
**House of Representatives**
November 29, 2000

2228 RAYBURN HOUSE OFFICE BUILDING
WASHINGTON, DC 20515
(202) 225–5341
FAX: (202) 225–1389

www.house.gov/morella

51 MONROE STREET
SUITE 507
ROCKVILLE, MD 20850
(301) 424–3501
FAX: (301) 424–5992

Mr. Robert Gary
2211 Washington Ave Apt 301
Silver Spring, Maryland  20910-2620

Dear Mr. Gary:

Thank you for your recent letters.  Please keep me up to date on what you hear from the Navy and please let me know if you need me to follow-up with whoever the next Secretary of Defense, and Secretary of the Navy may be!

As far as the controversy surrounding the Florida election, I can only say that this clearly illustrates the need for changes in our current voting system to bring us out of the 19$^{th}$ Century and into the 21$^{st}$ Century.  It is critical that we examine the electoral process to ensure that democracy, as established by our founding fathers, prevails.

I am currently supporting legislation to establish a five members bipartisan commission to study the current voting procedures, voting monitoring procedures, pending legislation and regulatory efforts which would affect voting procedures, and the cost of implementing standardized voting procedures for all fifty states and the District of Columbia.  Additionally, the Commission would be required to set up a web site to facilitate public comment and participation.  The purpose of this legislation is not be become involved in the current controversies, but to consider where we go from here, in order to try to prevent the kind of concerns and problems which we have at the present time.

Best regards.

Sincerely,

Constance A. Morella
Member of Congress

CAM:lb

**Robert Gary**
**2211 Washington Ave (#301)**
**Silver Spring, MD 20910-2620**

Mr. Leopold L. Targosz                    4 Dec 2000
Naval Criminal Investigative Service
716 Sicard Street SE, Suite 2000
Washington Navy Yard, DC 20388-5380

Dear Mr. Targosz,

It was a pleasure to speak with you today about a proximity control system to avoid repetitions of what happened to the USS Cole. I appreciate your work so far, which has been vigorous, and your taking the time to hear the outline of my designed system. Just to provide a written backup for what was said I would offer the following points:

1. The Volpe people are on the right track with their ground traffic control transponder concept. It's low power, short physical range, lateral RF oriented, and actually just perfect for what we want.

2. As a pilot, you know that the control tower gives you your transponder code numbers, and then you set them manually there in the cockpit. The analog in my design is that the Captain sends the code (4 digit, 6 digit, 9 digit, they are all OK) ashore and the code gets put into the wearable transponder boxes, and it's good for 72 hours, or 150 hours, or some fairly short period of time.

3. These wearable boxes need to go on the chests of trusted foreign nationals who will be the Chiefs of the tender boats. You want some sort of metalized strap here that's not easily removable. The voltage in the boxes is low, and the boxes are lightweight, so there's no jeopardy to the man by strapping it on him.

4. My system requires that the strapping on of the transponder box be face-to-face, eyeball-to-eyeball entrustment, (SEAL style, nice and simple, right there in realtime). If we can't find a few men we can trust in a foreign port, we have absolutely no business going there. If we can find them, then we can find an American who can put the Captain's "answer box" on their chests, so the ship knows they are authorized to come close.

5. Your 10 surface radar is all you need to detect the
approaching boat. CIC picks that up. Interrogates the small
craft. If the Chief man's transponder answers right, then nothing
happens. If there's no answer or a wrong answer the deck crew is
notified within less than 5 seconds.

6. What's needed on deck is a multi-step process that starts with
an angry-yelling loud hailer. Angry yelling is not something that
everyone can do. Bosuns do it much better, and much more
convincingly than Yeomen. It's a matter of projecting, through
sound, an angry and threatening message that basically says "Get
Back, Get Back Right now, Do it!!!" If the angry yelling man
simply doesn't have the personal capacity to do this act
convincingly then major repercussions follow, and they may be our
fault for not having the right man with the right character in
position to send a message for a US warship.

7. O.K. the small craft, that's not sqwauking back right keeps
coming. Now we need the flashbang man. I say it needs to be a
sharpshooter. That grenade has to blow up in exactly the right
place. It can't go over the approaching boat. It can't splash in
the water 50 feet from our ship. We have people that know how to
fire flashbang grenades. The folks that control the Grizzlies out
at Yellowstone are very good at it. We have a very few people in
law enforcement that are actually good with a flashbang grenade
launcher. Anyway the man on deck needs training and
familiarization fire and lots of it.

8. The rest of the levels of escalation are obvious, so I won't
bore you with them. The approaching craft is disabled with live
fire and if that's not possible it is sunk, and everyone aboard
is killed if that's what has to happen.

9. This brings me round to the issue of rules of engagement.
Navy's oath, just like at the State Department, is to protect the
US from all enemies foreign and domestic. Navy's obligation to
the parents of the servicemen and women is to place them at
measured risk in a reasonable way rather than uncontrolled risks
in a negligent way. What ports we visit and what the rules are
when we go into those ports, and who is locked and loaded on deck
with pre-delegated authority to "fire", should and must be 100%
our call and 0% the call of the State Department. It's not just
me that says this -- reality requires it -- I'm just the
messenger here. Navy must tell State where we are going and what
the rules are going to be. They can't be telling us. My design
requires this, and it requires that we take a fully functional,
and not always "gentle" or "maximally sovereignty respecting"
approach to the rules on engagement. Sometimes boatloads of well-
wishers with flowers and candies are going to get angrily yelled
at and even flashbanged, shot at, or sunk, in foreign ports by my
Navy's ships. This will be messy, embarrassing, bad Public
relations, and terrible diplomacy. Those are prices I have
foreseen and am willing to pay. As an international lawyer, (UCMJ

27 (b) certified by the Navy), I know the implications, and I
say, "Bring them on". Just no more bodies for Arlington, no more
parents that have to hear the worst thing a parent can ever hear.
So some people will be miffed and their feathers will be ruffed
up, we can send gentle people to mollify them using whatever
works. Let's take a SEAL approach to the realtime combat
situation. Then we can take a diplomatic and polite approach if
when we make a red mess in the water or a mistake, which is going
to happen, and which is fully factored in to my suggestions.
Better them than us. This is how warriors think. Navy ships are
not the Loveboat. Let our enemies beware -- beware!

10. There will be some unfriendly questions on Capitol Hill --
some hardballs. The right answer will not be "We are writing a
report, and here's the first five foot stack of documents which
will be included in our 10 foot high stack of final report."
Another wrong answer will be "We are conducting seminars and
panel discussions with experts to deeply research the full
implications of the total security environment of US warships."
Here's the only right answer: "We now have a very solid system in
development in the testing lab. We are conducting sea trials on
this system in the Spring of 2001, and full shakedowns in the
Summer of 2001. We are going to have a demonstration project
fully operational and deployed on three ships by the Fall of
2001." That is the answer which makes Navy look good. The
behavior that backs it up is the action that will make Navy
actually good, my Navy, the one I care about. Let's be able to
give the only right answer which reflects the right action.

11. You are well-begun on this track. Let me work with you as a
volunteer, as a patriot, as an unpaid systems design assistant to
get something substantive in place starting this Winter and
culminating in a operational demonstration project next Fall. I
bring to the project a sense of outcomes oriented design, combat
awareness, simplicity, and immediacy. These things can be very
helpful to the Navy under all the circumstances. I hope you and
Mr. Douglas Cavileer and Secretary Danzig will take advantage of
them. I look forward to your call on Friday December 8, 2000
between 3:00 p.m. and 9:00 p.m. so we can proceed to the next
step in this complex evolution.

Very Truly Yours,

Robert Gary

(301) 587-7147

2211 Washington Ave (#301)
Silver Spring, MD 20910-2620

Robert.Gary@prodigy.net

cc: Mr. Cavileer, Rep. Morella, Secr. Danzig

**Robert Gary**
**2211 Washington Ave (#301)**
**Silver Spring, MD 20910-2620**

Mr. Leopold L. Targosz                          12 Dec 2000
Naval Criminal Investigative Service
716 Sicard Street SE, Suite 2000
Washington Navy Yard, DC 20388-5380

Dear Mr. Targosz,

I was very pleased that you returned my call today and that we had a chance to chat about the matters that concern us both.

From our conversation, I understand that you are in contact with a SEAL (06) about this matter, and with the Volpe people in Cambridge. I would be guided by those people.

My questions for you at this point are really just matters of size and weight. What are the precise dimensions of the Chest Box which the Chief Boatman would wear? What is the cubic size and precise weight of the transponder interrogator that would have to go on the mast of a Navy warship. If possible please provide the Chest box size in cubic centimeters, and the Mast Unit size in cubic centimeters and kilograms. This is very critical information, it determines many other aspects of the total system.

From our conversation on this day, I see that there is a turf battle forming up on precisely which unit of the Navy will have cognizance of this matter. I also see that of the many high technology organizations that wish to proffer advice in this matter, each one wants to suggest that the technology system based on their propriety hardware and software is the ideal system which you should accept and adopt.

My modest proposal is that you reject all of them, and that instead you revert to the time-honored, and experience-based concept of having the Navy define precisely what it wants, in operational terms, and then issue a Request for Proposals, and look at the proposals that meet the specs, and take the one that incorporates the "best value" for the needs of the Navy.

I have told you that I want you to affirm what I want for the specs. I'm asking for your allegiance -- I do not deny that. When they ask you, "Should we take Robert's proposal for the initial system?" I want you to say, "Yes, that's exactly the one that you should take!" Does this mean that I don't realize that a far better system might be developed later? No! I do realize that. Someday a fuller, better, more capable system will be developed. After all the reports are written, after every four-star in the Navy has had his full opportunity to be heard, in every forum, on every subject -- yes, I think a fuller and better system might be devised.

But let me tell you this. The next attack will be harder to defend against. One thing we know with absolute certainly about Ossama Bin Ladin is that he always hits us where we are not ready. So the next attack will be from the air, or from a cigarette boat equipped with a bow mounted, impact-detonated, shaped charge, torpedo. In that case the response time will not be 8 or 10 minutes as it was for the USS Cole, but more like 15 or 20 or 30 seconds as it would be for a straight charging in torpedo boat.

In that amount of time there's no time for beanbags, or rubber bullets, or special ultra-high tech megaphones that simultaneously translate English to Arabic, or English to Chinese within fractions of a second, as if such a thing existed. You have one chance. You can send a message with "Emotional Conviction" in any language, English is good enough, and then you can fire to disable, sink, or kill, or you can fail to respond.

My system calls for a response. You send an angry message over the water using sound as your media. If that doesn't work, you fire flashbang grenades very accurately so that no approaching boat containing humans could fail to get the message. If that doesn't work, you shoot to kill on the theory that rules on engagement are in place and that American lives have value just as the lives of all other people do.

We Americans have the dubious benefit of knowing the fate of the HMS Sheffield. We understand about Exocet missiles, and we know that kamikaze small planes could be configured for similar strikes. I would like to see my transponder system set up so that it included the airspace from 0 to 5000 feet, and from 10 feet to 10,000 feet out. That would be ideal for a first cut solution. And I'm not offering anything more than a first cut solution. I'm ready for my whole "demonstration project" to step aside two or three years from now in favor of a far better and more sophisticated approach, if there is one. If your SEAL (06) asks me to back off, I'm ready to back off, and that's a fact, but he and I have the same motivation, the same intent, the same goal, and I'm ready to defer if there's better wisdom out there.

Know you enemy, love your enemy, learn from your enemy -- these are the key concepts of all true warriors, and we should heed them. In the practice of these ideas we need to get into a "Red Team -- Blue Team" Mode, like we did with the Soviets, and try to put ourselves into to shoes of our attackers.

By the same token, we should recognize that in 1972 we declared that those nations which provide sanctuary for anyone who attacks the USA are subject to our military response. Nixon and me went after Cambodia, and now it's time for our new President to go after the Taliban, to go after Afghanistan, and to have our reprisal at the level of 1000 to 1 which is the correct ratio, and only way we can deter the sort of thing that happened to the USS Cole in the future.

I have said in prior letters to you, Mr. Leo Targosz, and to Mr. Douglas R. Cavileer, and to SECNAV Honorable Richard Danzig, that this is an urgent matter, something that requires immediate and totally dedicated attention. I know you recognize this. I'm looking for some specific answers from you in the week of January 1, 2001, hopefully Tuesday, Wednesday, or Thursday between 3:00 p.m. and 9:00 p.m. After the New Year, I am prepared to come to Sicard Street or to the Pentagon and work with you to make the Navy look good and be good in this case.

Very Truly Yours,

/s/

Robert Gary, Esq.

CC: Douglas Cavileer
Connie Morella
Richard Danzig
} Priority Mail
(w/ original)

# DEPARTMENT OF THE NAVY

HEADQUARTERS
NAVAL CRIMINAL INVESTIGATIVE SERVICE
WASHINGTON NAVY YARD BLDG 111
716 SICARD STREET SE
WASHINGTON DC  20388-5380

December 13, 2000

5700
Ser: 07/0U083

The Honorable Constance A. Morella
U.S. House of Representatives
Washington DC 20525

**DEC 2 0 2000**

Dear Congresswoman Morella:

Thank you for your letter addressed to the Secretary of the Navy, The Honorable Richard Danzig, of November 7, 2000 concerning a proximity control system recommended by Mr. Robert Gary.

Mr. Doug Cavileer, Assistant Director for Law Enforcement and Physical Security, for the Naval Criminal Investigative Service (NCIS), provided the following information regarding proximity control systems.  As Mr. Cavileer indicated in earlier correspondence to Mr. Gary, the Navy is investigating radio frequency (RF) systems that will allow Commanding Officers to discern which vessels are authorized to be in close proximity to their ships and which are not. There are several commercial off-the-shelf systems currently available that may satisfy the need to identify friendly vessels and show promise for integration into existing and future shipboard systems.  These commercially available systems range in price from less than one hundred to several thousand dollars per deployable unit.

Additionally, on December 4, 2000, Mr. Leopold L. Targosz, Jr., Head, Security Technology Integration Division, NCISHQ, spoke to Mr. Gary about his proposal. Mr. Targosz, who chairs a Technology Working Group that supports the recently established Chief of Operations Force Protection Task Force, has recommended inclusion of transponder-like "identification of friend or foe capability" in the Coastal Area Protection System (CAPS) Advanced Concept Technology Demonstration (ACTD) currently being considered for funding. This "identification of friend or foe capability" is envisioned to allow for real-time proximity control in harbors and at anchorages.  The CAPS ACTD provides the mechanism to validate and optimize the overall concept.

We foresee that these RF identification devices coupled with appropriate tactics, techniques, and procedures for their employment will provide shipboard commanders with a useful tool to combat the asymmetric threat they face when operating in potentially unfriendly ports, anchorages, and restricted waterways.

Again, thank you for bringing Mr. Gary's concerns to our attention.  Please do not hesitate to contact me at 202-433-9543 if you have any further questions.

Sincerely,

Marilyn G. Hourican
Chief, Government Relations

**Robert Gary**
**2211 Washington Avenue (#301)**
**Silver Spring, MD 20910-2620**
**Tele: (301) 587-7147**

Senator John Warner                    January 16, 2001
Chairman
Senate Armed Services Committee
2120 RHOB
U.S. Senate
Washington, DC 20515

Dear Senator Warner,

After the bombing of the USS Cole, it was apparent that some sort of friend/foe identification system was needed for warships in dangerous ports. The logical approach would be to use a transponder based on the ship, and responding units would then be given to boatmen in small craft authorized to approach the ship, and thus it would be possible, at some distance to detect small approaching craft on radar and then interrogate them electronically and know within seconds if they were authorized to approach or if they might be unauthorized and potentially hostile.

I sent this idea to my Congresswoman, Connie Morella, who happens to be the Chairman of the Science and Technology Subcommittee of the House and she forwarded it, with a strong recommendation that it be given the most careful consideration to, the Secretary of the Navy. From there the idea seems to have been misrouted and it has been lost in the shuffle of the political changes that are occurring in Washington and which began around the time the USS Cole was bombed. Secretary Danzig sent the letter to the CNO who sent it to a group of detectives in an office on Sicard Street in the Navy Yard. These are people that have no resources and no authority to carry out my suggestion. They were kind enough to refer me to a site on the internet which turned out to be a public relations page for an innovative technology office in the Pentagon.

I would not raise the matter with you except for the fact that it was reported around the time of the USS Cole bombing that Ossama Bin Laden had plans to attack not just one but several U.S. Navy ships. The attack is very likely to be repeated on another ship, perhaps in the Med, perhaps in the Persian Gulf, perhaps near Oman or Yemen, where I have served on a visiting Navy ship seeking resupply. Failure to take reasonable physical security precautions, given the successful bombing of the USS Cole, might be regarded as a deficiency.

A very complex series of seminars and working group meetings has just culminated in a report issued by Secretary Cohen which I understand comes to the following conclusions: (1) The USS Cole was bombed (2) probably by a terrorist and (3) some better precautions might be taken in the future. These are all points that I agree are correct. The report also found that although many security precautions which might have been taken were omitted on the USS Cole, none of the officers are at fault because even if everything had been done by the book, and every precaution had been taken, it would have made no difference in preventing the successful attack. In other words, whatever negligence or omissions there may have been, that negligence and those omissions were not the proximate cause of the deaths and destruction which occurred. Furthermore, I understand that the report found the ship's Captain to be free from fault because he had not received adequate intelligence -- he had not been told that someone was going to bomb his ship -- and so he didn't know it was going to happen.

What the Navy needs to do now is to get some transponders, test them rigorously, put them on some small ships and do some tactical exercises to find out their precise operating characteristics, and then install them on three Navy ships as a demonstration project. These would probably be destroyers or cruisers out of Norfolk, bound for rotation to the Med or the Middle East sometime around January of 2002. This allows a full year for selection of the equipment, testing it, and for tactical exercises to develop a workable SOP. My suggestion also included, as a fully integrated feature the use of flashbang grenade launchers operated by trained members of the deck crew as a supplement to megaphone warnings delivered with emotional conviction -- not politely, not gently, but in a way that unmistakably says "Turn around, Get back -- Do it now!" Had such a system been present on the USS Cole, activated by transponder alert, and immediately followed up with angry yelling at the unauthorized boat and flashbang grenades launched directly to its bow, and if the small boat with the bomb on it kept coming closer, at least the deck crew would have known they were facing a potential military threat. Whether they would, in the 15 minutes available, have had time to unlock the weapons cabinet, load some weapons, aim them, and fire them is a matter about which one can only speculate. In the future, perhaps deck crews could be provided, in advance, with fully loaded weapons and the pre-delegated authority to use them under specified conditions to disable or sink unauthorized approaching craft (small boats and small planes) which fail to stop after emphatic verbal warnings and flashbang grenades. My military experience is confined to service as a Navy lawyer (JAGC) so I really don't know much about combat, but my SEAL friends have told me that readiness is an important part of combat success, and I can see intuitively that this might be true. From a legal perspective, the authority to act according to the SOP I have described should simply be written into the Rules of Engagement for the port visit.

In any case, the lives of U.S. Sailors and Marines are at least as valuable as the lives of foreigners in small boats, and if people around the world come to the view that it is a risky thing to drive one's small boat up to a U.S. Navy warship, that's probably as it should be. I do acknowledge that the approach suggested here will ruffle some feathers, and may result in some unfortunate casualties, with the corresponding loss of affection that other nations may feel toward the U.S. I have weighed that probability carefully and factored it in to the systems design suggested here. It's a balance. We owe our servicemembers a duty of care, and we owe that to their parents as well. Failure to take reasonable, feasible, and cost-effective precautions is a breach of that duty of care. The Navy is very lucky in this case to have found an expert who would say that, even so, there was no proximate cause in the case of the USS Cole. Without such a felicitous finding in the official records there might be persons who would feel that the case is one of such obvious and gross negligence, such heedless and reckless disregard of the most basic principles of readiness that the deaths and injuries sustained fall outside the scope the Feres Doctrine, and within the Federal Tort Claims Act, as a matter of established case law. But luckily no such persons will come forward now that the citizens can read in the official records that whatever negligence there may have been, was not the proximate cause of the injuries and deaths.

I would like you to bring new vigor to my idea and to create a pattern of <u>action</u> within the Navy -- genuine, real, action -- going and <u>getting some transponders</u>, testing them, doing tactical exercises, <u>putting them on three ships</u> by end of 2001, so we can gather real world data on how the system works when it is actually deployed in a dangerous environment. The next attack may very well be from the air, so the radar/transponder hookup should include 5,000 feet up and 10,000 feet out, easy enough to do with inexpensive <u>off-the-shelf commercial transponders of the sort used to control airport ground traffic</u>. Action is what's needed, because more talking simply lets time go by, time that cannot be recovered and which is built in to the risks future sailors and marines must face.

There seem to be two hitches which prevent action on this idea. First it's too cheap. The whole idea would only cost a million, or a few million to fully take to the three ship demonstration phase. Not enough constituencies will get a piece of the contract. Second, there's no money available in the Navy to spend on a <u>new need</u> that comes up. There are no available funds -- even at very low levels -- especially at very low levels. Everything is budgeted, everything is earmarked -- shaking loose a few million takes years and years of "office work". You could cut through that. Just tell them to do it, as <u>only you can</u>. I have faith in your responsiveness and initiative.

Sincerely,

Robert Gary

2211 Washington Avenue (#301)

Silver Spring, MD 20910-2620

(301) 587-7147

Lieutenant Chapman                         January 23, 2001
Office of the Chief of Naval Operations (CNO)
U.S. Navy
The Pentagon 20350

Dear LT Chapman,

I appreciate very much your candid and responsive telephone conversation with me this day. Perhaps you would let the CNO know that my goals are limited to the following points:

1. There should be a demonstration project for force protection on Navy ships that involves transponders for friend/foe identification and proximity control.

2. The transponders should be located on three ships, probably Norfolk based, and scheduled to rotate to the Med/Middle East in the Fall of 2001.

3. The transponder identification process is integrally connected with the megaphone and flashbang grenade launchers, the idea being that an ambiguous or hostile target needs an instant and totally unambiguous message, yelling first, flashbangs second, live fire third, all within a 30 second period. It is an integrated SOP not just an extra gadget on the mast.

As you say, NCIS has been very busy with the report for Mr. Cohen and with other vital matters related to the USS Cole. As I say, we are sending warships into very dangerous ports every day in the Med and Middle East and we are now 8 weeks after the USS Cole incident, so maybe it's time to make time to hear some ideas about force protection.

I see a very troubling pattern within DOD, and I know the Navy would be the last service to participate in such a pattern. It involves a sort of lack of care about the safety of servicemembers. We saw this in the Gulf War and in Kosovo with the use of depleted uranium ordnance that upon impact creates radioactive alpha emitting aerosols, that may be inhaled, and that may cause a variety of health problems. DOD says there's no provable proximate causal link between the extensively documented health problems and the DU ordnance. Then we have the case of the Osprey which crashes repeatedly, killing lots of Marines, none of whom signed up to be test pilots. And we find out that the

Lieutenant Colonel in charge of that program ordered falsification of maintenance records. DOD says there is no provable proximate causal link between the improperly documented maintenance and the lethal crashes. Now we come to the USS Cole where every indication is that the CO failed to take a number of security precautions that could have been and should have been taken. DOD says that even if everything had been done strictly by the book, and all the security precautions had been taken, the attack could not have been prevented, thwarted, or averted. In other words, there's no provable proximate cause between Navy negligence and harm to service personnel.

I know you see a pattern here. Perhaps it disturbs you as it does me. The Feres Doctrine, announced in 1950 by the U.S. Supreme Court says that servicemen and women have no claim under the Federal Tort Claims Act for actions or omissions by their military superiors in the course of military service. Whatever remedies they may have for injuries lie within the services or in the Veterans Administration. But this doctrine has exceptions in the case of heedless, reckless and gross negligence. Where those factors are present, and there is proximate cause, there may be a basis for a claim that would not be excluded by the Feres Doctrine. Now perhaps the pattern of the repeated concept "no provable proximate causal link" comes into sharper focus. We can see why these words are uttered by DOD with regard to Gulf War Syndrome, DU in Kosovo, the Osprey crashes, and the report that was prepared for Secretary Cohen concerning the USS Cole.

I don't sell transponders. I'm not connected with any company that sells them. I have been a member of the Federal Bar for 23 years and the Bar of the U.S. Supreme Court for 16 years. During that time I have handled incredibly sensitive cases, some nuclear related, some military, some security related. I have never disclosed any material fact to the press or written any article in any publication about a matter of Federal law or practice in which I was involved. So I probably won't do that now. You, Lieutenant Chapman, are the one I'm talking to, and through you to the CNO and to SECNAV and to SECDEF. You are the people that care the most about the issues that I raise. You are the ones that can do the most about them. I rely on you to brief your superiors up the chain of command, and to recommend that your associate Mr. Douglas Cavileer at least hear me out on the design and technology I propose. The CNO has tasked NCIS with coming up with force protection strategies, so maybe hearing some voice from outside the Navy would be O.K., they could consider what I say, if they can't support my demonstration project, they could say it to my face, and tell me why.

I was in Oman in 1981, around the time of the Iran Hostage Crisis, when the Omanis didn't like us much better than the Yemenis do now. I was a TAD JAG on the USS Constellation and the only JAG/International Lawyer to go ashore to observe the vertrep resupply (mostly fresh vegetables). I mention this because I feel compelled to speak about the USS Cole, and you

should know that my own stake in this matter is that it could
have been me that got blown up. I also served at the Headquarters
of the Navy Recruiting Command in Washington DC as the Deputy
Staff Judge Advocate. That gives me another stake in this matter.
I know what sailors sign up for, I know some of their parents, I
know what the People of this country expect in terms of care and
force protection -- I made the promises, it was my word, my bond.
Now I'm retired, so I ask you to be there for my word, to keep
the faith that I promised, and to assist in creating a memorial
through timely and appropriate action to the sailors and marines
of the USS Cole and to all in peril on the sea on behalf of the
USA.


Very Truly Yours,



Robert Gary
LT, JAGC, USN (Ret.)

**Robert Gary**
**2211 Washington Ave (#301)**
**Silver Spring, MD 20910-2620**

Tele: (301) 587-7147


Captain Rollin Lippert                         January 29, 2001
Room 4E514
2000 Navy Pentagon
Washington DC 20350

Dear Captain Lippert,

Enclosed are the documents relating to the transponder design
which I promised to send to you in our telephone conversation of
a few moments ago.

There may be an opportunity for me to present the design in
greater detail in your office there, and, of course I would be
happy to answer any questions that staff or technical people may
have, if I can.

There are 11 months left in this year, and if you create a
demonstration project around my basic design concept, and put it
on a fast track, it will be cheap to do, and will not interfere
with any other project underway or in the thought stages. Doijg
some tactical exercises with transponders would be needed under
any circumstance to develop a workable SOP. Why not start in the
Spring -- out on the Bay, and use a YP from the Naval Station,
and some Midshipmen in motorboats -- a sort of Red Team/Blue Team
exercise to discern the operating characteristics of the system
under some level of challenge. The thing will need sea trials on
a real ship -- that could be done in the Summer with active duty
servicemembers. Only if the system makes sense after all that,
would I suggest that it be bolted to the mast of three small
ships out of Norfolk bound for dangerous waters in the Med or
Middle East. Fam-Fire with the flashbang grenade launchers, and
skillful use of the megaphone with angry yelling are key
components. The intelligence work that supports the distrubution
of the wearable transponder boxes is another key element. All the
elements have to work together to effectively address the
friend/foe ID and proximity control problems. This is doable.
Let's do it, ASAP.


                              Sincerely,

                              /s/
                              Robert Gary

February 13, 2001

**FAX From Robert Gary to Meredith Moseley**

**Enclosed on the following 4 pages are my letter to Senator Warner about the USS Cole and my proposed transponder solution to prevent a repetition.**

**The last page is the letter I mentioned in our phone conversation which was sent by Rep Connie Morella to Secretary Danzig regarding my idea and that the Navy should take it seriously.**

**I request that Sen Warner send a one or two line note to the CNO Admiral Vern Clark urging that my idea be given adequate and prompt consideration. Below Adm Clark the persons that have responsibility for this type of countermeasure include Vice Admiral Tim Keating, Rear Admiral Select Holden, and Captain Lippert.**

**I would like to make about a 20 minute presentation at Navy Pentagon, and then answer whatever questions they may have. I would also like them to answer a few questions that I have about their attainments so far in responding to the USS Cole incident.**

Sincerely,

Robert Gary

# DEPARTMENT OF THE NAVY
### OFFICE OF THE CHIEF OF NAVAL OPERATIONS
### 2000 NAVY PENTAGON
### WASHINGTON, D.C. 20350-2000

IN REPLY REFER TO

February 26, 2001

Mr. Robert Gary
2211 Washington Avenue (#301)
Silver Spring, MD 20910-2620

Dear Mr. Gary:

On behalf of the Chief of Naval Operations, thank you for your letter regarding methods of protecting our ships while in port. It is always a pleasure to hear from a Navy veteran.

Your ideas for an integrated package of protection and responses are well-founded. To reiterate what Mr. Cavileer has stated in his letter to you, the use of positive identification techniques, warnings and escalating levels of response from non-lethal to finally lethal, i.e, Defense in Depth, follows very closely with the projects that the CNO's Task Force is implementing and testing in various programs. The Navy has already implemented many new procedures and fielded new technologies for use in the fleet.

We have already conducted demonstration projects to test many different emerging technologies and to develop the integrated tactics, techniques and procedures to be used by our Sailors in stopping potential intruders and terrorists. While much progress has been made, work must still continue for the foreseeable future to improve our tools and techniques. As a former naval officer you understand that many of these projects are classified or are proprietary and cannot be discussed beyond official channels.

Thank you again for your great interest in the protection and security of our Sailors, ships and aircraft of the Navy.

Sincerely,

J. M. ZORTMAN
Rear Admiral, U.S. Navy
Assistant Deputy Chief of Naval
Operations (Plans, Policy and
Operations) (N3/N5B)
Acting

**Robert Gary**
**2211 Washington Avenue (#301)**
**Silver Spring, MD 20910-2620**


J.M. Zortman                                    March 1, 2001
RADM, USN
Asst. Dep. CNO (N3/N5B), Acting
2000 Navy Pentagon
Washington, DC 20350-2000


Dear Admiral Zortman,


        Thank you very kindly for your excellent letter of
February 26, 2001. Let me address a few of the issues you raise.
First, on the subject of proprietary projects. It seems to me
that your argument, although plausible, is overbroad. Every
action of every part of the military involves some sort of
equipment or technology. If a citizen could be barred from
communicating with DOD based on the idea that there might be some
trade secrets or proprietary information that DOD needs to
protect on behalf of a third party (i.e. a contractor or vendor),
then this would vastly limit communications between the citizenry
and the DOD, which I think would not be a good thing. In my 23
years of federal legal practice, I have occasionally done
litigation support work in patent cases, so I understand the
monetary and profit focus of any holder of trade secrets or
proprietary information, and I support those feelings, and that
protective instinct. I think this matter could be set aside based
on my representation to you that I work for no business interest,
I have no desire to learn any proprietary information, and if, in
the course of communications with DOD, I should accidentally
learn some, I hereby undertake that it will not be communicated
to any other person or entity whatsoever except under court
order.

        Now on the subject of techniques, I realize that
conventional transponder technology may be behind the curve with
regard to what is possible now. I know about proxcards and about
shape sensitive radar technology both of which require no power
source in the responding unit. My design calls for transponders,
and the reason is because they are programmable, with codes that
can be installed or changed at the last moment.

        I am not interested in learning any information that
genuinely needs to be secure from a member of the federal bar,
whose integrity has never been questioned, and who keeps and has
kept many secrets, and always will. I am encouraged by the fact
that your letter does not preclude the possibility of a meeting
between myself and the Navy. As you may know, I have asked for a
**meeting with Vice Admiral Tim Keating and his staff**. My request
is supported by Connie Morella, my own Congressperson, and by
John Warner the Chairman of the Senate Armed Services Committee.
They both feel that if the Navy heard me out for 20 minutes in a
meeting, it would be difficult to see how that could be harmful
to the Navy. There would be no need for the Navy to disclose any
secrets or trade secrets.

        On the subject of the demonstration projects the Navy
has already conducted to test many different technologies to
protect Sailors and Marines, I would urge that you put a note of
caution in your representations. I'm a Navy vet. I'm friendly to
the Navy. I want it to shine. But let's assume that your letter
fell into the hands of a less friendly person. They might ask
questions like this: (1) When were the demonstration projects
completed? (2) On what ships were they conducted? (3) When would
it be convenient for a staff member to go to those ships and
interview members of the crew to discover their experience during
these demonstration projects? (4) What reports were written
summarizing the findings of these demonstration projects? (5) to
whom were these reports disseminated? (6) How were these
demonstration projects financed? and (7) If any of these
demonstration projects were conducted prior to the incident on
the USS Cole in Yemen, and if any of them indicated the existence
of an effective technology to perform friend/foe identification
integrated with a method to repel foes why was this technology
not available or not used effectively on the USS Cole?

        You see, that's what you have to face if you want to
take the position that the Navy has already done many
demonstration projects in the area of what I have proposed.
Someone is going to want to know the details, not me, I'll take
you at your word, but put some caution on what you say about what
the Navy has already done. There may be a strong desire to send
me a message that my overtures are unwelcome, futile, redundant,
and superfluous, but in the course of sending me that message,
you might say more than you can actually prove.

        By the same token there will be another category of
cynics out there, not including myself, who might feel that the
Navy is dragging its feet on making any improvements in this area
so that people won't say, "Well why wasn't that done before the
USS Cole incident?". In the law, we have a special rule of
evidence that excludes any evidence of post-accident repairs for
the simple reason that many hundreds of years of experience
indicates that people are very hesitant to make post-accident
repairs (or in this case technology upgrades) if they think that
it might be held against them at law.

My own feeling, as you know from my prior letters, is that the Navy is right on the razor's edge of negligence in the matter of the USS Cole. I do not put full confidence in the official report based on the so-called "expert" testimony to the effect that even if everything had been done by the book and every precaution had been taken perfectly the success of the terrorist bombing was utterly inevitable, and therefore whatever negligence there may have been, or whatever oversights or lapses of procedure may have occurred, were immaterial. They were not the "proximate cause" of the harm which resulted exclusively from the superseding, intervening, independent act of a pair of criminal terrorist agents. I think the official report is incorrect. However, on the Navy's behalf, I would also say that going to Yemen was utterly inappropriate, and it was mainly the result of White House and State Department manipulations in which a Navy warship was used as a pawn on a chessboard of international goodwill hunting. Compared to that colossal blunder, whatever errors the Navy may have made in the area of force protection were small, though obviously not insignificant.

You have wisely not refused to see me. Such a refusal would require that I seek a SECDEF Directive, or an Executive Order to accomplish my objective. My own idea is that the Navy <u>can</u> manage itself, and it can do it in a way that is flexible, enlightened, responsive, creative, and positive. Admiral Zortman, my initiative with regard to transponders is a challenge and an opportunity for the Navy and for you to rise to the occasion. My only objective is to get a three ship demonstration project using transponders, (or some equivalent or superior technology, if there is one) up and running, in the field by December 31, 2001. I am very mission oriented. <u>I want that specific goal to be accomplished</u>. After completion of my objective, you would be able to say which three ships the demonstration project was conducted on. Crewmembers could be interviewed about how it went. A report would be available showing the anticipated strengths of the system, and the unanticipated weaknesses discovered during the demonstration project. I would not ask to see a copy of this report. I would only ask that the Chairmen of the Senate Armed Services Committee see it, and that the Chairman Joint Select Committee on Intelligence see it. They represent me in this matter. If they tell me that the report is satisfactory, that's all I need to know. Apart from the National Command Authority and Executive Branch appointees, civilian control of the military is not direct. It flows through elected representatives by their oversight authority and by their appropriations authority. But it does flow -- the system does work -- at least in those cases where I have taken an interest, and as you accurately point out I have a great interest in preventing the USS Cole scenario from being repeated. Keep in mind that "Extremism in the defense of liberty is no vice ...", and that includes extreme commitment to the personal protection of those who defend liberty. I think these are motives you and I share completely. Now what we need to do is share a process of action.

        My instincts tell me that the root problem we face is
not secrecy, but lack of available discretionary funds. My
proposed demonstration project, using the very precise design I
have suggested, would run 2 or 3 million dollars. But the Navy
has no loose uncommitted funds. The money simply can't be found
within the narrowly cast "pots" that are for very specific
purposes. If this is the problem, again, it would be the course
of wisdom to talk to me, or at least hear me out. It may be the
case that our appropriations process is dysfunctional with regard
to responding in a timely manner to newly emerged threats. If
that's true, the more transparency we can have in government
about it the better. Get it out on the table -- maybe it can be
fixed. This is a time when government is being improved.

        For your convenience I am enclosing a draft copy of the
presentation I plan to give to Vice Admiral Tim Keating and his
staff, (which I assume in this case would include yourself). This
is just a draft version, I may include a little additional math.


                        Very Truly Yours,



                        Robert Gary, Esq.
                        LT, JAGC, USN (Ret.)

**Robert Gary**
**2211 Washington Ave. (#301)**
**Silver Spring, MD 20910-2620**

Tele: (301) 587-7147
E-mail: Robert.Gary@prodigy.net

Rep. Connie Morella                             March 5, 2001
(Attn: Lisa Boepple)                            <u>**CONFIDENTIAL**</u>
2228 Rayburn Building
Washington, DC 20515

Dear Rep Morella,

     The Navy is continuing to take a hard line in rebuffing my transponder initiative. Enclosed are three documents related to current business. The first is Rear Admiral Zortman's letter to me of February 26 2001. The second, is my letter back to Rear Admiral Zortmen dated March 1, 2001. The third is a draft of a proposed letter from Rep. Connie Morella to Rear Admiral Zortman asking for parts of the reports that have been done so far on transponders. Presumably he already has all these assembled in his office as part of his professional considerations in the weeks and months since the bombing of the USS Cole.

     A careful examination of RADM Zortman's letter reveals that he asserts (1) that many and various demonstration projects have been done involving different emerging technologies and (2) that the CNO is testing positive identification techniques. He does not say that any demonstration project has ever been done by the Navy involving transponders. In our new post-Clinton age, things need to be <u>parsed very carefully</u>. This man wants to avoid an untrue statement such as "We have already done a demonstration project involving transponders". Instead what we see is the inky black fluid in the water, the fuzzy camouflage of ambiguous language. When I was a defense counsel in the Navy's Judge Advocate General's Corps, I sometimes used that very same strategy on behalf of my clients. Please don't let it work on the Congress. The proposed letter draft is designed to make the Navy put up or be silent on the subject of transponder demonstration projects it has supposedly already done.

It is essential to be clear about this basic point.


               Very Truly Yours,



               Robert Gary, Esq.

My instincts tell me that the root problem we face is not secrecy, but lack of available discretionary funds. My proposed demonstration project, using the very precise design I have suggested, would run 2 or 3 million dollars. But the Navy has no loose uncommitted funds. The money simply can't be found within the narrowly cast "pots" that are for very specific purposes. If this is the problem, again, it would be the course of wisdom to talk to me, or at least hear me out. It may be the case that our appropriations process is dysfunctional with regard to responding in a timely manner to newly emerged threats. If that's true, the more transparency we can have in government about it the better. Get it out on the table -- maybe it can be fixed. This is a time when government is being improved.

For your convenience I am enclosing a draft copy of the presentation I plan to give to Vice Admiral Tim Keating and his staff, (which I assume in this case would include yourself). This is just a draft version, I may include a little additional math.


Very Truly Yours,



Robert Gary, Esq.
LT, JAGC, USN (Ret.)

**Robert Gary**
**2211 Washington Ave (#301)**
**Silver Spring, MD 20910-2620**
**Tele: (301) 587-7147**

Donald Rumsfeld                                    March 7, 2001
Secretary Of Defense
Office of the Secretary of Defense
The Pentagon
Washington DC 20350

Dear Secretary Rumsfeld,

Shortly after the bombing of the USS Cole in Yemen on October 12, 2000, I began analyzing the principle factors that might have prevented the success of that suicide attack. It comes down to two basic factors: (1) reliable friend/foe identification and (2) defensive measures beginning with non-lethal but rapidly escalating as the situation warrants to lethal defensive action.

Transponder technology, which is at least 35 years old, is the most logical way of assuring reliable friend/foe identification. Flashbang grenades are the most logical non-lethal force that can send a fully unambiguous message to an approaching small boat. Accordingly, for the past 16 weeks I have been trying to get the Navy to do a demonstration project involving transponders and flashbang grenades. As you can see from Rear Admiral Zortman's letter (enclosed) my efforts have come to no result. The Navy wishes to study this issue very thoroughly and to keep all of its options open in the area of new technology for force protection.

In the meantime, the Navy sends ships just like the USS Cole into ports that could be very hazardous on a weekly and monthly basis. The terrorists who bombed the USS Cole no doubt consider their action to be a success. It was very inexpensive to carry out. It did enormous damage to the U.S. Navy. They have a virtually unlimited supply to suicide bombers, high explosives, and the rudimentary technical skills required to build a shaped charge into a small boat. It is substantially likely, based on the reports that appeared in the major papers in October of 2000 that the terrorists connected with Ossama Bin Laden intended to bomb several U.S. Navy ships. Taking all of these factors into consideration, there is a significant chance that another attempt will be made to bomb a U.S. Navy ship within the next year or two. This likelihood may increase or decrease slightly based on the success or failure of Secretary of State Powell's efforts to achieve some stability in the Middle East, and specifically in Israel.

Accordingly, I respectfully request that you relieve the Navy of further responsibility for conducting discussions, seminars, study panels, or academic research on the subject of a transponder + defense in depth integrated approach. I request that you issue a Directive that the Navy shall forthwith begin concerted action designed to acquire three transponders for installation on small ships, and that these ships undergo sea trials of the total integrated system no latter than the Summer of 2001, and that they be deployed to the Mediterranean or the Middle East no later than December 31, 2001.

Even with this fast track timetable for the obvious logical technology, it will take at least two years to complete a demonstration project. During this time the Navy will be able to assess the strengths, and more significantly any unanticipated weaknesses in the approach being demonstrated. There is a certain amount of tactical knowledge that can emerge in the course of demonstrating a system, that could not possibly emerge around a seminar table. The complete integration of the system: hardware, software, wetware, and ordnance may contain hidden difficulties that can only be revealed in a demonstration.

Assuming the transponder units themselves cost no more than $100,000 apiece, and the installation process on the ships, and connecting the transponders to the equipment in the Combat Information Centers costs no more than $150,000 for all three ships, the entire demonstration project should be feasible within a budget of $2 to $3 million dollars. There are other pieces of hardware required, including an ashore coding unit, and several dozen wearable codable response units. There are training costs. There are costs associated with the flashbang grenade launchers, and with other on-deck readiness measures.

However, these costs can be allocated among all the services, and not borne entirely by the Navy. The system I have suggested has excellent inter-operability, and could, with very slight modification be used to defend a firebase on land, a column of tanks, a flightline (or hangar) of planes, or a civilian vehicle carrying a diplomat or other VIP.

Because of the long lead time, and the significant risk of a repeat attack such as the one made on the USS Cole, it is essential that the talking stop and the action start on this demonstration project at the earliest reasonable time. It is difficult to test a system like this in the Winter months in the Atlantic. If this coming Summer is a missed opportunity, the entire demonstration might have to be done in the Pacific, or it might not get underway until the Summer of 2002. This would mean that the crucial data would not be available until sometime in 2004. That's too long to wait. Transponders are a tried and true technology. They are the obvious choice for friend/foe identification. The risks of a repeat performance by suicide bombing terrorists are greater the more years go by. Furthermore, a Directive from you creating a fast-track demonstration project involving transponders and flashbang grenades, and heavier ordnance as the last step, would not interfere with the Navy's ability to conduct exhaustive research and detailed seminars about all the other measures that they may have under consideration -- the many different emerging technologies spoken on by Rear Admiral Zortman. My requested Directive adds to, and does not subtract from the Navy's pursuit of potentially viable options to solve its force protection problem.

By way of background information I would like to mention that I approach the Navy entirely as a concerned citizen, and as a Navy veteran, not as a lawyer, not as an inventor/designer, not as a transponder salesman. I have no business connection to any company that might be involved in any way in the proposed demonstration project, neither do I have any legal client with any interest in the USS Cole bombing or any other Naval issue, nor do I intend to seek such a client. I have no intent to develop any patentable technology for my own benefit, or to acquire any trade secrets, or national security secrets. My only concern is protection of the lives of men and women who are on the frontiers of freedom, guarding my liberty, some of whom I may have sent there my years as a Navy Recruiter. I don't need to see any of the reports that come back from the demonstration project. I would like to see it get underway at the earliest reasonable time, and it is my considered opinion, after 16 weeks of working with the Navy, that without a Directive from your Office, it will not do so. Thank you for your attention to this matter.


Very Truly Yours,


Robert Gary
LT, JAGC, USN (Ret.)


Enclosure: Letter from RADM Zortman dated February 26, 2001

**Robert Gary**
**2211 Washington Ave (#301)**
**Silver Spring, MD 20910-2620**

**Tele: 301 587-7147**


Admiral Vern Clark                              March 19, 2001
Chief of Naval Operations (CNO)
The Pentagon
Washington, DC 20350-2000

Dear Admiral Clark,

        Enclosed is my letter to Vice President Cheney which
requests that the President be prepared to exercise his authority
as Commander in Chief directly for the purpose of getting a three
ship demonstration project of transponders and flashbang grenades
for proximity control shaken down this Summer and deployed by
December 31, 2001.

        This approach was not my first choice. I take it after
18 weeks of waiting to speak with someone on your staff for 20
minutes. My appeal to the President is made only after my own
Congressperson Connie Morella, and the Chairman of the Senate
Armed Services Committee, Sen John Warner have interceded
unsuccessfully on my behalf with you. I continue to hope that you
will reverse the position that has been expressed on your behalf
by Cdr. P.J. Neher, JAGC (Ser3N5L/1U630303), to the effect that
the Navy cannot meet with me briefly on this matter. I do
understand how busy you are and I would like you to understand
that time is a factor in getting this very cost-effective
demonstration project underway. If the Summer window for
shakedown is missed a whole year of delay would ensue. This means
no meaningful research yield from the demonstration until 2004. I
think we can do better by the men and women of the Fleet. If it
takes an order from the President to make it happen, so be it.


                            Respectfully,



                            Robert Gary

Encl: Ltr to Vice President Cheney dated March 19, 2001 (w/out
      enclosures)

**Robert Gary**
**2211 Washington Avenue (#301)**
**Silver Spring, MD 20910-2620**

P.J. Neher                                    March 19, 2001
Commander, JAGC, U.S. Navy
Legal Advisor, (N3/N5L)
Office of the CNO
Department of the Navy
The Pentagon
Washington DC, 20350-2000

Dear Commander Neher,

Thank you for your letter (Ser3N5L/1U630303) of March 13, 2001 wherein you decline my offer to make a 20 minute presentation on the subject of force protection to Navy Pentagon officials. Having served as a Navy JAG myself, for a headquarters Command, and with responsibility for certain Congressional Inquiries, I have nothing but respect for your position, and will extend to every courtesy so that my efforts on this matter can come to a productive conclusion.

As can see from my letter to SECDEF (enclosed), my ship protection design has excellent inter-operability (page 2, paragraph 4), as this provides a basis for participation by SECDEF which might an entirely more receptive situation with regard to my proposed presentation. Senator Warner, who as you know Chairs the Senate Armed Services Committee has strongly supported my effort to be heard very briefly by Navy Officials, and his letter is on its way to Admiral Vern Clark. My letter to Secretary Rumsfeld is enclosed, as a courtesy to you. You will observe that I am suggesting that the Navy be relieved of the task of designing and demonstrating a transponder-based system because after 18 weeks since my initial suggestion, the time to get underway with sea trials this summer in the Atlantic is getting very short. If a Directive is issued by SECDEF to simply proceed and set three ships up with transponders, there could be a database from a completed demonstration by the year 2003. I don't know if this would be soon enough to prevent another successful terrorist sneak attack on a Navy ship in a foreign harbor.

I intend to abandon my effort to present my ideas to Navy Pentagon right after President George W. Bush refuses a request by the Senate Armed Services Committee that he directly exercise his authority as Commander in Chief by ordering three ships to be set up with transponders and sea trials to begin this summer with the idea of those ships being deployed by December 31, 2001. It is entirely possible that Secretary Rumsfeld will decline to take up this project, and that, in such a case, the President will

refuse to over-ride that decision. I can only do the best I can.
I can't do more. I'm not taking this matter to the public, as I
have never taken any matter to the public which I have worked on
as a matter of public interest. I try to be professional, and if
I'm defeated this time, it will not be for the first time, and my
feelings will be more in sorrow than in anger. I wish the Navy
could be more receptive to ideas from the outside. I'm not asking
to be put at the controls of a nuclear submarine during an
emergency blow -- I just want to give a 20 minute presentation
and possibly answer some questions about my design. I'm not
asking to be briefed on any aspect of any classified information
pertaining to force protection measures that may or may not have
been taken, or demonstrated, so far.

You will be a veteran yourself, at some point. You'll probably
still feel a lot of affection toward the Navy, and you'll want to
see it shine. So, just as I can understand your position, I trust
that you can understand mine.


Sincerely,


Robert Gary


Encl: Ltr to SECDEF dated March 7, 2001 (w/out encl)

**Robert Gary**
**2211 Washington Ave (#301)**
**Silver Spring, MD 20910-2620**

**Tele: 301 587-7147**

Vice President Richard Cheney                    March 19, 2001
The White House
1600 Pennsylvania Avenue N.W.
Washington, DC 20500

Dear Mr. Vice President,

I am writing you because of your familiarity with military matters, and your friendship with Secretary Donald Rumsfeld, and with Senator John Warner. It concerns the USS Cole and with some countermeasures that I am proposing to avert the possibility of a repetition of terrorist bombing of a U.S. Navy ship in a foreign harbor.

For the past 18 weeks, approximately since the time of the bombing of the USS Cole, I have been trying to get an opportunity to speak with Navy officials about a transponder and proximity control system to make sure that the next bombing attempt, if there is one, is not able to harm a Navy ship. My Republican Congressperson, Connie Morella, has been fully supportive of this effort, as has Senator John Warner, both of whom have written to the Navy on my behalf. In spite of these efforts, the Navy has decided that they can't take 20 minutes to hear what I have to say (see letter from Cdr Neher, enclosed)

Here's the gist of it, which I hope you will convey to Admiral Vern Clark or to whomever is appointed the new Secretary of the Navy. First, a land-based transponder system to control the entire harbor in a foreign port is not cost-effective. It requires a crew of at least eight, and their families must be supported, schooled, provided with medical care, and diplomatic assistance in 50 or 100 foreign ports. Adding it up it amounts to several thousand people permanently stationed overseas -- a very costly and not very effective solution. Therefore a ship-based transponder is obviously the way to go. The people manning the transponder are the right there on the ship, already on the payroll, and there's no need to play "telephone" with a shore based controller to get the results.

This means some sort of demonstration project to develop a ship based proximity control transponder system. Admiral Zortman (see his letter enclosed) says that many emerging technologies are being examined, and that the Navy has done many demonstration projects, but you will observe that he carefully does not say that the Navy has done a demonstration project involving transponders for proximity control in foreign harbors -- because it hasn't. It should, and the three ship proposal I have made would be inexpensive, not complicated, and information productive -- it would have a good "research yield".

The system I propose involves coded transponders for friend/foe identification, and flashbang grenades for proximity control. It is a very carefully designed system. I know that there are alternatives, for example water cannons might be used for proximity control. This would be an error for the simple reason that it takes between 15 and **45 minutes** to get a water cannon fully deployed, at full pressure, with all the hoses connected up, and the right nozzle in place, with the right man handling it. By contrast a flashbang grenade launcher takes 5 seconds to remove from the arms locker, 5 seconds to lock and load, and 5 seconds to aim for a total delay time of **15 seconds**, which I realize may be too long, and I'm looking for ways to cut it down.

The next real situation may occur with a bow mounted torpedo boat, at night, charging straight in, making no attempt at deception, ruse, or camouflage, and arriving around 11:45 p.m. on a foggy Christmas Eve night. That is the scenario around which realistic readiness plans must be framed. Assuming a small boat that can make 30 knots in the water, and that has some protection (i.e. steel plate) around the wheelhouse, the Navy ship would have 15 seconds to recognize its potential peril, 15 seconds to fire some flashbang grenades, and 15 seconds to fire enough lethal ordnance to stop and totally disable the oncoming craft. Inability to meet this challenge means that our surface Navy ships are just sitting ducks in foreign harbors, and that the USS Cole scenario is bound to be repeated until the U.S. comes to grips with this basic fact.

The system I am proposing has some chance of meeting that challenge, but **it's not a sure thing**. It needs shakedown, which means this Summer, on three small ships in the Atlantic. It needs a demonstration project which will take about two years to see how the hardware, software, wetware, and ordnance mesh together, if they do -- and that's a big if. **The main purpose of the three ship demonstration project is not to find the strengths of the system, but rather to identify its weaknesses**, and there are sure to be some -- that's why is takes 24 months to find them, that's why it takes real ships, on real deployments, in real foreign ports. I don't sell transponders by the way, nor do I stand to benefit in any way if this demonstration project goes forward.

Currently, my basic position has been forwarded to Secretary Donald Rumsfeld, after the Navy refused to meet with me for 16 weeks. He has it on his desk. I would respectfully request that you brief the President on this matter, and explore with him the possibility of his direct exercise of his authority as

Commander in Chief. <u>He could simply direct the Navy to put transponders on three ships and try out my idea</u>. Doing so would cost about $3 million, and doing it quickly would mean that those ships might do their shakedowns this Summer and be deployed by the end of this year. That would provide an experiential database from real operations no later than the end of 2003, at which point a decision about broader deployment might be possible. Even such a fast-track timetable might not be fast enough to avert a repetition of the USS Cole scenario, but it is the right thing to maximize whatever opportunity we may have for naval force protection in increasingly hostile foreign ports and in the absence of adequate underway replenishment and refueling capacity. If the President is willing to exercise his authority as Commander in Chief directly, this would be a very appropriate case for him to cut through the Pentagon red tape, and just get the proposed demonstration project underway forthwith.

I used to be a Navy Recruiter, actually a JAG at the Navy Recruiting Command World Headquarters. I played a pivotal role in hundreds of recruitments, and some of the men and women in the fleet today are probably my recruits. I've been on a Navy ship, and been ashore on behalf of that ship in Oman, right next to Yemen. So I have an interest as a citizen, as a veteran, and as a former recruiter in making sure that whatever can be done for naval force protection is done. I don't think that's happening now. I think the Navy is confused from a design perspective and organizationally paralysed. I think the President could open some windows, let in some fresh air, and make some new things happen. That's what we elected him to do, and expect he will do, with God's help in a pinch, but in the meantime, with yours.


Most Respectfully,


Robert Gary, Esq.


Encl: Letter from Admiral Zortman of 26 Feb 2001
      Letter from Commander Neher of 13 Mar 2001

**Robert Gary**
**2211 Washington Ave (#301)**
**Silver Spring MD, 20910-2620**
**(301) 587-7147**

Chairman Dan Burton                    March 29, 2001
Government Reform Committee
U.S. House of Representatives
Washington DC 20515

Dear Chairman Burton,

    I was pleased to hear the remarks of Governor Gilmore and General Clapper before the National Security Subcommittee of your Committee yesterday. I would like to add a few points to what they said.

    It is true that there are about 40 agencies of the government that would have some possible role to play in mass casualty emergencies. It is also true that each of those agencies stands on its own legislative foundation in the U.S. Code, and that asking them to form themselves into a one-stop shop for a Governor in an emergency is not a viable course of action unless the Committee for Government Reform acquires the power to delete a significant fraction of the laws of the U.S. Those 40 agencies would be fully prepared to conduct seminars with each other to determine jurisdictional boundaries for a very long period of time at taxpayer expense, but in the end, they would come out as they went in, each with their turf intact, each with their mandate and their programs. Much carbon dioxide would be created in this process -- very costly, but not very useful.

    Here's what I think is needed. Ask the 40 agencies what they could do that would be of some use in a mass casualty emergency. Tell them to state specifically, on one page, what they could do as of 8:00 a.m. on the morning of 29 March 2001. Who exactly could they help, and how could they help? Food, medicine, emergency housing, transportation, radiological monitoring, chemical monitoring, biological threat assessment, trauma care -- these would be examples of what I'm talking about. Now you have 40 pages of statements of what the agencies say they can do -- actually I think 25 agencies will evaporate with this first question -- so you will wind up with 15 pages. Now you send auditors out to verify that what the 15 agencies say they can do, they can actually do. If one says it can provide cots for 10,000 people, you send an auditor to look at the cots, and count them. If another says it can feed 100,000 people, you send someone to examine the emergency rations which were supposed to be on hand at 8:00 a.m. on the morning of March 29, 2001, and see if those emergency rations are actually in place and ready to go. Going through the list of 15 "Helpful Agencies" this way, I think you will winnow it down to about 5 or 6 agencies -- FEMA, DOD, CDC, and maybe three others, that could possibly do a Governor some actual good in a real situation.

If these half dozen agencies were put on a card, one through six with their phone numbers and their offered capabilities, that would be the ideal thing for a Governor to have in a real emergency. The Governors know what they need. If the Federal government answers the phone and can really deliver what it says it can the help would be very much valued.

My own experience includes 23 years of practice as an attorney in the Federal system, mostly focused on emergency management, and legal cases, and administrative matters arising therefrom. I also hold an MBA with a focus on General Systems Theory and Management. What I suggest seems highly simplistic, especially is relation to the detailed expert testimony that your Subcommittee has received, and to the ambitious goal of a one-stop shopping point for Federal emergency services. But I say that even though it sounds simple to make the card I suggest, it is actually so difficult I don't think it could be done. You may find, as you examine this matter that no agency of the Federal government is actually ready to commit in advance that they will do any specific thing in any emergency.

Let me offer one simple example to illustrate my point. You recall the Three Mile Island Nuclear Power Plant Accident in 1979. That was an accident where 85% of the core melted to slag and all during the accident, and for tens years after the accident all officials of every kind insisted that the radiation released was so minuscule and microscopic that it was utterly insignificant for all purposes. How many Curies are in 85% of a nuclear core, and where did they go? These are questions that the scholars will have to address in future ages. In 1992, I suggested that the Army trucks at Indiantown Gap be made available in the event of a future emergency at Three Mile Island to evacuate people from Harrisburg. There are several hundred trucks there. There are 50,000 people in Harrisburg with no Federal plan whatsoever to evacuate them in case of a future emergency. It seemed to me so obvious to use the Indiantown Gap trucks. DOD turned me down flat. Total snub. Straightarm.

I had the support of the Mayor of Harrisburg, and Senator Wofford, and Senator Specter. I met a stonewall. DOD was adamantine, granitic, obdurate. Nothing mattered to them except that I didn't have the authority to make them do what I was asking them to do. I couldn't give them a direct order. Lacking that power, I had no standing in their eyes to speak to them about any matter, particularly the use of DOD trucks.

Perhaps General Clapper has a more receptive sense for requests of this sort. I sense that there is some residual hesitation due to the Posse Comitatus Act, so let me address that issue. That Act was designed to prevent the use of military forces for civil law enforcement. It has no legislative history consistent with the idea that it forbids the use of military forces and assets for mitigation of mass emergencies whether civil of military. The intent of the Act was to allay fears that the U.S. would blur the lines between police authority and military authority. But in an emergency, when you need a ride out of town, you don't care what kind of truck picks you up.

There are a couple of other related issues that need mention in this context. First, as far as I can tell, in Pennsylvania, there is no specific number of rems per hour of radiation that triggers an call for evacuation. As a lawyer, with lots of experience in this area, I was pretty specific in questioning the folks at their Department of Natural Resources and the Pennsylvania Emergency Management Agency on this point -- and they all agreed on one thing -- "It depends". This I think is a terrible mistake. It means that the discussion of what radiation exposure rate should trigger an evacuation has to take place in the midst of an emergency, between 2 or 3 or 10 people instead of before an emergency in the public forum. As a practical matter, no mass evacuation has ever been ordered or facilitated anywhere in the U.S. by reason of nuclear radiation, although I can think of at least three cases where it was clearly appropriate to do so. When the 2, or 3, or 10 people get together, they always seem to decide that "It's Best Not to Panic People". One reason they decide this is because in any event, there is no evacuation plan, and the reason for that is that people like myself get stonewalled and straightarmed by DOD when we ask for a resource commitment. Your Committee can't change that. You have a million times more authority than I do, but still not enough to give a direct order to DOD. But you could tell the Governors that triggers for certain specific emergency responses should be publically and debated and then firmly arranged in advance so that people would know that an evacuation would definitely be ordered if the situation were really bad (at a quantifiable, gauge readable, level).

The last issue I would mention in this context is the issue of truthtelling in an emergency. I don't agree with the witnesses in the Subcommittee hearings who said that a nuclear mass casualty situation was unlikely in the U.S. in the next 20 years. I think it's likely. We are in potential conflict with the Chinese over the Taiwan issue, perpetual conflict with the Russians over the issue of Communism vs Capitalism, and perennial conflict with all of Islam over the issue of Western Decadence vs Moslem Purity. All it would take would be a Russian or Chinese bomb to get into the hands of a Moslem person seeking paradise by striking the Great Satan in the cause the Jihad, and you would have a 50 kiloton explosion in downtown Chicago, New York, or Seattle. It would be about as difficult as the bombing of the USS Cole. All the ABM systems in the world wouldn't stop it. No missile needed, no radar track acquired, no intercept possible, no source verified -- just a big BOOM! and then as task of "consequence management" something we know almost nothing about, and are utterly unprepared for. Would Federal officials tell the truth about radiation levels to the people under those circumstances? Not if history is a reliable guide. They would decide that it would be better not to panic people. They would decide to tell people downwind just to stay indoors, and close their windows. The effect of this well-meaning deceit would be to triple the loss of life and health from the blast. It would be beneficial if the government could somehow decide in advance that in a mass casualty emergency, whether nuclear, chemical, or biological it would speak the truth to the people utterly. Such a decision would have to be promulgated completely at all levels of government state and Federal, and there would have to be sanctions of some sort for non-compliance. Officials would have to know that they could be punished for making knowingly false statements in emergencies no matter how well-meaning they might be. This approach would create public confidence in Federal and state officials, which at present is regrettably but understandably dicey. If people know that they will get the truth, however bad it may be, they will behave more rationally in mass casualty situations.

My message to you boils down to the following points (1) simplicity in assessing what the Federal government can do to help -- put it on a card -- like a menu -- send it around to the Governors -- that would be a big help (2) triggers for evacuation determined in advance -- with public hearings -- in the open society -- lots of transparency -- and this includes radiation levels, parts per million of nerve gas -- parts per billion of biological agents/viruses and (3) official truthtelling as a firm commitment backed up by real sanctions.

In law the fundamental rule for life and death mass emergencies is "sauve qui peu" which means that those who can save themselves should do so. The fundamental concept of government should be to not get in the way of this principle. Be helpful in concrete ways, be prepared to order reasonable countermeasures, and tell the truth about how bad things are and where the toxic plume is going. This is useful because it keeps people from fleeing into the plume. If the government in Washington could just do these simple things, the Governors and their people in the 50 states could face whatever comes with better hopes for survival.

Feel free to include this letter with the testimony that has been placed in the record by the witnesses before the subcommittee. All statements contained in this letter are true to the best of my knowledge information and belief, and I so affirm.

Very Truly Yours,

/s/

# DEPARTMENT OF THE NAVY
OFFICE OF THE CHIEF OF NAVAL OPERATIONS
WASHINGTON, DC 20350-2000

IN REPLY REFER TO
Ser3N5L/1U630303
March 13, 2001

Mr. Robert Gary
2211 Washington Avenue (#301)
Silver Spring, MD 20910-2620

Dear Mr. Gary:

This responds to your letter of March 1, 2001 to Rear Admiral Zortman, which I understand to be the seventh letter you have written to Navy/DoD officials on the subject of force protection in the aftermath of the attack on USS Cole. In your letter, you offer to meet with senior Navy officials to make a presentation on methods by which Navy can improve force protection

We must respectfully decline your offer, but thank you again for your interest in this subject.

Sincerely,

P. J. NEHER
Commander, JAGC, U.S. Navy
Legal Advisor, (N3/N5L)

# Presentation on Transponders
## by
## Robert Gary
## for
## Navy Pentagon

My design requires a shipboard transponder located on the mast with a connection an integrated radar/transponder screen in the Combat Information Center (CIC) which in turn has instantaneous communication with the deck security detail.

The idea is that small transponder response units are distributed the lead boatmen in all small craft that are authorized to approach the US warship. These small units, about half the size of a carton of cigarettes are physically strapped onto the chests of the authorized lead boatmen. This is a very important aspect of the design. It requires direct physical contact with the trusted lead boatmen, which provides a full opportunity to recognize them, establish their identity, and their state of mind, to a degree. This attachment of the response units would be done by someone ashore -- perhaps the U.S. military liaison, or perhaps an advance detail Marine Security Unit, or perhaps an U.S. intelligence officer, or U.S. military policeman.

My system calls for a programmable transponder code system, which could be thought of as a sort of PIN number. It's really quite simple, just 9 digits, nobody knows them except the Captain, he sends them ashore 90 minutes before the ships arrives in harbor, so the PIN number for the transponder response units arrives on a just in time basis, and is personally made up, or picked out of a random number table, by the Captain as part of the SOP for this system's design. It's not necessary or desirable that anybody else in the chain of command know the PIN number. The higher ups don't need to know it. The Sailors and Marines aboard ship don't need to know it. So in the interest of keeping things simple, which is always a fundamental design principle in security matters, the Captain can just put the number in his safe, once his signals people can sent it ashore. It should be a scrambled burst transmission, of course, and on a frequency that can only be received by the security unit ashore that will program that PIN number into the wearable transponder response units.

The response units can be wired so they will only accept an interrogation signal once per second, and therefore can only sqwauk back a PIN number bearing response once per second. Thus it is exceedingly unlikely that in less than 72 hours an enemy could break the PIN code by rapid electronic trial and error. Since the PIN code is only valid for 72 hours, and then needs to be updated with a different code, the 9 digit approach is very likely to be secure enough.

The other important point about the transponder interrogator on the ship's mast is that it see's out to 10,000 yards and at that range up to 5,000 yards in altitude. It's basically a lateral oriented unit, but it does have some vertical scope, which means that it can detect and interrogate a small plane entering the security envelope from about 2 miles out. In some circumstances the Navy may wish to have authorized small planes in the vicinity of warships in port, and this sort of transponder feature would allow that.

It is assumed in this design that the U.S. can tell for a fact that the trusted chief boatmen are indeed trustworthy. If this isn't true, then it is better to refuel and resupply at sea than to come into port. Making this true requires months and years of personnel work by intelligence agencies and security specialists. They need to do the vetting, and it has to be right. That way when our military liaison straps the transponder response unit to the chest of the fully vetted, fully identified chief boatman, the Captain of the ship can rely on that man's being a "friend" rather than a "foe" or potential foe. Reliance on the transponder response units is only as good as the vetting and identification of the trusted lead boatmen that those gadgets are attached to.

3

So far I've just covered the transponder angles of the overall system, the purpose of which is friend/foe identification which was the first crucial element missing in the USS Cole security disaster. Friend/foe ID is a necessary but not sufficient cause of ship security. The other critical element, also missing in the USS Cole disaster, is the ability to repel a potential foe.

Let me turn now to that aspect. My system calls for some sort of yelling through loud hailers which may be accompanied by tapes in the native language of the potential foes. My initial instinct as a designer is to keep the process natural and realtime, so my inclination is to opt of angry yelling in English by someone with a Voice of Command, through the loud hailer, over the water, accompanied by waiving of arms, and clear gestures that say Get Back! Turn Around! Go away! Do it now! We're not kidding!. The emotional content of the message is what counts -- not the semantic content of the words. So one furious Bosun is worth a thousand Arabic tapes as far as my initial design instinct leads me. But I have been brought to somewhat better thinking by a naval officer who tells me that "Before you kill a man, you should warn him in his own language." As a lawyer, I can see the sense in this position, and therefore the initial design concept could be augmented, it now seems to me, by adding some tapes in Arabic, or whatever the local language is, so that the legal, and possibly moral issue can be satisfied correctly.

However the yelling and tapes phase cannot be designed so that is must of necessity last more than 10 seconds. It's O.K. depending upon the speed of approach of the potential foe for the yelling phase to exceed 10 seconds, but under some circumstances it must be compressible into no more than 10 seconds, assuming that it can start when the potential foe is at least 100 yards out.

If the potential foe approaches in the face of live angry Bosun yelling and Arabic tapes, then my design calls for the use of flashbang grenades. This is a simple technology, but one the Navy would have to learn. It is used at Yellowstone to repel Grizzlies from places they shouldn't be. It works very well on bears, and probably would work even better on Arabs. The charge in a flashbang grenade can blind of deafen a human being if the thing goes off too close to their head. It could even, in a very rare circumstance, even kill someone. So the grenade launcher needs to be operated by service personnel who have plenty of fam-fire experience and can put that grenade exactly where it needs to go. The idea is to send a message that is 100% unambiguous, but to do it non-lethally. The grenade should detonate 20 feet from the bow of the approaching potential foe.

This will send the message but hopefully not disorient the boat driver so completely that they lose control of the their small boat. Ideally you want to fire 3 to 10 flashbang grenades if necessary and if there's time. In the real world it would be safe to assume the enemy is in a cigarette boat that can do 40 knots, and is mounted on the tip of the bow with a 1000 pound semtex torpedo that detonates on contact. No shaped charge, no ceremonial salutes, just a straight in ramming charge with the idea that Paradise is seconds away. This is the worst case scenario for a surface attack, and it's the one that any effective design must address. This means that your grenade launching team has only got 5 or 10 seconds to do their work. So three grenades is what they are likely to get off in that time if they work skillfully.

If the potential foe is still coming, and coming fast, you have to open up with live fire. The rounds have to be heavy enough to disable or stop the approaching foe. 50 caliber is probably not sufficient. A Phalanx Gun is almost certainly sufficient, but they are not universally available on US warships, and they take some fairly sophisticated radar and programming to get them on target. The ideal gun would be something like a Boeffers cannon. It fires rapidly, accurately and fairly heavy shells. You could probably get off at least 3 rounds in the final 40 yards of enemy approach. If the enemy was killed by these he might be deflected or set up for a sure kill

with the 50 caliber or a smaller weapon such as an M-16 or a
combat shotgun.


There is no foolproof system against kamikaze
terrorists. My design is as robust as it can be within the
constraints of low cost, simplicity, and not doing terminal
diplomatic damage at every port we go into. All of these factors
have been weighted. Not only is this design not foolproof as a
set of protective measures, but it's also not error proof as a
set of behaviors that might cause the loss of innocent life of a
foreign person, or several. Common sense has got to be fully
integrated into the SOP so that where a less lethal path can be
followed, that's the one we always choose, automatically, in the
fog of war, in the stress of the moment. We've had a captain
shoot down a civilian airliner trying to protect his ship.
There's a lesson in that experience, and the lesson is to have a
plan, follow procedure, but have the clearest and most definite
evidence of the need to proceed to a more lethal level before
doing so. In a USS Cole type situation, the difficulty would be
compounded if the attack came on a moonless night, in a heavy
harbor fog, on a day like Christmas Eve, at around midnight. I
think my design could cope with that, but perhaps not, perhaps no
reasonable design could.

Rules of engagement are crucial of course. They are slightly beyond the scope of my comments here. Suffice it to say that security is a tightrope between the legal and the dead. We need to be sure that all the ports we go into are places that the Navy, and no one but the Navy has chosen for us to visit. We need to be sure that all the rules of engagement are determined by the Navy, and by no one else. If a status of forces agreement or a treaty is in place that makes it impossible for the Navy to frame reasonable rules of engagement, then refuel and resupply at sea -- build more Oilers -- that's better than being a diplomatic pawn on someone's chessboard of international goodwill, and it's better than accepting rules of engagement that are unsatisfactory in allocation of risk between Navy personnel and foreign people. If they want our cash for oil and food resupply they have to accept the occasional flashbang in their harbor, and the occasional body in their morgue. This is bound to happen if my design is adopted, and it's a terrible thing, especially when the designer can see it coming, and the only worse thing is to not adopt my design or some similar one that gives a decent level of security to US warships in dangerous foreign ports.

# Technical Specifications for Proposed Transponder
# and
# Related Internet Search (Annotated)
# by
# Robert Gary
# March 31, 2001

The ideal transponder arrangement for a Navy ship, for proximity control (RFID) in harbor situations is something that plugs directly into to "10" radar units in the Combat information Center. All incoming transponder data shows up on one of those screens, fully integrated with the data from the regular radar sweep. We might call this a combined, or overlay image.

Creating a separate transponder station would be less than ideal. It would be in the way, it would require SOP modifications for the CIC personnel, and it would be what in electronics is called a kludge -- an extra box hanging off the side of equipment into which it's function could easily have been integrated.

Obviously, there's going to have to be a new box on one of the masts, and a pair of wires running down to CIC. But ideally, within CIC the data from the new box on the mast should feed through a modular plug-in card that fits into an empty socket on the "10" radar. This minimizes costs, as well as work process re-engineering, both of which need to be minimized to keep this demonstration project cheap and simple.

The key datapoint that needs to be tested is that an RFID transponder (whose feed is displayed on a "10" radar screen in CIC), could pick out a non-responding small boat in a group of small boats moving all around a Navy ship. The test would involve setting the technology up on some dummy craft maybe a Yard Patrol Boat to simulate the ship, and some rubber inflatable speedboats to simulate the assorted small boats. You give all the speedboats a transponder except one. You scramble them up. You have them approach the ship on complicated courses, and see if the fellow reading the "10" can pick out the non-responder. If this experiment fails, there's no point in going further with the demonstration project. If the system can't do what it needs to do, it's not going to work any better on a real Navy warship than it would on a YP, so there's no point in installing it, at great cost, on a real mast, and getting it through sea trials.

If but only if the system works in a mini-trial out on the Bay, does it make sense to go ahead and buy (or lease) three copies, and take them through sea trials. If but only if those three copies work as well on the ships as the mini-trial indicated they might, and also make it through their sea trials (i.e. not fall off the masts, get rusty with salt water, or succumb to vibration and rough handling), we arrive at the go/no go decision point for an actual deployed demonstration project in which the Navy will place some <u>limited</u> reliance on this system to safeguard the lives of service personnel.

The internet search recovered a total of 19 pages from the computer, and in those pages the following five datapoints have been identified:

<u>Datapoint A</u>: Was found on page GR-6 -- <u>The RFID Handbook</u> -- looks like a very authoritative source -- the Verlag and John Wiley connection is known to be a consistent provider of the highest quality information on technical subjects -- this book published in 1999 is up to date -- the cost is estimated at less than $100 delivered.

<u>Datapoint B</u>: Was found on page GR-8 -- we find at least six companies that seem to have a security connection in their RFID transponder applications including (on page GR-9) <u>ReaDX Global</u> that does design and applications work, as well as supplying the equipment.

<u>Datapoint C</u>: Was found on page GR-10 -- where we observe that <u>Philips Semiconductors</u> and <u>Micron Technology Inc</u>, which are both

very substantive firms are in the RFID business. This is important information. The requirements in this case are difficult enough so that it would be cost-effective to start right out with a very experienced and substantive company (as distinct from a recent upstart entrepreneur whose is trying to extract value from a specific patent). We need transponders that can be recoded, that will work at some distance -- a mile, perhaps two, that will cover some airspace if necessary, and that can be configured so they integrate with what we already have on the ships, on a plug in basis, and not as a kludge. A big company can tackle this kind of assignment much better than a shoestring operation. Turning to page GR-11 we are pleased to see that <u>Motorola</u> and <u>Texas Instruments</u> are also in the RFID business.

<u>Datapoint D</u>: Was found on page GR-14 -- we find the name and address of <u>Mr Mike Marsh</u> -- who appears to be a transponder enthusiast and expert. It is possible that with the right handling this fellow would provide very valuable overall systems design guidance, for free, or for a very low exchange value -- for example a new subscription or two to his Newsletter. This sort of cognoscenti who pursue a subject for the love of it often have much better design sense for what is really practical, and what would work, than people trying to sell a specific product.

<u>Datapoint E</u>: On page GR-15 -- Having run an advanced search for Proximity AND Control AND Security, we got a 100% hit on the name <u>ReaDX Global Ltd</u>. This is not conclusive of anything, but suggests that this particular company may have some prior experience with RFID transponders for proximity control. This does not mean that they would or would not be a good source for DOD. They might be too small or otherwise unqualified. But they might be worth contacting for their expertise, on an informal basis, just to pick their brains, look through their product catalog, find out what they done for other customers, find out who they are, and what they say they can do. Turning to page GR-17 we find that <u>they are located in Boulder Colorado</u>, with their address, FAX, Telephone and e-mail -- and that they specifically claim to provide "RFID proximity systems for the security access control market" (whether this includes, or could include transponders with a 1-2 mile range, we don't know, but that information could be gotten in 15 minutes with a phonecall to Colorado).

It is noted here that one proposed alternative design modality would involve <u>placing the transponder ashore</u> and operating on some sort of "harbor control" basis. This is regarded as <u>totally impractical</u> for three reasons.

First, it would mean some sort of installation ashore in 50 harbors. Let's say that each installation takes 8 men, for 24 hour coverage in three 8-hour shifts -- now you have their wives, and their children, so you have to build housing, and schools, and hospitals, supply and diplomatic service centers. Figure that this all runs $10 million/year in addition to salary -- so that's half a billion dollars a year for 50 harbors. By contrast, if the transponder is on the ship, then wherever the ship goes you have a transponder right there in that harbor, manned by people who are already on the payroll, and whose wives and kids are not with them.

Second, it's better not to play telephone if you don't have to. "Keep it simple" is the core concept of good design. That is particularly true in a case like this where you may have 30 seconds to effectively respond. There's no time to play telephone with a harbor control master ashore. Paradise Seekers are unlikely to flinch or hesitate in any way at the last moment -- so when I say 30 seconds is your lead time in a worst case scenario, that's what I mean -- which implies there's no time to play telephone.

Third, putting people ashore with their families to man 50 harbor control stations worldwide just exposes more people to terrorism than are already exposed. It puts America's most vulnerable people in the worst kind of harm's way.

We need less exposure, not more, simpler systems, not more complex ones, cheaper systems not more expensive ones, and systems that respond faster rather than slower.

There are things apart from transponders that can play a role in hazard mitigation in refuelling situations. One idea is to scrap the concept of tender boats altogether. Let Americans, and American Sailors go get the refuelling lines and bring them out to the ship. It's sort of the difference between "Full Service" and "Self-Service" at the local gas station. We need to switch to "Self-Service" -- we go get the refuelling hoses, and we turn on the pump. Don't buy gas from harbors that won't permit "self-service". Foreign aid is a separate matter. If the U.S. has a desire to give money to foreigners, just give it to them. But allowing them to render contract services that have the inevitable effect of endangering Navy ships is improvident, unwise, and unnecessary.

Picket boats are another item that needs to be upgraded. We need to patrol the water around our ships as long as they are in port. The rules of engagement must specify a generous exclusion zone at all compass points around a Navy ship at every moment it is in the harbor. Picket boats should aggressively enforce this exclusion zone using all means necessary and possible.

Lethal and non-lethal ordnance is another factor for careful analysis. The water cannon approach as a non-lethal measure is too slow, too cumbersome, too hard to deploy quickly at high pressure. Flashbang grenade launchers take 5 seconds to remove from the arms locker, 5 seconds to lock and load, and 5 seconds to aim. This 15 second readiness delay is within the permissible time. And they are highly effective, especially if manned by a marksman, sharpshooter, or sniper.

All the flashbang does is change Navy's legal status, it doesn't change a terrorist's intent, capability, speed or momentum. It enhances Navy's legal right to follow on with lethal fire, but it's not even going slow down, a true Paradise Seeker. To do that you need a shell weighing about 25 pounds, and you may need 2 or 3 of them to stop a cigarette boat dead in the water. If you stop the oncoming boat, the suicide bomber will try to escape, they will not blow themselves up. The idea is to live to try another day. Dying gloriously for the Paradise Seeker means making it count -- killing lots of supposed enemies. Once the possibility of doing so is physically removed, the mission is over, and the secondary mission is to survive, evade, resist, and escape.  Thus, to stop the boat is to end the mission and to avert the explosion. If anyone is alive when the boat is disabled they will jump overboard and try to swim away.

For lethal ordnance, a Phalanx Gun is probably the
wrong answer. First of all it's got DU shells which will only get
the U.S. into more trouble. If the Depleted Uranium shells were
replaced by tool steel and titanium alloy the stopping power even
at 600 rounds per minute would be questionable. There are wire or
radar or laser guided shoulder fired anti-tank missiles which are
worthy of consideration. They are cheap, light, and deploy
extremely fast -- (within our 15 second time horizon). Another
alternative is something like a Boeffers Cannon, with a 50mm 25
pound shell. The problem is that it can't be fired except from a
bolted down fixed mount, which would have to be a new addition to
the deck of the ship -- and again a kludge -- an item that's in
the way -- not designed in, hard to get operational quickly, and
needs specialize training to use effectively. The Navy and
Marines have plenty of people that can fire a shoulder mounted
anti-tank weapon -- they can get it ready fast and they can fire
it fast. I don't think we have people that are good with a
Boeffers Cannon.

The lethal force must have real stopping power and must
be deployable very fast -- 15 seconds, and should be consistent
with the basic design principles of (1) working with what's
there, (2) doing things simply, and (3) good cost-effectiveness.
If that final piece can be put in place by a warrior with more
knowledge than this designer has about ordnance, then the overall
system should provide good value as a security upgrade for

avoidance of a repetition of the USS Cole scenario.

Acceptance of this entire design is no guarantee against a successful repeat attack. It's good value -- it enhances our security posture -- but that's all it is. Security really depends, not just on gadgets but on warrior instinct, and gut-level awareness, cunning and skill. Without this, there are no secure ships. With it, ships can be secure without any gadgets. Transponders are certainly no panacea. They can, however, be one cost-effective way to significantly reduce the risk of being taken by surprise in the complex environment of a foreign harbor.

U.S. Sailors and Marines aren't asking to be "safe". They just want their superiors to do what can be done to make them as safe as possible consistent with completion of their mission and with their continued voluntary membership in the inherently hazardous profession of arms -- those in peril on the sea ask only this, but they deserve nothing less.

All statements made in this presentation are true to the best of my knowledge, information, and belief, and I so affirm.

Silver Spring Maryland                    Robert Gary, Esq.

March 31, 2001

**Robert Gary (#301)**
**2211 Washington Avenue**
**Silver Spring, MD 20910-2620**

Tele: 301 587-7147

Vice-Admiral Tim Keating                    April 18, 2001
Room 4E592
Navy Pentagon
Washington DC 20350-2000

Dear Admiral Keating,

        This is my report to you of my final conference with
the professionals at NCIS regarding my concerns about the USS
Cole. As you may know, Admiral Vern Clark (CNO) advised that this
meeting should occur based on correct and adequate
considerations.

        Enclosed is my e-mail message of this day to Mr. Leo
Targosz at NCIS. I regard the meeting as an overall success. I
have no idea what impact it might have. Some persons within the
scope of Navy are warriors, and some are not. This is a simple
fact. I was very positively impressed by your man Mr. Doug
Cavileer. He was deeply knowledgeable and very open to my ideas.
My sense is that he will make good use of the insights that came
out of that meeting.

        I rely on you to supervise the process. You understand
that I will continue to take an interest and will follow up long
term on what gets done regarding my proposals. I'm a public
interest lawyer. I've represented veterans for 23 years. I'm
retired Navy -- a former Navy Recruiter. I can't claim to
represent the men and women in the Fleet because they haven't
authorized me to do that, but I'm saying this "They didn't sign
up to lead safe lives, all they want from you is the best safety
that you can give them within the context of lives that
inevitably are going to be at hazard. John Paul Jones is their
leader, hearts of oak are in their breasts, but just let the
Admirals do their part, and all will be well."

                        Very Truly Yours,




                        Robert Gary, Esq.

Encl: E-mail to Mr. Leo Targosz dated April 18, 2001

**DEPARTMENT OF THE NAVY**
OFFICE OF THE CHIEF OF NAVAL OPERATIONS
2000 NAVY PENTAGON
WASHINGTON, D.C. 20350-2000

IN REPLY REFER TO
2 May 01

Mr. Robert Gary
2211 Washington Avenue (#301)
Silver Spring, MD 20910-2620

Dear Mr. Gary:

This is in reply to your letter to the Secretary regarding your proposal for development of a proximity control system to prevent future attacks on U.S. Navy ships.

We appreciate your interest and enthusiasm for protecting the men and women of the U.S. Navy. For this reason, Mr. Douglas R. Cavileer, Deputy Director, Antiterrorism/Force Protection Division on my staff, and Special Agent Thomas Shelko and Mr. Leopold L. Targosz, Jr. from the Naval Criminal Investigative Service met with you on 17 April 2001 at the Washington Navy Yard to further discuss your proposals. I understand that you were provided information on the Physical Security Equipment Action Group and the Technical Support Working Group, the latter an organization that affords the private sector and academia an established means of proposing solutions to physical security and force protection challenges.

If we may be of further assistance, please to not hesitate to contact us.

JOSEPH J. KROL
Rear Admiral, U.S. Navy
Assistant Deputy Chief of Naval
Operations (Plans, Policy and
Operations)

BARBARA A. MIKULSKI
MARYLAND

SUITE 709
HART SENATE OFFICE BUILDING
WASHINGTON, DC 20510–2003

(202) 224–4654
TDD: (202) 224–5223
http://mikulski.senate.gov/

## United States Senate
WASHINGTON, DC 20510–2003

May 3, 2001

Mr. Robert Gary
2211 Washington Avenue, Apt 301
Silver Spring, Maryland  20910-2620

Dear Mr. Gary:

Thank you for forwarding me a copy of your letter to Senator John Warner regarding your idea to identify friend/foe for warships after the USS Cole incident.

This is obviously a matter of great concern to you and I wanted to let you know that I appreciate your efforts to keep me informed of your views and actions regarding this matter.

Again, thanks for keeping in touch with me.  Please let me know if I may be of assistance to you in the future.

Sincerely,

Barbara A. Mikulski
United States Senator

BAM:cg

**CHIEF OF NAVAL OPERATIONS**

8 May 2001

Dear Congresswoman Morella,

Thank you for your letter regarding
Mr. Gary's proposal for a proximity control
system to prevent future attacks against U.S.
Navy ships.

Mr. Gary has been in frequent written and
verbal communication with the Navy since the
tragic USS COLE incident.  We also met personally
with Mr. Gary on 24 April 2001.  We are prepared
to submit his proposal to our technical experts
for system validation and cost analysis.

We appreciate Mr. Gary's interest and
enthusiasm for protecting the men and women of
the U.S. Navy.

Sincerely,

VERN CLARK
Admiral, U.S. Navy

The Honorable Constance A. Morella
U.S. House of Representatives
2228 Rayburn House Office Building
Washington, DC 20515

OFFICE OF THE VICE PRESIDENT

WASHINGTON

July 26, 2001

Dear Mr. Gary:

The Vice President has asked me to reply to your letter providing your views and suggestions on issues related to our nation's defense.

I can assure you that the Administration is committed to providing the nation the best possible defense against the threats of today and those that may arise in the future. To fulfill that commitment responsibly, we must ensure that the nation gets the best return for each defense dollar. We simply cannot afford to commit additional dollars before we clearly understand where they are most needed.

To that end, the President has directed a comprehensive review of defense strategy and policy. The results of that review will be used to build a defense budget that makes sense and meets the needs of our nation. It would be premature for me to address the specifics of any defense issue until the review is complete.

The Vice President appreciates your sharing your views on this matter.

Sincerely,

Eric Edelman
Principal Deputy Assistant to the Vice President
For National Security Affairs

Mr. Robert Gary
2211 Washington Ave. #301
Silver Spring, Maryland  20910-2620

Faxed to 202-225-1389 75
12 SEPT 2001
1330 hRS EST

**Robert Gary**
**2211 Washington Ave. (#301)**
**Silver Spring, MD 20910-2620**

Tele: (301) 587-7147
E-mail: Robert.Gary@prodigy.net

Rep. Connie Morella                              September 12, 2001
(Attn: Lisa Boepple)
2228 Rayburn Building
Washington, DC 20515

Dear Rep Morella,

        A good Congress feeds on good ideas. You know that since my involvement with the **USS Cole** matter, with your kind assistance, I have urged the Navy to use transponders to protect their ships in dangerous foreign ports of call. Let me give you three ideas related to the World Trade Center Attack that was perpetrated yesterday.

**First:** I agree with John Nance of Tacoma Washington, (our leading authority on airplane matters) that the door between the first class cabin and the flightdeck cannot be a bank vault type door with a time lock. The reason for this has to do with sudden depressurization and the need to permit rapid pressure equalization on both sides of that barrier. So <u>here's my idea</u>: a triple mesh Kevlar screen that is set so that it can be pulled across on a metal track behind the flightdeck door after it closes, and once pulled across can be locked in position with a timelock. This would provide the functional equivalent of a bank vault type door, and it wouldn't have the depressurization problem, and it would be very light, and fairly inexpensive. With two securing hooks on each side of the door, it would keep the door from opening. It would be very hard to cut or shoot through. When the flightdeck is secure, as it would be with such a device, there would be no repetition of the World Trade Center Disaster.

**Second:** Although I approve of the idea of federalizing airport security and having very high quality uniformed federal personnel do it, I don't think that, by itself, will solve the problem. The Trade Center terrorists used boxcutting knives with 2 inch blades. Pocket knives with 4 inch blades are legal to carry on a U.S. flight. So even a fully trained screener would have let the boxcutting knives onboard in the pockets of passengers. The main weapon was a ruse. A bag was held up and said to be a bomb. The little knives were probably just used to kill the flightdeck crew and wound a few flight attendants to make an impression of seriousness and have the bomb threat taken seriously. So <u>my solution would be</u> to vet all passengers wishing to fly in the U.S.A. The vetting would have to be done by a firm with personnel analysis experience, like an insurance agency, or a credit agency, or the F.B.I., or even a new branch of the F.A.A. It could take 6 months. It might require interviews, background checks, identity verification etc. The pass seeker could pay, say $500.00 toward reimbursing the government for part of these costs. If that seems inconvenient, they could just take a train, or a bus, or go by car. It's far better for Lady Liberty to lose a finger, than to lose an arm, or a child. We, her children, are going to have to sacrifice some liberty to maintain our security. But since the days of Roosevelt we have been taught that there's no trade-off ever needed -- we can have all our liberty and all our security. That is a false teaching, and one from which we must now disenthrall ourselves. Carefully and fairly pre-vetting all airline passengers and giving them picture identity cards, which they help pay for, is more reasonable than focusing exclusively on last minute carry-on baggage and pocket checking at the airport, even if it's done skillfully.

**Third:** Shooting missiles at Kabul or Baghdad or even at terrorist training camps in Afghanistan, Pakistan, Lebanon, Iraq, or Iran is not likely to be helpful. It won't make the U.S. or its citizens more secure. We can only neutralize enemies like Bin Laden and his organization <u>by operating at the rate and in the place that good intelligence comes in</u>. If we sent a division of Special Forces to Afghanistan with the idea of setting up a firebase in a protectable location, they could be re-supplied indefinitely from amphibious carriers in the Indian Ocean, or in the Mediterranean. We tell the Taliban that whatever part of their "sovereignty" is being violated by the firebase within their borders is suspended for reasons of State (Raison D'Etat), and that the purpose of the firebase is to provide a center of operations from which we can kill Bin Laden and his organization when we get reliable intelligence concerning his whereabouts. We go into the field and we will stay until the job is done. This could take five or ten years, but it would send a strong message to Saddam Hussein, or to the Hezbulla, or the Mullahs in Iran. The message is "If you harm us, we will suspend your sovereignty for the purpose of hunting down terrorists from a firebase within your "sovereign" borders, and we stay for as long as it takes. This is far better than launching $1,000,000 tomahawks to destroy $100 puptents in the badlands of Afghanistan, based on sketchy or no intelligence. It is far better than blowing up some Taliban office buildings in Kabul, or some of Saddam's palaces in Iraq. Those approaches disclose our unwillingness to go into the field and kill our enemies. It's not likely that long-range missiles will disenable, disempower, or even seriously effect our committed mortal foes, like Bin Laden.

You are my Congressperson, and perhaps the smartest, most scientific, and sensible member of Congress. So please, look over these three proposals, and **if you like them, put them forward to the GOP Caucus.** I fear that our response to the World Trade Center Attack will be political, gestural, unhelpful, and amount to little more than paper tiger tactics. I fear that without seasoned guidance the Administration may fail to frame an effective response to this vicious and cowardly attack. An ineffective response will lead to a grim future. My understanding of security matters might perhaps be of some small value in shaping a course toward a more secure future for this country -- the home of the brave, the place where democracy does not, and will never, mean weakness -- e pluribus unum!

Your hopeful constituent,

Robert Gary
LT, JAGC, USN (Ret.)

# Part B


# The 9/11 Attack and Cockpit Access Controls for Commercial Airlines in USA

# (17 Sep 2001 - 16 Jul 2002)

**Robert Gary**
**2211 Washington Ave. (#301)**
**Silver Spring, MD 20910-2620**

Tele: (301) 587-7147
E-mail: Robert.Gary@prodigy.net

Chairman John Duncan                          September 14, 2001
House Aviation Subcommittee
2251 Rayburn Building
Washington, DC 20515

Subj:           1. __Barrier to Assure Flightdeck Security__

                2. __Background Checks for Passengers__


Dear Chairman Duncan,

The door between the first class cabin and the flightdeck cannot be a bank vault type door with a time lock. The reason for this has to do with sudden depressurization and the need to permit rapid pressure equalization on both sides of that barrier. So <u>here's my idea</u>: a triple mesh Kevlar screen that is set so that it can be pulled across on a metal track behind the flightdeck door after it closes, and once pulled across can be locked in position with a timelock. This would provide the functional equivalent of a bank vault type door, and it wouldn't have the depressurization problem, and it would be very light, and fairly inexpensive. With two securing hooks on each side of the door, it would keep the door from opening. It would be very hard to cut or shoot through. When the flightdeck is secure, as it would be with such a device, there would be no repetition of the World Trade Center Disaster.

Although I approve of the idea of federalizing airport security and having very high quality uniformed federal personnel do it, I don't think that, by itself, will solve the problem. The Trade Center terrorists used boxcutting knives with 2 inch blades. Pocket knives with 4 inch blades are legal to carry on a U.S. flight. So even a fully trained screener would have let the boxcutting knives onboard in the pockets of passengers. The main weapon was a ruse. A bag was held up and said to be a bomb. The little knives were probably just used to kill the flightdeck crew and wound a few flight attendants to make an impression of seriousness and have the bomb threat taken seriously. So <u>my solution would be</u> to vet all passengers wishing to fly in the U.S.A. The vetting would have to be done by a firm with personnel analysis experience, like an insurance agency, or a credit

agency, or the F.B.I., or even a new branch of the F.A.A. It
could take 6 months. It might require interviews, background
checks, identity verification etc. The pass seeker could pay, say
$500.00 toward reimbursing the government for part of these
costs. If that seems inconvenient, they could just take a train,
or a bus, or go by car. It's far better for Lady Liberty to lose
a finger, than to lose an arm, or a child. We, her children, are
going to have to sacrifice some liberty to maintain our security.
But since the days of Roosevelt we have been taught that there's
no trade-off ever needed -- we can have all our liberty and all
our security. That is a false teaching, and one from which we
must now disenthrall ourselves. Carefully and fairly pre-vetting
all airline passengers and giving them picture identity cards,
which they help pay for, is more reasonable than focusing
exclusively on last minute carry-on baggage and pocket checking
at the airport, even if it's done skillfully.

My own experience in the course of 20 years of legal
practice has included some work on a transponder concept to
prevent situations like the USS Cole, and some investigation of
the Personnel Reliability Program within the Department of
Defense. I would be happy to discuss the two ideas I offer the
Congress today, with you or with a staff member, at your
convenience. You will, no doubt, receive many suggestions. Please
give some time to these and consider them with care. As an
attorney, I am of course deeply aware of the privacy issues
involved in the second suggestion, however these devices and
procedures would be the minimum necessary to effectively address
the threat that we now know exists. Please make the House
Aviation Subcommittee aware of the two ideas I'm offerring, and
this letter may be included in any record of proceedings if you
see fit to do so.

Very Truly Yours

Robert Gary
LT, JAGC, USN (Ret.)

2 PAGE     FAX TO CHERYL 80
202 225 4629
4 OCT 2001
1715 hrs EST

**Robert Gary**
**2211 Washington Ave. (#301)**
**Silver Spring, MD 20910-2620**

Tele: (301) 587-7147
E-mail: Robert.Gary@prodigy.net

Rep. John Mica                              September 14, 2001
House Aviation Subcommittee
2251 Rayburn Building
Washington, DC 20515

Subj:           1. **Barrier to Assure Flightdeck Security**

                2. **Background Checks for Passengers**


Dear Rep. Mica,

        The door between the first class cabin and the
flightdeck cannot be a bank vault type door with a time lock. The
reason for this has to do with sudden depressurization and the
need to permit rapid pressure equalization on both sides of that
barrier. So <u>here's my idea</u>: a triple mesh Kevlar screen that is
set so that it can be pulled across on a metal track behind the
flightdeck door after it closes, and once pulled across can be
locked in position with a timelock. This would provide the
functional equivalent of a bank vault type door, and it wouldn't
have the depressurization problem, and it would be very light,
and fairly inexpensive. With two securing hooks on each side of
the door, it would keep the door from opening. It would be very
hard to cut or shoot through. When the flightdeck is secure, as
it would be with such a device, there would be no repetition of
the World Trade Center Disaster.

        Although I approve of the idea of federalizing airport
security and having very high quality uniformed federal personnel
do it, I don't think that, by itself, will solve the problem. The
Trade Center terrorists used boxcutting knives with 2 inch
blades. Pocket knives with 4 inch blades are legal to carry on a
U.S. flight. So even a fully trained screener would have let the
boxcutting knives onboard in the pockets of passengers. The main
weapon was a ruse. A bag was held up and said to be a bomb. The
little knives were probably just used to kill the flightdeck crew
and wound a few flight attendants to make an impression of
seriousness and have the bomb threat taken seriously. So <u>my
solution would be</u> to vet all passengers wishing to fly in the
U.S.A. The vetting would have to be done by a firm with personnel
analysis experience, like an insurance agency, or a credit

1

agency, or the F.B.I., or even a new branch of the F.A.A. It could take 6 months. It might require interviews, background checks, identity verification etc. The pass seeker could pay, say $500.00 toward reimbursing the government for part of these costs. If that seems inconvenient, they could just take a train, or a bus, or go by car. It's far better for Lady Liberty to lose a finger, than to lose an arm, or a child. We, her children, are going to have to sacrifice some liberty to maintain our security. But since the days of Roosevelt we have been taught that there's no trade-off ever needed -- we can have all our liberty and all our security. That is a false teaching, and one from which we must now disenthrall ourselves. Carefully and fairly pre-vetting all airline passengers and giving them picture identity cards, which they help pay for, is more reasonable than focusing exclusively on last minute carry-on baggage and pocket checking at the airport, even if it's done skillfully.

My own experience in the course of 20 years of legal practice has included some work on a transponder concept to prevent situations like the USS Cole, and some investigation of the Personnel Reliability Program within the Department of Defense. I would be happy to discuss the two ideas I offer the Congress today, with you or with a staff member, at your convenience. You will, no doubt, receive many suggestions. Please give some time to these and consider them with care. As an attorney, I am of course deeply aware of the privacy issues involved in the second suggestion, however these devices and procedures would be the minimum necessary to effectively address the threat that we now know exists. Please make the House Aviation Subcommittee aware of the two ideas I'm offering, and this letter may be included in any record of proceedings if you see fit to do so.

Very Truly Yours

Robert Gary
LT, JAGC, USN (Ret.)

**Robert Gary**
**2211 Washington Ave (#301)**
**Silver Spring, MD 20910-2620**
**Tele: (301)587-7147**

Vice President Richard Cheney                    September 17, 2001
Attn: Mr. **Richard Edelman**
The White House
1600 Pennsylvania Avenue, N.W.
Washington, D.C. 20500

Dear Vice President Cheney,

There are three relatively low risk but highly effective things
that the government might do right now to increase national
security.

Neutron detectors need to be employed at our border, particularly
our border with Mexico. The NEST team has some experience in this
area but I think the work would be more effectively done by
private contractors. Airports also need to be covered, and
seaports as well. The fewer the number of Federal employees
involved in this work the more chance it can be done covertly and
not telegraphing our search effort to the enemy. Private
companies operating on a bounty hunter basis with substantial
Federal funding through contracts with D.I.A. would probably be
the ideal arrangement to keep this monitoring low profile and
staffed with highly competent people.

The Bin Laden businesses in Saudi Arabia, Sudan, Egypt, and
elsewhere need to be taken down to zero cash balances, zero
capital, zero inventories, and zero credit. This is "unfair and
disempowering" to "innocent" family members, and it may cause
strains in our relations with the Saudis, but it is necessary to
cut Osama Bin Laden off from all access to hard currency, gold,
or any valuable resources. His power has been abused.

Arabs in the U.S. who arrived after 1990, and are male, and are
under 65, and are not presently U.S. citizens should be declared
"persona non grata" in the U.S. and asked to leave. Again this is
potentially unfair to a significant percentage of this group but
it is entirely lawful, it is in the interests of Americans, and
it would cut Osama Bin Laden off from his personnel resources,
and some of his funding, in the U.S.

As I'm sure you know I have worked intensively since the bombing
of the USS Cole to get a proximity control transponder
demonstration project up and running within the U.S. Navy. I've
communicated with **Rep. Morella, and Sen. Warner**, who were good
enough to facilitate a technical meeting between myself and
representatives (at NCIS) of the CNO. Mr. **Eric Edelman**'s letter
to me of July 26, 2001 indicated that it would be "premature to

address the specifics of any defense issue", and this means that the transponder project is set back by at least three years, and that nothing truly effective will be done to prevent a recurrence of what happened to the USS Cole until around 2005.

In light of repeated security difficulties, perhaps it's time to start thinking outside the box a little. If you want to think outside the box, you have to go to some people who are outside the box. It's not sensible to keep going back to the same insiders/experts, expecting that after a long series of security failures that they will suddenly know how to prevent the next one. The instinct in government, as in the teaching "profession", always seems to involve going to those who have been in place holding official positions for a long time, no matter how often they have failed or how costly their failures. Fresh thinking is needed. People outside the box might be helpful with that.

I have been a public interest attorney for 20 years, much of which has been spent in the security, emergency management, and nuclear fields. I don't know who is truly qualified to speak for all of the American people on the subject of whether they wish to have young Arab male non-citizens in this country at their sufferance. I cannot claim to speak for each and every American citizen in that regard. But I think I speak for many when I say that young Arab aliens are here on revokable licenses from the INS and we just don't need them here right now. We don't have enough tax dollars to pay enough investigators to track their every movement, phonecall, and e-mail. Americans can do things that are in their own interests for that reason alone. This used to be called raison d'etat. My President, of whom I am very proud, says we are in a true war. So, let's put our tax money into effectively prosecuting that war and not playing cat and mouse games with foreign nationals who are here at our discretion, and who have no Constitutional or legal rights to be here. If we declare non grata 100 people for every 1 prospective suicide bomber that we expel, that's a good enough ratio to make this expulsion plan worthwhile as an effective security measure that is low risk, low cost, totally legal, and comparatively humane. This measure, if adopted, will be tested in the U.S. Supreme Court, no doubt, and as a member of the Bar of that Court, I will be there to file Amicus Curiae briefs in favor of this measure because it is vital, reasonable, and necessary. I told **Senator Lugar** back on October 28, 2000 that there was a theoretical danger of a nuclear bomb carried by speedboat from Green Bay to the base of the Sears Tower in Chicago. He was busy with his campaign. I realize this issue is complex and busy people have many things to do. I hope we can do something effective, and not just put on a show in our war of terrorism.

Very Truly yours,

cc: Shelby, Warner, Lugar
    Morella, and Cox

## *Publications of Robert Gary 1970 - 1998*

### 1998:

**Greek Tragedy**
Comment on the Tobacco Settlement in April 1998
Rollcall (The Newspaper of Capitol Hill Since 1955) Vol 43,
Number 75, Monday April 30, 1998, Page 4 (Washington D.C.)

### 1997:

**The Case Against MOX** (The Proposed Mixed Oxide Fuels Program of
the Department of Energy), Robert Gary,
The George Washington University Jacob Burns Law Library
Catalog Number: KF3948 .A75 C37 1997. (Washington, D.C.).

### 1995:

**Collected Documents in Support of Suits Concerning the Effects of
Exposure to Radiation on Servicemen in the 1950's who were on
Active Duty at Camp Desert Rock Nevada**, Robert Gary, The George
Washington University Jacob Burns Law Library (rare book
collection), Catalog Number: KF1321:b.C65. (Washington D.C.)

### 1994:

**Selections from the Harrisburg Papers on the Ten Mile Rule:
selected documents in docket no. 50-289 license no. DPR-50
petition under 10 CFR 2.206, including DD-94-03 to obtain an
emergency evacuation plan for the people of Harrisburg
Pennsylvania.**

Published: Silver Spring, Md.: PICA, (The Pennsylvania Institute
for Clean Air) 1994. Subjects: Three Mile Island Nuclear Power
plant (Pa.); evacuation of civilians -- Pennsylvania --
Harrisburg; metropolitan area; statistics.

CALL NUMBER Pennsylvania State Libraries: 363.179 Se48
Location Room 102, Main Open Stacks.

CALL NUMBER Catholic University of America Judge Kathryn J.
DuFour Law Library
Catalog Number: TK1345.H37 S45 1994. (Washington, D.C.)

**Legislative Efforts to Obtain Fair Compensation for the Nuclear
Veterans: A Chronicle Spanning 15 Years**, Robert Gary, Catholic
University of America Judge Kathryn J. DuFour Law Library
(government publications section)
Catalog Number: KF7745.A25 G37 1994. (Washington, D.C.).

*1994 Cont.*

<u>Calculating Compensation for Radiation Victims Based on a Retrospective Probability Analysis</u>, Robert Gary, Congressional Record of the United States, June 29, 1994 (introduced into the record by Hon. Joseph P. Kennedy, II), pages E1351 to E1353.

*1992:*

<u>Cost-Effective Ways to Comply with the New Clean Air Act</u>, Gary Associates, Pennsylvania State Library Catalog Number: KF3812.G3 (Harrisburg, Pennsylvania).

*1991:*

<u>Interactive Multimedia Industry Blueprint</u>, Gary Associates, unpublished document done on a research contract and distributed to private clients.

<u>The Future of Interactive Multimedia for Education</u>, Gary Associates, unpublished document done on a research contract and distributed to private clients.

*1990:*

<u>Who Owns Railroad Rights of Way?</u> Robert Gary, a series of eight legal opinions written for inclusion in seminars given by the Rails to Trails Conservancy and sponsored by the National Park Service. (Washington, D.C.)

*1986:*

<u>The Foundations and Effects of Antitrust Policy Under the Reagan Administration and Some Suggested Alternatives</u>, Robert Gary (MBA Thesis), The George Washington University, Gelman Library (special collections), Catalog Number: AS 36 .G3 1986. (Washington, D.C.)

<u>The Theory of Retrospective Causality for Assessing Cases of Toxic Exposure such as Radiation</u>, Robert Gary, testimony before Committee of Veterans' Affairs, U.S. House of Representatives, Serial #99-52, volume 1, pages 206 et seq, 99th Congress, 2nd sess, Government Printing Office, (1986:Washington DC).

*1982:*

<u>The Feres Doctrine</u>, Robert Gary, unpublished, a formal lecture given at the Navy Legal Service Office, Subic Bay, Republic of the Philippines on 25 October 1982 to fellow members of the Navy JAG Corps, and to members of the NAVMAR TRIJUDIC.

_1980:_

<u>Plaintiff's Reply Brief in Punnett v Carter</u>, unpublished but the case is cited at 621 F 2d. 578 (3rd Cir. 1980). This major brief addressed the issue: Should Injunctive Relief be Granted to Protect the Health and Safety of Veterans Exposed to Radiation at the Nevada Test Site? The brief was defeated by the Acting Assistant Attorney General of the U.S., and the court did not grant injunctive relief as sought in the brief, and oral argument. (Philadelphia, Pennsylvania)

<u>Plaintiff's Reply Brief in Johnsrud v. Carter</u>, unpublished but the case is cited at 620 F 2d. 29 (3rd Cir. 1980). This major brief addressed the issue: Does a Federal District Court Have Subject Matter Jurisdiction to Order the Government of the United States to Provide Funds to Provide a Truthful Health Effects Warning and to Evacuate People From the Areas Surrounding Three Mile Island During a Nuclear Emergency? The brief prevailed over the Acting Assistant Attorney General of the U.S., and the court found that jurisdiction did exist in the U.S. District Court as argued in the brief, and oral argument. (Philadelphia, Pennsylvania)

_1979:_

<u>Statistical Estimation of Retrospective Causality in Radiation Cases, and Victim's Compensation Models</u>, Robert Gary, testimony before the Veterans' Affairs Committee of the Senate of the United States, Serial# CIS S761-2.7, pages 295 et seq., 96th Congress, 1st Session, Government Printing Office 1979 (Washington, D.C.)

_1972_

<u>A Bill to Amend the Maryland State Code Concerning Selection Methods for Liberal Arts Professors in Maryland Universities</u>, H.R. 1178, Introduced and debated March 6, 1972, but not enacted, Maryland House of Delegates. (Annapolis, Maryland).

**Robert Gary**
**2211 Washington Ave (#301)**
**Silver Spring, MD 20910-2620**
**Tele: (301)587-7147**

President George W. Bush                    September 17, 2001
The White House
1600 Pennsylvania Avenue, N.W.
Washington, D.C. 20500

Dear President Bush,

Last year I wrote to Senator Lugar and to Vice President Cheney
in connection with transponders to prevent a repetition of the
USS Cole incident. In that letter I described an attack not very
different from what happened at the World Trade Center except
that in my hypothetical scenario the attack happened at the base
of the Sears Tower, using a nuclear weapon (W-88) in a speedboat,
and it killed 3 million people within 60 minutes.

I've worked in the military, as a Navy JAG, and in emergency
management, in security-related matters, as a public interest
attorney, for about 20 years. I have a few basic steps that the
U.S. could now take to increase its security in light of the
September 11, 2001 events.

First, it makes sense to focus on the issue of who gets on
planes. In Israel, all passengers boarding El Al flights are
pre-screened by Israeli intelligence long before they arrive at
the airport. At the airport they are closely interrogated to
ensure that no false names or disguises have been used. We could
phase in a similar arrangement in the U.S.A., starting with
business people. We could use I.D. cards with retinal imaging,
voiceprint, fingerprint and pictures on them. Taking the process
layer by layer starting with the easiest, we could get the whole
U.S. flying public in the system within 5 years at a cost of  a
few Billion dollars. Once it's possible to know who is on the
plane, the personnel reliability aspect of the problem is solved.

Second, behind the flimsy door into the cockpit, you need a
triple thick Kevlar mesh screen that can be pulled across on a
steel track, hooked to the back of the door, and secured with a
timelock. Triple mesh Kevlar of the sort used in bulletproof
vests is hard to cut through, even with a torch, and impossible
to shoot through, but since it is porous, it has the advantage of
not creating a de-pressurization hazard. The need to accommodate
rapid pressure equalization within the fuselage is the reason why
cockpit doors are so flimsy. The Israelis again have a system
similar to what I've described and they also have a secret system

within the cockpit to immobilize and intruder instantly just in case their barrier is compromised. Just buying the technology from El Al would make sense. Cockpit security goes hand in hand with personnel reliability and together the highjack risk is reduced as low as reasonably achievable.

Beyond the highjacking issue we need to look at recently arrived young males of Arab descent in the U.S.A. For starters, they shouldn't be taking flight lessons here. Those that do not have ironclad legal rights to be here such as citizenship or credentials of a diplomatic nature, should not be here at all. There is not enough money in the U.S. Treasury to hire enough F.B.I agents to listen to every phonecall, follow every young Arab, decipher every coded e-mail, keep track of every possible cell of El Queda in the U.S. We don't have the manpower, the cash, the time, the technology, or the warrants. It is no crime for the citizens of the U.S. to do things that are in their own interests. It would be in the interest of our citizens to declare all male Arabs under 65 who are not citizens or diplomats and who arrived in the U.S. after 1990 "persona non grata". It would not be necessary to say any unkind things about them, or to accuse them of anything, or to assert any particular suspicion. We could simply say that we don't have the investigative powers to sort out terrorists from ordinary people in that category (which is obviously true -- we clearly don't have that ability). The legislators of this country, along with yourself, and the Supreme Court can take an action for the general welfare for reasons of state (Raison D'Etat) and that is no crime. Such a law would be tested in our highest Court. The civil libertarians must have a full and fair opportunity to be heard.

There's a profound paradox at the center of our thinking about the World Trade Center attack. On the one hand we say that it is a transforming incident, that it will change everything, that we are now embarked on a war against terrorism, but on the other hand we say that if it causes us to change any fundamental thing about the way we do business, then the terrorists have won. Both of these ideas cannot be true. If we are truly at war, then we must change some fundamental things. When we were truly at war against Japan, we rounded up Japanese who were actually citizens and put them in detention camps. My suggestion does not go nearly that far. I'm talking about non-citizens, and I'm talking about declaring them persona non grata not detaining them in any way. From a security perspective it makes no difference where they go, as long as they are not here among us. It would, no doubt, be unfair to 75% or maybe 95% of them, but then, life isn't fair, as 5000 Americans found out on September 11, 2001.

The persona non grata option is reasonably necessary to meaningfully reduce the risk of terror on our soil. In other words, without being a panacea, it would be an effective part of a more comprehensive solution. Beyond being effective it disempowers, disprivileges, and disenables a group of people whose power privileges and ability have been abused by a small but unidentifiable contingent among them. The persona non grata option is reasonably related to the objective of prevention under the real world condition of imperfect knowledge and limited investigative resources, and it is humane in the sense that no one is killed or physically harmed or even detained. It is inexpensive compared to playing cat and mouse with a few very smart but extremely vicious mice hidden among lots or ordinary look-alikes. It obviously amounts to "doing something", and thus it might satisfy the public's deep need to see something done.

To fully appreciate the persona non grata option, it must be compared to the viable military options. It is much better than launching cruise missiles at Kabul, or Baghdad, or puptent training camps in the badlands of Afghanistan. It is much better than forming an alliance with Pakistan, the nation whose intelligence service created the Taliban, set them up in Afghanistan, and has used them in its campaigns in Kashmir. Such an alliance may have worked well for us in the days of the Soviet occupation of Afghanistan, but the world has changed very greatly since then, and today such an alliance would be highly unreliable, and worse than useless from an intelligence and military perspective. Going into Afghanistan, as the Soviets did, is probably not an ideal option even with Division strength special forces, even with massive air support, even with ground based target designation for targets to be hit by cruise missiles launched from standoff B-52's or Navy guided missile cruisers. The problem is that of collateral damage. When we tried to go in for Aideed in Somalia he just disappeared into the people and by keeping himself surrounded by women and children at all times he assured that any attack which might kill him would inflict massive collateral damage which could then be used for propaganda purposes. If we couldn't extricate Aideed in Somalia, (partly due to the protection he got from Bin Laden), our chances of extricating Bin Laden himself from Afghanistan, or getting a clean kill, are very low. If history is any guide, our chances of taking significant casualties on the ground there are very high.

Going after Bin Laden's money by direct on the ground action against banks, individuals, and businesses in Saudi Arabia, Egypt, Sudan, Yemen, Qatar, and elsewhere, would be far less risky, and far more effective. Without money, especially gold and hard currency, Bin Laden would be another angry face in the vast crowd of extreme militant fundamentalist America haters. Without money or agents in the U.S. his face in the crowd would have no more meaning than the others.

Knocking down some buildings in Kabul, and maybe some palaces or Chemical/Biological/Nuclear research and storage centers in Iraq would be a useful part of the total response equation for the reasons eloquently stated by Secretary Eagleburger. We need to strike hard and make the Taliban and other harborers pay a big price for what has been done to 5000 Americans. Today's predicament arises directly from the abject failures of the CIA, State, and DOD under President Bill Clinton. From 1992 till your Inauguration, we never had the right information, we never did the right things, and we never put security first.

Going in on the ground is a grim option that makes sense only if all else fails. If we must go in let's not do it with the "assistance" or "permission" of Pakistan, and let's not do it with the idea of "bringing Bin Laden to justice" We should go with the idea of suspending the sovereignty of Afghanistan until an acceptable government can be constituted. The country may need to be De-Talibanized before any kind of democratic rule would be sensible. It could take 5 or 10 years of essentially American military occupation there. It would be an example to other rogue states like Iraq, but a costly exercise for our already overstretched and underfunded military. Less ambitious ground missions would be dangerous way out of proportion to their marginal value, <u>even if we captured or killed Bin Laden</u>.

Beyond all of this we need imagination -- the kind of imagination that terrorists have. We need to start thinking about who we sell biological germ incubators, pesticide component chemicals, and blueprints to our nuclear facilities to, the same kind of precaution that we failed to take on flight training to needs to be applied in 20 other areas. If we can catch El Queda or other terrorist cells while they are preparing to strike that would be significant to our security. This is more a matter of monitoring and analysis than covert human intelligence as practiced overseas. We will need to amend or repeal the Posse Comitatus Act so that the F.B.I. and C.I.A. can work closely on a routine basis on cases related to terrorism. Civil libertarians must have their opportunity to try to strike down in the Courts whatever actions this Democratic Republic takes to increase its security. In the meantime however, legislation should proceed guided only by <u>what is reasonably necessary for the public good in these new circumstances</u>. The Justices will sort out the Constitutional issues by weighing all the variables, realities, and rights. Things change, laws change -- we have a living Constitution. Not one of the Founders would have wanted our laws to be a straightjacket under circumstances such as the present. If they were still in charge, they would make big changes, as <u>when they were, they did</u>. We are here now in their stead, and must do what's right <u>for our time</u>.

Very truly yours,


Robert Gary

4

**Robert Gary**
**2211 Washington Ave (#301)**
**Silver Spring, MD 20910-2620**
**Tele: (301)587-7147**

Hon Norm Mineta                                    September 18, 2001
Secretary of Transportation
U.S. Department of Transportation
400  7th  Street, NW
Washington, DC 20590

Dear Secretary Mineta,

After the USS Cole incident I worked intensively for about a year to get a transponder system up and running the protect Navy warships. I have a few technical suggestions that might be implemented through the FAA to prevent another attack like that which occurred on September 11, 2001 on the World Trade Center Towers.

As a basic line of defense the isolation of the cockpit from intruders is obviously required. My suggestion is along the lines of measures already taken by El Al. First, you need a Kevlar mesh screen that can be pulled across on a bolted down metal track. This would be the same triple thickness Kevlar used in bulletproof vests for policemen. It does not create a pressure equalization problem but it does positively stop intruders with a barrier that can be hooked to the back of the door on both sides and locked in place with a timelock. This sort of material is light, flexible, and fairly inexpensive compared to complete redesigns of the cockpit door arrangement. The Israelis have a second line of defense in the cockpit that is secret. I can only speculate, but what I know is that if somehow an intruder got into a cockpit of an El Al plane he would be instantly immobilized and rendered incapable of further action.

There are three ways to do this. Stun gun technology, pepper spray technology, and nitrogen asphyxiation technology. Each of these ways has virtues, and each has drawbacks. Stun gun is the quickest. If I were designing such a system I would put the stun projectors in the deckplate so they would strike upward

1

from below into the lower legs and thighs. 400,000 volts at low amperage would incapacitate an intruder in a tenth of a second, and for at least 5 minutes. This would give the flightcrew time to put the cuffs on the attacker. The drawback of this technique is the hazard created by releasing electrostatic electricity anywhere inside of a plane in flight. That danger could be mitigated by using cathodic protection methods.

Pepper spray would have to be of a sort that would penetrate any ordinary respirator. We can assume that the flightdeck personnel have access to bottled air. If the intruder does not have such access, a device that would fill the flightdeck with pepper spray, might be adequate. The drawback of this method is the fact that passengers would also be affected, and possibly killed by exposure to strong pepper spray which inevitably would find its way into the passenger areas.

Nitrogen asphyxiation would again require that the flightdeck crew have access to bottled air. If the flightdeck were flooded with nitrogen, the intruder would have no warning whatsoever, they would simply black out and keel over. There is no respiratory distress with nitrogen asphyxiation -- no warning of oxygen deprivation -- just sudden blackout, similar to finger pressure on the jugular and just as quick. The drawback here is the need to protect the passengers, which I think can be overcome by pumping outside air at low pressure into the passenger compartment. The pressure has to be lower than the pressure of the nitrogen flooding the flightdeck so the intruder has no access to oxygen. To foil this method would require intruders to bring their own bottled air. No other sort of respirator would be of any value. But bottles of compressed air could be detected at the airport, even assuming that the screening system does not get significantly better, which I think in fact it will.

Apart from the issue of flightdeck intruder security, which I think is the most basic and obvious step you can take to prevent a repetition of the events of September 11, 2001, the next level of improvement would be in the area of passenger assessment from the perspective of security risk. Every passenger on an El Al flight receives a clearance from Israeli intelligence long before they get anywhere near the airport. This clearance is given based on a very thorough background check and identity verification process. El Al performs searches and interrogations at the airport just prior to boarding, but it does not rely exclusively on looking in people's bags and in their pockets. We must, I think do the same.

This involves two steps, both of which would be anathema to civil libertarians, but both of which are necessary under present conditions for the general welfare, and thus Constitutional and lawful. Identity/Security cards should be issued to the U.S. flying public based on comprehensive background checks and security analysis. This could be done in five years, for a few billion dollars and the card recipients could bear part of the costs, say a third, with the airlines putting in a third, and the government putting in a third. I would start with the business travellers -- they are the easiest to work with, and their cooperation would create familiarization with the process for the other members of the flying public. Assuming that comprehensive background checks take six months to do and cost around $1,500 per person, and assuming that 50 million people need to be cleared and given very secure I.D. cards with retinal imaging, fingerprint data, photos, holograms, etc, it would take five years to get a system in place that would reduce the probability of a highjacking by 95% from where it is now.

The second part of this approach would be to alter the Posse Comitatus Act so that local police, the F.B.I., the D.I.A., and the C.I.A. could all work as a unified team to accomplish the security clearances. Another piece of law that would have to be changed, would be the law of common carriers, some of which amounts to Constitutional law. Airlines would have to be completely free at their own discretion to declare any potential customer "persona non grata" for any reason, or for no reason. Giving the airlines this freedom would be one of the necessary steps to assure that the people who board planes in the U.S. are highly unlikely to be terrorists. Maintaining a common carrier concept when there are hundreds of thousands of persons in the U.S. whose backgrounds and intentions cannot be discerned with any real reliability is imprudent, and it would represent a victory of misguided egalitarianism and civil rights emphasis over good sense. People that are differently situated may be treated differently when necessity requires it. Emergencies and conditions of war create new necessities. We cannot reasonably take the position that if terrorists can make us change any fundamental things about the way we do business, then they have won. That position puts abstract metaphysics above security for innocent life and it's just not reasonable under current circumstances. In a new situation we regretfully must disenthrall ourselves from some of our traditional ideas and ways of doing things prior to September 11, 2001. If the events of that day change everything, and put us into a true war against terrorism, then some things will have to change. We must not take the position that if we change anything then the terrorists have won. Even with significant but necessary changes, we will still be the greatest Democratic Republic history has ever seen.

The suggestions made here are as moderate as they can be while still being effective. The Founders of this country, when they were in charge, made far bigger changes. This is our time, and circumstance, and we must reshape our laws to meet our current and future needs.

Civil libertarians will have a fair opportunity to seek to strike down some or all of these suggested measures by taking them to the U.S. Supreme Court. That's part of our system, and it's a good part. I have been a member of the Bar of that Court since 1985, and I am confident that it will do what is reasonable (which might include slightly amending some of the ideas presented here). The details of how the Court will balance the right to life and security against the right to privacy and travel cannot be predicted at this time. DOT should take a hard line on security and leave it to the Court to sort out, with the assistance of the Solicitor General, Civil Libertarians and filers of Amicus Curiae briefs.

If you wish any further information, I live nearby and would be happy to serve in any way that is possible and appropriate. Enclosed is a publications list to indicate my experience in the emergency management, public interest, and security areas. It does not include my recent work on a transponder system to prevent a re-occurrence of the USS Cole incident. This work was done on a volunteer basis, as a public interest attorney, in consultation with NCIS and the Chief of Naval Operations, and with the approval of several members of Congress. It is too sensitive to publish at this time, however it is available for you to examine if you wish.

Very truly yours,


Robert Gary
LT, JAGC, USN (Ret.)


Encl: Publications List for Robert Gary 1970 to 1998

**Robert Gary**
**2211 Washington Ave (#301)**
**Silver Spring, MD 20910-2620**
**Tele: (301)587-7147**

George Tennet                                    September 18, 2001
Director of Central Intelligence
Central Intelligence Agency                      <u>**URGENT & SENSITIVE**</u>
Washington DC 20505

Dear DCI Tennet,

I am an attorney in the Washington area, and have some experience with security and emergency management matters, but more to the point I have the ability to listen very closely to remarks.

Former President Clinton was on T.V. today doing his first interview about his thoughts concerning the World Trade Center Terror attack and Bin Laden in general.

Here is part of what he said. He said that when the U.S. launched the cruise missiles against the Bin Laden training camps in Afghanistan several years ago --- "we told the Pakistanis at the last minute .... and according the reports we got back later we barely missed Bin Laden ... and got some of his close lieutenants". 20 years as a lawyer has taught me to listen very closely and for meaning.

I would ask Clinton:

1) What is the **precise** meaning of the term "the last minute"? Things that are considered "the last minute" between nations might actually be a matter of 15 minutes or even 30 minutes in real actual time. I would want to find out from Clinton immediately what "the last minute" meant when he made that remark -- how many seconds precisely, was it more than 60 seconds, was it more than 5 minutes, was it as much as 15 minutes?

2) How far can a man in Bin Laden's physical condition run in whatever time it actually was? Is it 50 yards? Is it 100 yards? is it a quarter mile, or a half mile?

3) What was the kill zone of the cruise missiles that were launched, considering the terrain in which they landed, and the defilade (shielding) factor of that rough terrain? And considering the ability of a trained man to take effective cover? Was it 50 yards, 100 yards, a quarter mile?

These questions are **urgent** right now because we are in
the process of considering trusting General Musharif of Pakistan
with information that will be pivotal should we decide to take
action in Afghanistan. If the Pakistanis sold us out during the
Clinton cruise missile strike, aren't the chances even greater
that today they would telegraph every move we reveal to them to
our target -- Bin Laden -- in Afghanistan?

Tomorrow's Presidential Daily Brief might be enhanced
if there were some discussion of these questions there. <u>I don't
need to know the answers</u>, although I hope you will do me the
courtesy of acknowledging receipt of this letter.

I earnestly hope that you inquire, get precise
information, from Clinton and others, and include some analysis
of your findings in the report you provide to my President George
W. Bush as soon as reasonably possible. With the initiatives that
are in process by **<u>Senator Biden</u>** and by **<u>Secretary Colin Powell</u>**, it
seems to me that we need to analyze the past, in light of
Clinton's remarks of today, to provide some valuable guidance for
the future of any disclosures that we might make to anyone in or
from Pakistan, for any reason, at any time. It seems apparent
that the last time we struck there our cause was lost before we
began, probably only half an hour before we began, but a miss is
as good as a mile, and in that case a miss may have been by about
a mile. If today we can figure out that we made mistakes in the
past maybe somehow we could avoid repeating those precise and
identical mistakes in the very near future.

There's a lot at stake this time. We need to know who
is on our side. This is a skill area that we do not seem to have,
probably because of our idealism and very positive view of human
nature. But the failure of a surprise surgical missile strike
this time may require a ground assault down the road and
consequent loss of American lives. We should be very careful
about who we share information with if we feel that a successful
surgical missile strike requires the element of **total** surprise --
not almost surprised, not 15 or 30 minutes away from being
surprised, but totally surprised -- the kind of surprise that
proves lethal even to a wily, trained, and physically fit fellow
like Bin Laden, and even in very rugged terrain that provides a
high defilade (shielding) factor.

Very truly yours,


Robert Gary
LT, JAGC, USN (Ret.)

cc: Sen **Biden**, Sen **Shelby**, Secretary **Powell**

**Robert Gary, Esq.**
**2211 Washington Ave (#301)**
**Silver Spring, MD 20910-2620**
**Tele: (301) 587-7147**

Senator Arlen Spector                     September 20, 2001
U.S. Senate
Washington DC 20510

Dear Senator Spector,

      You and I worked together as lawyers in Philadelphia back in the late 1970's, and you worked with me again in 1994 on my effort to get the nuclear emergency evacuation plan for the city of Harrisburg Pennsylvania which was joined by Sen Harris Wofford. I hope you will recall my work, and the fact that I have 20 years of experience in the law as it applies to nuclear matters, emergency management, and security.

      Today I heard the hearings of the Subcommittee on Appropriations of the Joint Senate and House Transportation Committee, and my attention was drawn specifically to your comments and those of Rep Harold Rogers.

      Thinking the unthinkable in regard to air travel safety I have developed a plan that would require background checks and air travel security I.D. cards for 50 million members of the U.S. public who fly at least once a year. This plan could be voluntary for the air traveller -- if they don't want to have a background check, and be pre-screened they can decline to pursue an I.D. card. We have an expression in the law volenti non fit injuria -- the things we voluntarily do are not injuries done to us. So the issue of privacy is a non-issue in a voluntary program. The cost of the pre-screenings would be around $1,500 per person, a third of which cold be borne by the individual seeking the air travel security I.D. card, or his company. It could take 2 to 6 months for private firms to do the background checks -- I would suggest credit card companies and insurance companies already have the skills and much of the required information. FBI, NSA, CIA, and DIA could play a role, as could state and local police data centers. The Posse Comitatus Act is likely to be one of the casualties of the September 11, 2001 terror attack as well it should be. New circumstances require new recourses, and even some diminution of old liberties, privacies and niceties of separation of government functions.

1

The program could be phased in over 5 years, perhaps working through 10 million people a year, and starting with the easiest which would be the executive business passengers who are Americans and who work for American companies. Once the work process is up and running, the program might extend out to active duty military, military veterans, and finally to other American citizens. The idea here is to pre-screen as many passengers as possible so that whatever is done at the airport in terms of the baggage and pocket searches and the CAPS (Computer Assisted Profile System) can concentrate on the few individuals who are not pre-screened. There are circumstances where the airlines should have the right to obviate their general obligation as common carriers and, in the interest of public safety, and at their sole discretion, for any reason, or for no reason, they should be able to deny boarding to anyone. They should be able to declare certain individuals "persona non grata" on all their flights. And they should be able to offer less drastic measures such as a tyvek suit, and hand and leg restraint, and a no-carry on option so that they have a full range of measures that can be applied in proportion to the perceived risk of carrying a specific passenger. Some human dignity, and some sense of equality are also going to be casualties of the terror attack on September 11, 2001. I am the first to be appalled that we would have to pay such prices. After 20 years as a Constitutional lawyer, I do understand our traditions, and their unique value in creating the enterprise called USA. However, as a public interest lawyer in the security field, I'm hardheaded about what needs to be done -- what would be effective -- what would make a difference. Knowing who is on the plane is vital. It's not a substitute for pocket and bag checks, and it's surely not a substitute for a Kevlar reinforced cockpit door, but it is a sine qua non of any effective security system -- and it's something we just don't have now.

I was not pleased in listening to the hearing at most of the remarks that were made by most of the people that were there. The extensive and repetitious praise of the FAA for what a wonderful job they have done struck me as untrue, and unnecessary, and really quite stupid. If there's one thing that clear as crystal it's that the FAA has done a terrible job, and so have the airlines in the area of air security. This is true even after the Gore Commission Report on Airline Security and the excellent work of Mary Sciavo the I.G at FAA which brought to light glaring deficiencies, the same ones we are talking about today, five years ago. Interbranch diplomacy, and inter-agency office politics are probably called for in some situations but the effusive praise of the FAA under these circumstances was simply unwarranted. Americans can hear what's phoney. It's better to keep it real, I think.

Another very disturbing element in the hearing was the repeated insistence by Administrator Jane Garvey that certain matters be discussed only in closed session. The FAA does not want to publicly discuss the security measures it is taking, or is thinking about taking. This would be a very reasonable position in any government except a democratic republic where every new measure gets hashed out in public before it is authorized, and certainly before any funds are appropriated for it. I think we should go the other way right from the start and say, "There can be no non-public public safety countermeasures for air security." This creates much greater accountability at FAA. They will have to do intelligent things, and without undue delay, and with competent execution on their plans, or the transparency of the process will bring their deficiencies to public attention and to responsive and corrective action by you the Senators and Congresspersons. Letting the FAA operate behind an cloak of hush hush security secrecy means letting them get away with another few decades of incompetence, confusion, mismanagement, and downright stupidity. I wish there were a nicer way to say this. The only things that should be kept fully secret are onboard combat tactics by crew and equipment and maneuver. There's no need for that information to be public knowledge prior to the moment of its use. But broad strategies for passenger screening, and pre-screening, and information gathering related thereto, are radical changes made necessary by the horrific air terror event, and if we are to put them in place they might as well be part of our public forum of debate. To try to make the sort of intelligence upgrades that need to be made in secret is to give the FAA license to drag it feet and botch the job, and it would give the kneejerk civil libertarians an opportunity to conduct a veritable Donnybrook of legal challenges down to road. As a person who expects to write some Amicus Curiae briefs when the airline security countermeasures issue makes it to the U.S. Supreme Court, I would like to line the ongoing and future facts up so that my arguments have some appeal and seem wise and reasonable to that Court. I'm in favor of taking fairly radical steps if they are the most moderate effective solution. Israeli intelligence already does full field background checks and pre-screens every passenger that boards an El Al plane. If we decided to do these on a voluntary but wholesale basis in the USA for the air travelling public, we could do the whole thing in 5 years for less than $10 Billion. The airlines could pay a third, the passengers could pay a third, and the government could pay a third. Those passengers who want to opt out could come to the airport 3 hours ahead of time, board in tyvek suits, with no carry ons, sit next to an air marshall (possibly in some form of restraints), or just drive or take the train. Everybody can exercise their liberty in their own way, but keep in mind that the other passengers have a right to life which is involved here, and the government has a right to national security and the protection of people on the ground (public safety). Whatever the law may have been with regard to the "duty" for tort purposes of

the airlines and the government prior to September 11, 2001, it's
is now very different. The duty of a reasonable airline and the
duty of a reasonable government is to take effective steps to
minimize the risk that major air terror happens again in the USA.
The risk must go down to "as low as reasonably achievable".
Transparency in deliberations about most of the ways to do this
and the progress and outcomes pursuant to the FAA's plans is
vital. Let's not try to make major changes behind closed doors,
and lets not confine ourselves to such minor changes that they
have virtually no impact on the security threat. Wars are
conducted in public. That's where the action happens. That's
where the plans should be deliberated. We all have to understand
and participate. It's not just a matter of recruiting foreign
allies to join us, we need to recruit the American people into
some significantly new ways of doing business. This process of
orientation and societal re-alignment is the crux of any
significant increase in our air security posture. It is a sad day
for America. Lady Liberty may lose a finger in the ensuing
changes. But it's better that she lose a finger than an arm, or a
child. What is necessary, is proper.


Very truly yours,

Robert Gary, Esq.


P.S. Feel free to use excerpts from this letter in any documents
or publications if you feel it might be useful, helpful, and
appropriate. Because of the unavoidable critical tone of some
wording in this letter, it might be better not to publish the
entire text verbatim.


Enclosure: Publications List as background FYI, and to remind you
of the projects we worked on together in the past

**Robert Gary, Esq.**
**2211 Washington Ave (#301)**
**Silver Spring, MD 20910-2620**
**Tele: (301) 587-7147**

Co-Chairman Harold Rogers                    September 20, 2001
Sub-Committee on Appropriations
Joint Committee on Transportation
U.S. House of Representatives
Washington DC 20510

Dear Chairman Rogers,

Today I heard the hearings of the Subcommittee on Appropriations of the Joint Senate and House Transportation Committee, and my attention was drawn specifically to your comments and those of Rep Harold Rogers.

Thinking the unthinkable in regard to air travel safety I have developed a plan that would require background checks and air travel security I.D. cards for 50 million members of the U.S. public who fly at least once a year. This plan could be voluntary for the air traveller -- if they don't want to have a background check, and be pre-screened they can decline to pursue an I.D. card. We have an expression in the law "Volenti non fit injuria" -- the things we voluntarily do are not injuries done to us. So the issue of privacy is a non-issue in a voluntary program. The cost of the pre-screenings would be around $1,500 per person, a third of which cold be borne by the individual seeking the air travel security I.D. card, or his company. It could take 2 to 6 months for private firms to do the background checks -- I would suggest credit card companies and insurance companies already have the skills and much of the required information. FBI, NSA, CIA, and DIA could play a role, as could state and local police data centers. The Posse Comitatus Act is likely to be one of the casualties of the September 11, 2001 terror attack as well it should be. New circumstances require new recourses, and even some diminution of old liberties, privacies and niceties of separation of government functions.

The program could be phased in over 5 years, perhaps working through 10 million people a year, and starting with the easiest which would be the executive business passengers who are Americans and who work for American companies. Once the work process is up and running, the program might extend out to active duty military, military veterans, and finally to other American

1

citizens. The idea here is to pre-screen as many passengers as possible so that whatever is done at the airport in terms of the baggage and pocket searches and the CAPS (Computer Assisted Profile System) can concentrate on the few individuals who are not pre-screened. There are circumstances where the airlines should have the right to obviate their general obligation as common carriers and, in the interest of public safety, and at their sole discretion, for any reason, or for no reason, they should be able to deny boarding to anyone. They should be able to declare certain individuals "persona non grata" on all their flights. And they should be able to offer less drastic measures such as a tyvek suit, and hand and leg restraint, and a no-carry on option so that they have a full range of measures that can be applied in proportion to the perceived risk of carrying a specific passenger. Some human dignity, and some sense of equality are also going to be casualties of the terror attack on September 11, 2001. I am the first to be appalled that we would have to pay such prices. After 20 years as a Constitutional lawyer, I do understand our traditions, and their unique value in creating the enterprise called USA. However, as a public interest lawyer in the security field, I'm hardheaded about what needs to be done -- what would be effective -- what would make a difference. Knowing who is on the plane is vital. It's not a substitute for pocket and bag checks, and it's surely not a substitute for a Kevlar reinforced cockpit door, but it is a sine qua non of any effective security system -- and it's something we just don't have now.

A disturbing element in the hearing was the repeated insistence by Administrator Jane Garvey that certain matters be discussed only in closed session. The FAA does not want to publicly discuss the security measures it is taking, or is thinking about taking. This would be a very reasonable position in any government except a democratic republic where every new measure gets hashed out in public before it is authorized, and certainly before any funds are appropriated for it. I think we should go the other way right from the start and say, "There can be no non-public public safety countermeasures for air security." This creates much greater accountability at FAA. They will have to do effective things, without undue delay, and with competent execution on their plans, or the transparency of the process will bring their deficiencies to public attention and to responsive and corrective action by you the Honorable Harold Rogers. The only things that should be kept fully secret are onboard combat tactics by crew and equipment and maneuver. There's no need for that information to be public knowledge prior to the moment of its use.

Israeli intelligence already does full field background checks and pre-screens every passenger that boards an El Al plane. If we decided to do these on a voluntary but wholesale basis in the USA for the air travelling public, we could do the

whole thing in 5 years for less than $10 Billion. The airlines
could pay a third, the passengers could pay a third, and the
government could pay a third. Those passengers who want to opt
out could come to the airport 3 hours ahead of time, board in
tyvek suits, with no carry ons, sit next to an air marshall
(possibly in some form of restraints), or just drive or take the
train. Everybody can exercise their liberty in their own way, but
keep in mind that the other passengers have a right to life which
is involved here, and the government has a right to national
security and the protection of people on the ground (public
safety). Whatever the law may have been with regard to the "duty"
for tort purposes of the airlines and the government prior to
September 11, 2001, it's is now very different. The duty of a
reasonable airline and the duty of a reasonable government is to
take effective steps to minimize the risk that major air terror
happens again in the USA. The risk must go down to "as low as
reasonably achievable". What is necessary, is proper.


Very truly yours,



Robert Gary, Esq.


P.S. Feel free to use this letter in any documents or
publications if you feel it might be useful, and appropriate,
including the hearings record.



Enclosure: Publications List

**Robert Gary**
**2211 Washington Ave (#301)**
**Silver Spring, MD 20910-2620**
**Tele: (301)587-7147**

Honorable Bob Graham                    September 20, 2001
Chairman Senate Intelligence Committee
524 Hart Senate Office Building
Washington DC 20510

Dear Chairman Graham,

There are **three relatively low risk but highly effective things** that the government might do right now to increase national security.

**(a) Neutron detectors** need to be employed at our border, particularly our border with Mexico. The NEST team has some experience in this area but I think the work would be more effectively done by private contractors. Airports also need to be covered, and seaports as well. The fewer the number of Federal employees involved in this work the more chance it can be done covertly and not telegraphing our search effort to the enemy. Private companies operating on a bounty hunter basis with substantial Federal funding through contracts with D.I.A. would probably be the ideal arrangement to keep this monitoring low profile and staffed with highly competent people.

**(b) The Bin Laden businesses** in Saudi Arabia, Sudan, Egypt, and elsewhere need to be taken down to zero cash balances, zero capital, zero inventories, and zero credit. This is "unfair and disempowering" to "innocent" family members, and it may cause strains in our relations with the Saudis, but it is necessary to cut Osama Bin Laden off from all access to hard currency, gold, or any valuable resources. His power has been abused.

**(c) Arabs in the U.S.** who arrived after 1990, and are male, and are under 65, and are not presently U.S. citizens should be declared "persona non grata" in the U.S. and asked to leave. Again this is potentially unfair to a significant percentage of this group but it is entirely lawful, it is in the interests of Americans, and it would cut Osama Bin Laden off from his personnel resources, and some of his funding, in the U.S.

I have worked intensively, since the bombing of the USS Cole, to get a proximity control transponder demonstration project up and running within the U.S. Navy. In light of repeated security difficulties, perhaps it's time to start thinking outside the box a little. If you want to think outside the box, you have to go to some people who are outside the box.

As a public interest attorney for 20 years, much of which has been spent in the security, emergency management, and nuclear fields, I don't know who is truly qualified to speak for all of the American people on the subject of whether they wish to have young Arab male non-citizens in this country at their sufferance. I cannot possibly claim to speak for each and every American citizen in that regard. But I think I speak for many when I say that young Arab aliens are here on revokable licenses from the INS and we just don't need them here right now. We don't have enough tax dollars to pay enough investigators to track their every movement, phonecall, and e-mail. Americans can do things that are in their own interests for that reason alone. This used to be called raison d'etat.

My President, of whom I am very proud, says we are in a true war. So, let's put our tax money into effectively prosecuting that war and not playing cat and mouse games with foreign nationals who are here at our discretion, and who have no Constitutional or legal rights to be here. If we declare non grata 100 people for every 1 prospective suicide bomber that we expel, that's a good enough ratio to make this expulsion plan worthwhile as an effective security measure that is low risk, low cost, totally legal, and comparatively humane. This measure, if adopted, will be tested in the U.S. Supreme Court, no doubt, and as a member of the Bar of that Court, I will be there to file Amicus Curiae briefs in favor of this measure because it is vital, reasonable, and necessary.

I told Senator Lugar, in graphic terms, back on October 28, 2000 that there was a theoretical danger of a nuclear bomb carried to the Panama Canal and then across the US-Mexico border and finally by speedboat from Green Bay to the base of the Sears Tower in Chicago. A W-88 devise weighing about 400 lbs, and easily transportable in a steamer trunk, would kill 3 million people in the Chicago area in about 60 minutes after detonation in the waterways of Chicago. This is the sort of thing that we may face in the next round of terrorism on American soil, as Secretary Cohen well knew and warned us about at least 50 times in public speeches.

As an Navy veteran, my hope is that we can go beyond the Kabuki of political showmanship -- the Mikado of the Schmoos, as it were, and actually do something effective to combat terrorism on our shores. The steps that I have proposed are not politically correct, nor are they multiculturally correct, but they are the most moderate steps that would be effective. They are the least we can do. Perhaps they would be a minimal common ground on which we could come together.

Very Truly yours,


Robert Gary, Esq.

**Robert Gary**
**2211 Washington Ave (#301)**
**Silver Spring, MD 20910-2620**
**Tele: (301)587-7147**

Vice President Richard Cheney                September 20, 2001
Attn: Mr. **Eric Edelman**
The White House
1600 Pennsylvania Avenue, N.W.
Washington, D.C. 20500

Dear Vice President Cheney,

There are three relatively low risk but highly effective things that the government might do right now to increase national security.

Neutron detectors need to be employed at our border, particularly our border with Mexico. The NEST team has some experience in this area but I think the work would be more effectively done by private contractors. Airports also need to be covered, and seaports as well. The fewer the number of Federal employees involved in this work the more chance it can be done covertly and not telegraphing our search effort to the enemy. Private companies operating on a bounty hunter basis with substantial Federal funding through contracts with D.I.A. would probably be the ideal arrangement to keep this monitoring low profile and staffed with highly competent people.

The Bin Laden businesses in Saudi Arabia, Sudan, Egypt, and elsewhere need to be taken down to zero cash balances, zero capital, zero inventories, and zero credit. This is "unfair and disempowering" to "innocent" family members, and it may cause strains in our relations with the Saudis, but it is necessary to cut Osama Bin Laden off from all access to hard currency, gold, or any valuable resources. His power has been abused.

Arabs in the U.S. who arrived after 1990, and are male, and are under 65, and are not presently U.S. citizens should be declared "persona non grata" in the U.S. and asked to leave. Again this is potentially unfair to a significant percentage of this group but it is entirely lawful, it is in the interests of Americans, and it would cut Osama Bin Laden off from his personnel resources, and some of his funding, in the U.S.

As I'm sure you know I have worked intensively since the bombing of the USS Cole to get a proximity control transponder demonstration project up and running within the U.S. Navy. I've communicated with **Rep. Morella, and Sen. Warner**, who were good enough to facilitate a technical meeting between myself and representatives (at NCIS) of the CNO. Mr. **Eric Edelman**'s letter to me of July 26, 2001 indicated that it would be "premature to

address the specifics of any defense issue", and this means that
the transponder project is set back by at least three years, and
that nothing truly effective will be done to prevent a recurrence
of what happened to the USS Cole until around 2005.

In light of repeated security difficulties, perhaps it's time to
start thinking outside the box a little. If you want to think
outside the box, you have to go to some people who are outside
the box. It's not sensible to keep going back to the same
insiders/experts, expecting that after a long series of security
failures that they will suddenly know how to prevent the next
one. The instinct in government, as in the teaching "profession",
always seems to involve going to those who have been in place
holding official positions for a long time, no matter how often
they have failed or how costly their failures. Fresh thinking is
needed. People outside the box might be helpful with that.

I have been a public interest attorney for 20 years, much of
which has been spent in the security, emergency management, and
nuclear fields. I don't know who is truly qualified to speak for
all of the American people on the subject of whether they wish to
have young Arab male non-citizens in this country at their
sufferance. I cannot claim to speak for each and every American
citizen in that regard. But I think I speak for many when I say
that young Arab aliens are here on revokable licenses from the
INS and we just don't need them here right now. We don't have
enough tax dollars to pay enough investigators to track their
every movement, phonecall, and e-mail. Americans can do things
that are in their own interests for that reason alone. This used
to be called raison d'etat. My President, of whom I am very
proud, says we are in a true war. So, let's put our tax money
into effectively prosecuting that war and not playing cat and
mouse games with foreign nationals who are here at our
discretion, and who have no Constitutional or legal rights to be
here. If we declare non grata 100 people for every 1 prospective
suicide bomber that we expel, that's a good enough ratio to make
this expulsion plan worthwhile as an effective security measure
that is low risk, low cost, totally legal, and comparatively
humane. This measure, if adopted, will be tested in the U.S.
Supreme Court, no doubt, and as a member of the Bar of that
Court, I will be there to file Amicus Curiae briefs in favor of
this measure because it is vital, reasonable, and necessary. I
told **Senator Lugar** back on October 28, 2000 that there was a
theoretical danger of a nuclear bomb carried by speedboat from
Green Bay to the base of the Sears Tower in Chicago. He was busy
with his campaign. I realize this issue is complex and busy
people have many things to do. I hope we can do something
effective, and not just put on a show in our war of terrorism.

Very Truly yours,

cc: Shelby, Warner, Lugar
    Morella, and Cox

Terror Attack -- September 11, 2001
General Systems Considerations
and
Thinking the Unthinkable
by
Robert Gary, M.B.A., J.D.
September 24, 2001


What happened to the World Trade Center buildings on September 11, 2001 is called pancaking. Our challenge at this time is to prevent our whole society from pancaking.

Let's start by examining the pancaking process. It is a catalyzed process, in this case by heat which melted the beams at 2000 degrees thereby releasing the stored potential energy in the upper floors of the building. This stored potential energy became kinetic energy which then destroyed the buildings floor by floor in a pancaking process, which is a sort of chain reaction, not different in some respects from an atomic chain reaction where each pair of released neutrons goes on to enable the release of potential energy and the production of further free neutrons.

Is there a possibility that our whole society will implode based on the catalyzing event of the destruction of the World Trade Center by two commercial airliners? What would the scenario look like for a chain reaction of devastation that would encompass the whole of USA by releasing pent up potential energy and converting it into destructive kinetic energy in a vast complex chain reaction?

Let's examine some of the potential energy. There are two areas that come to mind. The tendency of our Congress to overspend, and the tendency of our society to over litigate. These are dangerous propensities that are always lurking just beneath the surface of "good times" and which, if they are released can tear America apart at the seams.

On September 10, 2001 the big issue in Congress was whether we could go into the social security lockbox to find about 9 Billion to balance our accounts for this year and avoid a trainwreck in the last quarter. On September 14, 2001 Congress cut a check for $40 Billion right out of the lockbox and its just a down payment and it's not clear how this money will be used. Supposedly half is for repairs and half is for action to root out terrorism starting with Osama Bin Laden.

On September 10, 2001, our Courts were clogged as usual, and our insurance and capital markets were operating fairly close to the margin as usual. On September 14, 2001 our Courts may be facing 6000 new cases, our insurance industry is about to take a huge hit and several airlines are out of business. The ones that are still in business cannot attract capital or retain their workforces -- they are letting people go by the tens of thousands. The same is happening in the aircraft production business, and the hospitality and travel industries.

What's happening is that the physical attack and destruction at the World Trade Center on September 11, 2001 is becoming a catalyst for a chain of reactions which may, if left unchecked, destroy our government, our industry, and our financial markets (including capital and insurance). Just like is a nuclear reaction that has gone critical the key is to insert moderators, or control rods, or neutron absorbers fast enough to get the reaction cooled down and under control.

A country tipping on the verge of recession can be shoved into a major depression by a runaway chain reaction of economic and government events. Mass unemployment, creating a drop in consumer spending, and a need for government assistance is one aspect of the problem. The other aspect is runaway spending by the Congress, where every single Senator and Congressman uses the terror attack as a premise to add either on the defense side, or on the social welfare side, spending that breaks the budget, destroys the surplus, and cripples the Treasury.

What are the control rods? There are three. The first is to get control of the litigation. This "act of war" may or may not vitiate some normal commercial insurance contracts. Often there is a clause in such contracts excluding "acts of war". All the litigation in this matter needs to be brought into one Court as a massive common facts complex litigation. It probably will require a team of judges divided into panels specializing in various aspects of the claims. Federal legislation that is intelligent, simple and that streamlines the process would be very helpful. It would be helpful if there were caps on damages awards and no jury trials for these cases. This would be a good case for a common payer, probably the U.S. Treasury, so that all suits are by law required to be brought against the U.S. government, which then seeks indemnity from the insurers and corporate cross-claim defendants (i.e. the airlines, the developers, architects and realty firms, the airport security firms, and the insurers).

Once the litigation is on a track so that it can be handled efficiently and with reasonable caps on individual recoveries, then the danger to capital and insurance markets is brought under control and can be rationally factored into all new premium arrangements and lending agreements. The market can balance the disruption out, but only after its size can be rationally approximated. If the legal claims are inestimable they will kill off a lot of the American economy by creating a climate for business that is unfriendly to investment in the USA. Capital will go overseas. Insurers will pull up stakes, wind up their operations, and take their chips off the table.

The second control rod is fiscal policy. Runaway spending by the Congress is going to wreck the tax cut and cause a trainwreck in government and a shutdown at the worst possible moment -- when we have troops overseas and unemployed millions in our streets. Given their opportunity, the liberals will want to decorate the Christmas tree of every bill that is written to alleviate this emergency. If something is going to be given to the corporations, they will want something for displaced employees. If money is going to he appropriated for airline safety, they will want cross subsidies for rural air service, as we have already heard to our disgust from Senator Robert Byrd (D-West Virginia). If money is to be spent on a military response, they will want money spent on welfare in the U.S. and humanitarian actions abroad, perhaps all over the world. Every bill will be a bonanza. The Treasury becomes the great Pinyata -- every legislator there with his stick trying to break it open and get some of the goodies to bring home. Fiscal discipline once lost results in a trainwreck and the government closes down. Welfare and Medicare checks don't go out. The population gets harder and harder to control. Finally the thin blue line breaks, and we have pandemonium in our streets, no different from Chad, Biafra, Kabul, or Beirut.

Once Congress takes the spending bit in its teeth there is no Constitutional mechanism to bring it under control. Impoundment of funds was tried by Nixon and didn't work. The fiscal restraint control rod will be the hardest one to insert because it depends upon the good sense and good will of people who are not legally required to have or to exercise those qualities, and who in many cases, don't. Some sort of cap on all outlays in response to the terror attack for all reasons might be agreed to by all parties and players. There could be a decision to put a cap of 100 billion on the response and then hold all legislation of every sort: defense, social, compensatory, and preventative within that cap. This would mean the Congress would agree in advance to make choices, to make trade-offs, and not to spend, using the terror attack premise, on a "lid off" basis. No part of our Constitution compels Congress to be reasonable about this. It would have to be an agreement on a bi-partisan basis affecting the rules committees in the House and Senate, with the concurrence of the President, and at least the tacit approval of the Supreme Court. A lot of people would have to be reasonable, all at the same time, to create a fiscal control rod. But without such a control rod be could blow all the way through the $150 billion Social Security surplus and wind up in a real deficit spending mode for 2001, and possibly for 2002 as well. This would be deficit spending of the unified budget -- under the old accounting rules before anyone thought of the lockbox. Such deficit spending would put the social security system in jeopardy, it would put pressure on the dollar, and it might create a sudden catastrophic loss of faith in our paper money.

The third control rod is creating a favorable climate for business by monetary and regulatory policy. A nation can soak up a lot of unemployed people if the interest rate is low enough and the regulatory burden on business is kept to a true bare bones minimum. If the Federal funds rate went to 1% and regulatory compliance paperwork was cut by 90% and business taxes including capital gains were cut in half, the new business activity generated by this stimulus package would offset the business cutbacks in airlines, travel, hospitality, etc. It's hard to imagine a stimulus package that would be too bold. The Japanese have cut their interbank rate to 0%, and it hasn't been a panacea for them. Obviously we could not cut environmental compliance regulations beyond a certain point or we would be right back to the days of Rachel Carson's <u>Silent Spring</u>, in about a week. The toxic dumpers would kill the planet if they weren't held in check by enforceable regulations, which means monitoring, which means compliance paperwork. But keeping this in place, we could still cut government compliance paperwork by 90%. A lot of it is nonsense anyway and the country as a whole would be better off without it. People can pursue their diversity, sexual politics, and multicultural rights through other channels instead of by Federal regulation of business. The market can respond to monopolistic tendencies and market power by other means than the vague and whimsical application of 100 year old antitrust laws by a power abusing Justice Department. If we stop victimizing our productive businesses by loading upon their backs every person with a political agenda, career ambition, or personal ax to grind they would be free to deploy more capital productively within the USA and to provide employment for more people. The monetary and regulatory changes that create a positive climate for business in the U.S. are a vital part of preventing a pancaking of our whole economy and society as a chain reaction result catalyzed by the terror attack on the World Trade Center.

It is my earnest hope that all of the possible negative consequences foreseen here are purely in my imagination and have no possibility of occurring in the real world. But if they are not in my imagination, but are real dangers, then my next hope is that I have failed to see about a dozen available control rods that would be far more effective than the ones I propose and far easier to insert to stop the runaway chain reaction. But if those other control rods do not exist, my next hope is that the ones I have described are not nearly as hard to deploy as they appear in my description. They would not require as much good sense, good will or intelligence to use as I thought. They could be employed easily, smoothly, effectively, with little fuss and no bother. But if their easy availability and use is not part of the picture in this world, then the last part of my prayer is that we can insert the three control rods whatever it takes to do so.

**112**

**Robert Gary, Esq.**
**2211 Washington Ave (#301)**
**Silver Spring, MD 20910-2620**
**Tele: (301) 587-7147**

Rep. Paul Kanjorski                              September 26, 2001
(Attn: Liza Ackerman)
U.S. Capitol
2353 Rayburn Building                            FAX: (202) 225-0764
Washington, DC 20515

Dear Rep. Kanjorski,

I heard your comments in the insurance hearing today and I had a sense that you, like myself, have a desire to protect the interests of American taxpayers in the matter of compensation for the World Trade Center attacks. I have a specific suggestion.

First of all let me say that after 20 years of legal practice and an MBA (most of which has been as a public interest attorney), I am astonished that the House bill (H.R. 21??) seems to treat the attacks for compensation purposes as if they were torts committed by the taxpayers of the USA. The victims and their families apparently will have a new open-ended uncapped entitlement to make tort claims which will include loss of earnings and pain and suffering. For a single prosperous young bond trader who died in the attack, the claims by his family could well run to several Billion dollars, paid out of the U.S. Treasury, by the US taxpayer, who committed no tort and performed no attack on anybody. There could be 7000 claims, not all that large, but many of them in that range. I think the Bill was approved in haste, improvidently, and based on an untenable legal premise, which may be ultra vires with regard to Congresses power to spend from the U.S. Treasury. But let's assume I'm wrong about that, and that the Bill becomes law, and the claims are paid out.

Here's an old common law solution that fits this case. It's called the cross-claim. The U.S. Treasury should have a cross-claim against the states that sponsor terrorism -- as a group, like suits against asbestos companies or tobacco companies. The mass tort was collectively caused by the nations that sponsor terror in the world, of which there are three or four that have any assets. We should take their assets, using military means to seize gold, hard currency, securities, and other valuables held by banks in Iran, Iraq, Afghanistan, and Egypt. We are over there anyway with a vast armada of ships and planes, and few high value targets worth a cruise missile. Seizing assets is a much more humanitarian way of getting

1

Ltr to Rep Paul Kanjorski from R. Gary, 26 Sept 2001, page 2.

restitution than killing people en masse where most of the dead will be women and children, sometimes called "collateral damage". What we need to do is some targeted damage, and targeting hard financial assets would disempower those four nations who have abused their power. It would disable them from further participation in the modern world. This would be as close to justice as could be attained and a far better alternative than paper tiger airstrikes combined with making the U.S. taxpayers pick up the whole tab for this attack. People who are poor in good sense, and common decency, should be poor in gold, and hard currencies. We have a right to take back from the state sponsors of terror what circumstances compel our Treasury to pay out to the victims of terror. We should do this taking without hesitation, by pure military force, and without extended judicialization of the matter. It is an act of pure justice done for reasons of state and without seeking justification or validation by any third party, international tribunal, united nations, or world court. This is what great nations do. It's what the Romans did, to precisely these same people. It's what the crusaders did. What we have here is a clash of cultures, which may have no military solution long-term. To disable and disempower our foes may set them back enough to give us time to get organized.

Politicians who follow my suggestion here will be heros to about 280 million American citizens. They will certainly be heros to all the victims families who get compensated -- and generously compensated. But they will also be heros to the other citizens who just pay their taxes, and now because of this plan, do not have to be out $35 Billion from the U.S. Treasury for this one incident of terror attack (when there may well be others coming). I cannot claim to speak for each and every American on this matter, but after 20 years of experience as a public interest lawyer (with a libertarian slant, not to the left, not to the right), I think I speak for a lot of hardworking people here.

My sense is that of all the people who were in the hearing today, you are the one closest in spirit to my concern for the U.S. Taxpayers, and how they come out of this whole matter. I could not expect that Members of Congress to the left of you would support my solution, but you might. It is radical. It will take a Congressman of courage to put it forward through channels to the leadership. You might be that profile in courage. I can offer more arguments for this plan, but probably not better ones than are here in this letter. I live nearby and would be prepared to meet with you or Mr. Tod Harper, at any convenient time.

Robert Gary, Esq.

2

JOHN WARNER
VIRGINIA

COMMITTEES:
ARMED SERVICES, SENIOR REPUBLICAN MEMBER
ENVIRONMENT AND PUBLIC WORKS
HEALTH, EDUCATION, LABOR, AND PENSIONS
RULES AND ADMINISTRATION

225 RUSSELL SENATE OFFICE BUILDING
WASHINGTON, DC 20510-4601
(202) 224-2023
senator@warner.senate.gov
www.senate.gov/~warner/

CONSTITUENT SERVICE OFFICES:

4900 WORLD TRADE CENTER
101 WEST MAIN STREET
NORFOLK, VA 23510-1690
(757) 441-3079

MAIN STREET CENTRE II
600 EAST MAIN STREET
RICHMOND, VA 23219-3538
(804) 771-2579

235 FEDERAL BUILDING
P.O. BOX 887
ABINGDON, VA 24212-0887
(540) 628-8158

1003 FIRST UNION BANK BUILDING
213 SOUTH JEFFERSON STREET
ROANOKE, VA 24011-1714
(540) 857-2676

## United States Senate

September 28, 2001

Mr. Robert Gary
Apartment 301
2211 Washington Avenue
Silver Spring, Maryland 20910-2620

Dear Mr. Gary:

Thank you for contacting me regarding the recent terrorist attacks on the United States. I appreciate your thoughtful comments.

September 11, 2001 was indeed one of the most tragic days in America's history. While our lives will never be the same, I know that we will be better and stronger as a nation.

Regrettably, these loathsome, cowardly acts of terrorism have deeply wounded our country, but they have not, and will never dull, the spirit and resolve of the American people. My thoughts and prayers are with those who lost loved ones on that horrific day. My thanks and deep appreciation go out to the many thousands who stepped up in the face of danger to assist in the devastating aftermath, and who continue to work tirelessly at the Pentagon, World Trade Center and Pennsylvania crash site.

The Congress has come together -- speaking with a unified bipartisan voice -- in support of our President and his determination to punish the perpetrators of these attacks, as well as their sponsors. The Senate has unanimously approved a joint resolution, S.J.Res.22, condemning in the strongest possible terms the terrorists who planned and executed the September 11th attacks, and those who provided assistance to the terrorists.

This resolution was followed by unanimous Senate approval of an Emergency Supplemental Appropriations bill providing an initial $40 billion response to the September 11 attacks, and funding requested by the President for counter-terrorism, transportation security and military purposes. The Senate also passed a resolution authorizing President Bush to use "all necessary and appropriate force" against those responsible for or aiding in the attacks.

Our President, the Congress, and the men and women of the armed forces all over this world stand ready not only to defend this nation from further attack, but to take such actions as are directed in the future in retaliation for these terrorists acts.

In addition, during this time of crisis, it is important that we come together as a nation, regardless of ethnic or religious differences. Any violent action against our fellow Americans, whether they are Jewish, Muslim, or Christian, will not be tolerated and would only weaken the very fibers of this nation of which we are so proud.

September 28, 2001
Page 2

In the coming weeks and months, Congress will be addressing many of the concerns highlighted by your letter.  Please be assured that I will keep your comments in mind as we work to ensure the safety and security of the United States.

Thank you for your patriotism and keep the flag -- our symbol of freedom -- flying high.  God Bless America.

Note: the Federal Emergency Management Agency (www.FEMA.gov) has many useful phone numbers for volunteers, families, and victims regarding the terrorist attacks of September 11, 2001.

With kind regards, I am

Sincerely,

John Warner

JW/mlm

**Robert Gary, Esq.**
**2211 Washington Ave (#301)**
**Silver Spring, MD 20910-2620**
**Tele: (301) 587-7147**

```
Rep. Paul Kanjorski                         October 4, 2001
(Attn: Karen Feather Chief of Staff)
U.S. Capitol
2353 Rayburn Building                       FAX: (202) 225-0764
Washington, DC 20515
```

Dear Rep. Kanjorski,

The enclosed document is a follow-on to my letter to you of
September 26, 2001, and my FAX to Karen Feather, while she was at
Wilkes Barre on September 28, 2001. It contains a fuller and more
detailed statement of my legal opinion regarding the
Constitutional infirmity of the Airline Bailout Act, because of
the uncapped and indeterminate nature of the tort theory payouts.

It also contains the factual and legal premises for my theory of
a viable cross-claim to be made by the U.S. against the real
tortfeasors, those who conduct the ultrahazardous activity of
religious brainwashing of young men, training them to be
terrorists, and then setting them loose on the world. The Saudis,
in my view are the primary fountainhead of violent religious
fanaticism and are engaged in a criminal enterprise that has cost
the U.S. and will cost the U.S. a total of $250 Billion over the
past three decades, including but not limited to the most recent
attack on the World Trade Center. We have RICO statutes that
apply to international criminal enterprises and that would reach
promoters, indoctrinators, harborers, and funders as well as the
actual terrorists, who with the exception of Bin Laden are
judgment proof. We could take our damages using military means,
and we could take them in the form of cash, gold, or oil. This
would make the American taxpayers whole and it would send a
message to this sort of scheme in other places. The message is
that all conspirators, helpers, fanatic creators, brainwashers,
and religious school funders will be held liable if the people
they set loose on humanity are human timebombs. If an American
father raised his son to be indoctrinated into the idea of
killing a certain group of people, in the name of God, and then
trained that boy in firearms and bombing, and the boy went out
and killed thousands of people, we would hold that father
accountable at law for having conducted an ultrahazardous
activity in the raising of his son.

Sincerely,

Encl: Legal Considerations 3 Oct 01
      Publications List

Legal Considerations Regarding Terror Attack on September 11 2001
by
Robert Gary, Esq.
October 3, 2001


Within a few days of the attack on the World Trade Center Congress passed a Bill which became law for the purpose of preventing the airlines from going bankrupt due to prospective liability. Capital was drying up, there was talk of 7000 lawsuits against the airlines, based on a strict liability theory, and it was clear that without some intervention the airlines would go under and possibly take down a substantial part of the U.S. economy, like floors of a skyscraper pancaking on each other.

The Restatement of torts section 402 A does provide for strict liability, and one of the theories that may bring a case under strict liability is that the defendant was engaged in an "ultrahazardous activity" at the time that the plaintiff sustained an injury or loss. Once strict liability has been established as a matter of law the plaintiff's burden of proof really comes down to the issue of damages.

The Airline Bailout Act essentially established that the airlines would not be sued for damages, and instead the U.S. Treasury would pay the damages based on tort suits brought by the plaintiff family members for wrongful death, loss of earnings, pain and suffering etc. These suits are to be handled by special Masters. There are no caps on the amounts recoverable. A young bond trader in his early 30's making $50 million a year, with an expected worklife of 20 more work years, might cost the U.S. Treasury $1 billion just for the lost earnings, just for that one case. There were hundreds of people in very high earnings brackets who died in the attack. The uncapped recoveries that will be paid out to their families are not capable of being estimated with any certainly or limitation.

The Constitution of the United States provides that no payment shall be made by the U.S. Treasury except pursuant to an appropriation made by the U.S. Congress. It is true that the Federal Emergency Management Agency maintains a budget for the specific purpose of making payments to assist disaster victims but that budget is based on appropriations made by Congress, and it is fixed in the amounts appropriated and subject the oversight, investigation, scrutiny, debate, and deliberation, and the President's veto pen. It's also true that the Federal government may be sued, under the Federal Tort Claims Act, under the Court of Claims Act, and under several other statutes. When it is sued, if it loses in Federal Court, it pays out of the Treasury to the successful plaintiff. But these are cases in which the government of the U.S. has been adjudicated to be in the wrong, and liable, for some negligence or intentional harm.

Hardship cases have traditionally been brought directly in the U.S. Congress which on many occasions has passed special Bills to relieve some individual or group of individuals. But these Bills have fixed dollar amounts, and they are passed by the Congress and enacted into law. So there is little precedent for what has been done in the Airlines Bailout Bill, where the government was not liable, the amounts are not capped or fixed, and the Congress does not make an appropriation prior to a payout by the U.S. Treasury. The Airlines Bailout Bill may be ultra vires, unconstitutional, and beyond the power of Congress because it is an improper delegation of Congressional power, and because it is an open-ended new entitlement with no way to know what the draw on the U.S. Treasury may be. Congress can write checks on the Treasury but it can't hand out blank checks with the idea that some Special Master will fill them in. Allowing the victims families to recover on a tort theory would have been reasonable against the airlines, who arguably are in some way liable for what occurred, due to lax security in the face of repeated reports and warnings over the past ten years, but it is not reasonable to employ tort theory recovery as a basis for claims against the U.S. Treasury, when the U.S. is in no way responsible for the harms that occurred.

Unless the Bill is repealed or declared unconstitutional it is the law of the land and we have to live with it. I would argue that flying commercial jets hasn't been an ultrahazardous activity since the 1950's, and that it is a good deal less hazardous per passenger mile travelled than driving on the highway, which is not designated "an ultrahazardous" activity per se.

I would further argue that if a tort theory is going to be employed and the wholly innocent U.S. Taxpayer is going to pay the damages, then the U.S. Taxpayers should have an enforceable cross-claim against the real tortfeasors. The Taliban and Ossama Bin Laden are the direct tortfeasors, but the real tortfeasors include a much wider circle of parties.

Furthermore, it seems to me that all the these tortfeasors are engaged in a criminal enterprise, and thus are covered by our RICO Statutes. It's not just the bombers, and the planners, and the moneymen but its also the conspirators, promoters, harborers, and indoctrinators that all work together to produce the agent of terror and his bomb, with the mindset and the coordinated timing to make strikes such as occurred.

The Wahabi Moslems are the people that come to mind in this regard. Every one of the 19 terror bombers was a Wahabi, as is Ossama Bin Laden, and his lieutenants. The ultrahazardous activity is not flying commercial jetliners but running religious training schools that take young men and turn them into suicidal fanatics. They then proceed to Bin Laden's camps to be trained, and then go on the cells of Al Queda in 50 countries around the world. The global center of the enterprise is in Saudi Arabia, which exports religious fanaticism, and which uses its oil money to pay for religious studies in Wahabism. The suicide bomber is made from the religious school graduate. The terror cells are made from the terror training camp graduates. The truly ultrahazardous activity behind the deaths of approximately 6000 people at the World Trading Center is creating suicidal religious fanatics with bombs or in this case boxcutters. It's a combination of indoctrination (religious school) training (camp) and placement (cells). These are vicious creatures raised up to be vicious and capable of great harm, inspired until they are willing to give their lives in that act, and then set loose on the world. Saudi Arabia is the primary fountainhead of this international criminal enterprise, with secondary springs in United Arab Emirates, Egypt, Libya, Sudan, Iran, Iraq, Pakistan, Syria, Russia, Germany and other places. But teaching the Wahabi religious viewpoint of radical fundamentalist belief accompanied by the concept of martyrdom for Allah and violence against all "infidels" to purify the world and make it right, that is the true ultrahazardous activity.

That's where we should make our cross-claim. We should take every penny's worth of gold and hard currency out of Saudi Arabia, Egypt, and the United Arab Emirates until the U.S. is made whole for the harm done by the terror attacks of September 11, 2001. If these three don't have enough to cover the damages, we should go after Iran, Iraq, Libya, and Syria, until the damages are paid in full.

There was a man, just a regular U.S. citizen, whose daughter was killed in a bus in Israel by a fanatical bomber sent there by Hezbulla, paid for by Iran. This distraught father tried to sue Iran in a U.S. Federal Court to recover for the wrongful death of his daughter. The U.S. government opposed that suit, and used the Justice Department and State Department lawyers to ensure that the father's claims were thrown out of Court. Permitting such claims would be a violation of Treaty and would subject American assets to the prospect of seizure overseas, so they said.

We just don't want to make waves in the Arab world. We don't want to rock the boat. The U.S. wants to make sure that even in our present situation we have no gripe against Islam, it's only terrorists that we have a score to settle with. I think this is in one sense a form of cynical realpolitik (based of oil access and nuclear fears), but in another sense its a form of self-delusion and denial of the obvious truth about how the world is and what's happening in it. Ossama Bin Laden is like the Mahdi. He is the sword of Allah. Wahabism is his creed, and that of his followers, some of whom are formally trained, and hundreds of millions of whom are well-wishers, kindred spirits, fellow enthusiasts for the idea of bringing the U.S. down, making it weak, killing its people, crippling its economy, embarrassing its military, destroying its legitimacy in the world.

But we don't seem to understand that we are not facing a man, we are facing a movement, in a culture five times as old as the U.S. Wahabism is a growing movement that will outlive Bin Laden and which reaches into 50 countries. If we don't want to be bitten by this snake, again and again, we must kill it or defang it so that it has no ability to harm us. By taking the Saudi money, and that of several other nations that are wellsprings of militant Moslem belief we impoverish them, disempower them, disable them. Their ability to harm us becomes similar to ability of Biafra, or Bangla Desh, or Chad, or Haiti, or Rwanda. It's very rare that we have to worry about people from those countries. We don't worry what they think, or what they might dream of doing to us. It's not a problem, because they have no fangs -- they are not empowered, they are not able, they are not privileged. If the center states of the Wahabi movement, who are the true masterminds of the global criminal enterprise were defanged by becoming dirt poor subsistence level places we would have much less the worry about from them.

Also, we speak of justice. Closing the liability loop back on the conspirators, promoters, and harborers would be justice. I'm not talking about randomly looting these countries, or taking more from them than the damage that they've done in the U.S., and to the USS Cole, and to our Embassies in Africa. No, I just want a cross-claim in the correct amount, for the full damages, and I want the cross-claim to be enforced by seizure backed by military force. No one has to get killed, or even injured. This is a matter of justice, and the clear and immediate presence of overwhelming military force might be adequate to deter any resistance to the seizure process. $250 billion might be about right for the cross-claim. I think the Saudis could pay it with oil revenues, or with oil. We protect their oil anyway, and have from the start, when we easily could have brushed them aside in the 1930's and just taken possession of their oil areas. We have respected their property for 75 years which is why they are rich, and because they have abused their wealth by creating human timebombs and setting them loose on innocent humanity, we should now take enough of that wealth to cover our damages resultant from their ultrahazardous activity. The karmic lesson here might sink in to their minds as it has to many tortfeasors and criminals in the past -- you can't do wrong and get by. If they are weak for the next decade or so that would give us time to get organized to take whatever steps we need to take to assure our security, our way of life, and the continuance of our Constitution and the nation it informs, shapes, and directs.

**Robert Gary, Esquire**
**2211 Washington Avenue (#301)**
**Silver Spring, MD 20910-2620**
**Tele: (301) 587-7147**

Ms. Mary Dorman                                    October 9, 2001
Assignment Desk
NBC News
FAX (202) 362-2009

Dear Ms. Dorman,

The incident on October 8, 2001 where a deranged man broke into
the cockpit of an American Airlines plane and began to wrestle
with the co-pilot indicates clearly that cockpit security is not
an accomplished fact in the U.S. at this time.

Alaska Airlines somehow managed to retrofit all their cockpit
doors with reinforced steel bars that absolutely prevent
unauthorized entry by force and they did this within 7 days of
the WTC incident which happened on September 11, 2001 -- 28 days
before the American Airlines incident.

The issue now is "What is the deadline for making cockpits
secure?" It looks like the FAA has given the airlines a year to
make the cockpit doors stronger. Congress is now writing a Bill
on airliner security, which may include a shorter deadline. But
the only reasonable deadline for these fixes to be made is
November 30, 2001. After that "no secure cockpit -- no fly"
should be the rule.

How could this be achieved. The FAA could take the initiative,
but it probably won't. Tom Ridge could take the initiative, but
he won't. It could be done but statute enacted on an expedited
basis, but clearly that is not going to happen. The last
possibilities is Executive Order from the President of the U.S.,
or by Court Order from a Federal Court. These last two are real
possibilities. A short deadline for some sort of interim fix
could save lives, and certainly it would instill much needed
confidence, and prevent a loss of credibility in the government's
ability to actually do anything of significance on a timely
basis. One way to make this happen would be for the news agencies
to monitor the government every day (Mineta, Mica, and Bush)
asking for progress reports. It is possible that this elementary
step, that everyone agrees must be done on a **priority** basis, will
otherwise **not be done for a year or so** at most airlines.

                                   Very truly yours,

**Robert Gary, Esquire**
**2211 Washington Avenue (#301)**
**Silver Spring, MD 20910-2620**
**Tele: (301) 587-7147**

```
Phil Horton, Esq.                    October 10, 2001
Arnold & Porter                      FAX 202 942-5999
Attn: Pro Bono Committee
```

Subj: Cockpit Door Security (Mandamus or Injunction Action)

Dear Mr. Horton,

Thank you very kindly for taking the time to speak with me today about my request for pro bono assistance from Arnold & Porter.

I'm interested in getting cockpit doors on commercial airliners physically secured with some sort of interim barrier, like steel bars, by November 30, 2001. This would prevent having thousands of unprotected cockpits in U.S. skies during the Christmas season of this year. My efforts so far have come to naught in spite of exhausting every avenue of communications with the FAA, the Aviation Subcommittee in the House, the office of my own Congressperson, and the White House. The intent seems to be to secure the cockpit doors, in about a year or so, which would give Congress time to hold hearings for 6 months or so, and then commission an outside study, maybe by a technical consulting firm around the beltway, and then submit that report to a blue ribbon commission whose findings would go to DOT, FAA, and the new Homeland Security Chief.

Alaska Airlines put steel bars behind the cockpit doors on all its planes within a week of the World Trade Center attack on September 11, 2001. Twenty-eight days after that attack, the cockpit of the American Airlines jet bound for Chicago was invaded by a deranged man who tried to wrestle the co-pilot out of his seat. The Ossama Bin Laden terrorists have clearly stated on October 9, 2001 that they intend more airline highjackings and more building collisions. And they can clearly see from the case of the deranged man on October 8, 2001, that no precautions have been taken to create a physical barrier that prevents entry by force into cockpits in the U.S. The way is open to them to do it again.

In the meantime, the government creates new costumes, makes new hats, suggests new hearings, and new budgets, names new officials, creates ever better coordination and liaison between agencies -- and in short does nothing, except maybe now they really look in one's pockets, and at one's carry on bag at the airport -- that's their vigorous way of waging war against terror in our skies. The obvious critical factor of a physical barrier to prevent people barging into U.S. cockpits got lost in the

shuffle even though in the first week after the World Trade
Center attack it was universally recognized as the most logical,
effective, and high priority measure that could be taken to make
a repetition of that scenario impossible. They still plan to do
it, but in about a year or so.

I have sent a design for a Kevlar mesh screen to FAA which would
be light, ride on tracks, slide across behind the door, and
create really excellent security -- but this is an ideal
engineered solution, and I don't have a final production
blueprint, so it could take a year to get such equipment produced
and installed. But in the meantime, two steel bars, one high, one
low, would be an excellent interim measure that could be taken
very cheaply by November 30, 2001, and I think the airlines would
be grossly negligent to omit this obvious safety measure in light
of all the circumstances. Omission here would not be excusable by
pleading compliance with FAA regulations. It would be a failure
of a duty of due care that runs directly between the carrier and
the passenger (and people on the ground).

I recognize that there may be conflict considerations in seeking
a Federal Court order against an airline, but what about a
mandamus order against DOT, FAA, the President, or the Homelands
Security Director? The benefit to the airlines would be very
great in any case. They could use the retrofit in their
advertisements, and probably get their money back for these
interim fixture installations. If they were forced to do the
retrofits by Court Order, then the fixtures would not be capital
equipment but rather expenses incident to a loss in litigation so
they would be fully deductible, as if they were casualty losses.
In any event if these retrofits were ordered through a Court or
Federal agency they could be paid for by the $15 Billion airline
security and bailout Bills. So the airlines would come out ahead,
at least from where they are now. They might be able to recover
some of their business, and to avoid additional liability in
which they would be characterized as grossly negligent.

Time is the factor that makes me come to you and ask for help. I
could do this case alone, but not in six weeks. I need
administrative support. I'm willing to play any role or no role
in the proceedings ranging from client, to witness, to consulting
counsel, to co-counsel, to counsel of record. Whatever makes the
case proceed best -- that's what my role should be. The only
payoff for Arnold & Porter is to protect and serve the People of
the U.S. at a time of national emergency and with regard to a
matter of life and death. The possibility exists that precisely
because of its contacts with the airlines the firm could
negotiate a non-judicial and amicable agreement between the
airlines and myself. They would meet the deadline and there would
be no need to obtain a Court Order.

Very Truly Yours,

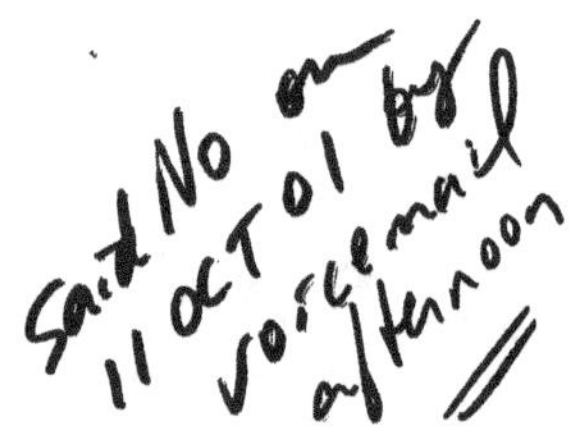


**Robert Gary, Esquire**
**2211 Washington Avenue (#301)**
**Silver Spring, MD 20910-2620**
**Tele: (301) 587-7147**

Jan Flack, Esq.                              October 10, 2001
Covington and Burling                        FAX 202 662-6291
Attn: Pro Bono Committee

Subj: Cockpit Door Security (Mandamus or Injunction Action)

Dear Ms. Flack,

Thank you very kindly for taking the time to speak with me today
about my request for pro bono assistance from Covington and
Burling.

I'm interested in getting cockpit doors on commercial airliners
physically secured with some sort of interim barrier, like steel
bars, by November 30, 2001. This would prevent having thousands
of unprotected cockpits in U.S. skies during the Christmas season
of this year. My efforts so far have come to naught in spite of
exhausting every avenue of communications with the FAA, the
Aviation Subcommittee in the House, the office of my own
Congressperson, and the White House. The intent seems to be to
secure the cockpit doors, in about a year or so, which would give
Congress time to hold hearings for 6 months or so, and then
commission an outside study, maybe by a technical consulting firm
around the beltway, and then submit that report to a blue ribbon
commission whose findings would go to DOT, FAA, and the new
Homeland Security Chief.

Alaska Airlines put steel bars behind the cockpit doors on all
its planes within a week of the World Trade Center attack on
September 11, 2001. Twenty-eight days after that attack, the
cockpit of the American Airlines jet bound for Chicago was
invaded by a deranged man who tried to wrestle the co-pilot out
of his seat. The Ossama Bin Laden terrorists have clearly stated
on October 9, 2001 that they intend more airline highjackings and
more building collisions. And they can clearly see from the case
of the deranged man on October 8, 2001, that no precautions have
been taken to create a physical barrier that prevents entry by
force into cockpits in the U.S. The way is open to them to do it
again.

In the meantime, the government creates new costumes, makes new
hats, suggests new hearings, and new budgets, names new
officials, creates ever better coordination and liaison between
agencies -- and in short does nothing, except maybe now they
really look in one's pockets, and at one's carry on bag at the
airport -- that's their vigorous way of waging war against terror
in our skies. The obvious critical factor of a physical barrier
to prevent people barging into U.S. cockpits got lost in the

shuffle even though in the first week after the World Trade Center attack it was universally recognized as the most logical, effective, and high priority measure that could be taken to make a repetition of that scenario impossible. They still plan to do it, but in about a year or so.

I have sent a design for a Kevlar mesh screen to FAA which would be light, ride on tracks, slide across behind the door, and create really excellent security -- but this is an ideal engineered solution, and I don't have a final production blueprint, so it could take a year to get such equipment produced and installed. But in the meantime, two steel bars, one high, one low, would be an excellent interim measure that could be taken very cheaply by November 30, 2001, and I think the airlines would be grossly negligent to omit this obvious safety measure in light of all the circumstances. Omission here would not be excusable by pleading compliance with FAA regulations. It would be a failure of a duty of due care that runs directly between the carrier and the passenger (and people on the ground).

I recognize that there may be conflict considerations in seeking a Federal Court order against an airline, but what about a mandamus order against DOT, FAA, the President, or the Homelands Security Director? The benefit to the airlines would be very great in any case. They could use the retrofit in their advertisements, and probably get their money back for these interim fixture installations. If they were forced to do the retrofits by Court Order, then the fixtures would not be capital equipment but rather expenses incident to a loss in litigation so they would be fully deductible, as if they were casualty losses. In any event if these retrofits were ordered through a Court or Federal agency they could be paid for by the $15 Billion airline security and bailout Bills. So the airlines would come out ahead, at least from where they are now. They might be able to recover some of their business, and to avoid additional liability in which they would be characterized as grossly negligent.

Time is the factor that makes me come to you and ask for help. I could do this case alone, but not in six weeks. I need administrative support. I'm willing to play any role or no role in the proceedings ranging from client, to witness, to consulting counsel, to co-counsel, to counsel of record. Whatever makes the case proceed best -- that's what my role should be. The only payoff for Covington and Burling is to protect and serve the People of the U.S. at a time of national emergency and with regard to a matter of life and death. The possibility exists that precisely because of its contacts with the airlines the firm could negotiate a non-judicial and amicable agreement between the airlines and myself. They would meet the deadline and there would be no need to obtain a Court Order.

Very Truly Yours,

**Robert Gary**
**2211 Washington Ave. (#301)**
**Silver Spring, MD 20910-2620**
Tele: (301) 587-7147
E-mail: Robert.Gary@prodigy.net

Jane Garvey                                          October 12, 2001
Administrator FAA
Federal Aviation Administration
800 Independence Avenue, S.W.
Washington, DC 20591

Subj: **Emergency Petition for Cockpit Security Bars**

1. **This emergency petition is to be responded to within 10 working days.**

2. Whereas on September 11, 2001 four planes were hijacked and massive damage was caused because the cockpit doors on those planes were not secure, and whereas on October 8 a deranged man broke into the cockpit through an unsecured door and threatened the co-pilot on an American Airlines flight to Chicago, it is now apparent that security bars need to be placed on all commercial planes to ensure the security of the cockpits.

3. The security bars to be installed under this petition are intended as a partial interim stopgap measure, and not as a comprehensive, final, perfect solution. It is expected that within one year a better way of securing cockpits will be designed, engineered, acquired and installed.

4. It is requested that the FAA shall issue an emergency order to all commercial air carriers in the U.S. that security bars to block unauthorized cockpit access must be installed by November 30, 2001. Commercial planes in the U.S. without security bars or equivalent cockpit door reinforcement shall not be permitted to fly after November 30, 2001.

5. It is requested that the FAA shall issue the emergency order immediately without further delay, on this day, 31 days after the World Trade Center and Pentagon, and Pennsylvania attacks, and 4 days after the October 8, 2001 incident.

Signed,

Robert Gary (Petitioner)

**Robert Gary**
**2211 Washington Ave. (#301)**
**Silver Spring, MD 20910-2620**
Tele: (301) 587-7147
E-mail: Robert.Gary@prodigy.net

Rep. Connie Morella                                          October 12, 2001
**(Attn: Lisa Boepple)**
2228 Rayburn Building
Washington, DC 20515

Dear Rep Morella,

In an attempt to be fair to Administrator Jane Garvey of FAA, and
in an effort to exhaust my administrative remedies prior to
possibly seeking an injunction in a Federal Court, I have
formally petitioned the Administrator on this day. My petition is
enclosed for your information. I'm also sending a copy to Rep
John Mica but you might forward a copy to him from your office as
well if you think his attention should be called to this
petition.

I have not been able to line up a major lawfirm to take the case
on a pro bono basis. I will not go to Court against the
government without such support. There is one major lawfirm that
is still considering my request for assistance.

I must tell you, frankly I think Jane Garvey should be fired. The
reasons are obvious. There is no excuse for letting 28 days go by
after the September 11, 2001 hijacking attacks and having planes
in American skies with unfortified cockpit doors. I realize that
the FAA Administrator's job is a complex one and many details get
lost in the shuffle, but **this was no detail.** This was the one
thing that was universally agreed on and recognized a vital
emergency requirement in the first week after September 11, 2001.
Ms Garvey should have issued an emergency order no later than
September 20. Had that been done American Airlines might well
have complied in time to prevent the October 8, 2001 incident. We
don't need to wait any longer to know that this particular
Administrator is not competent for that appointment. Someone is.
They should be quickly identified, recruited, and appointed.


                                        Very Truly Yours,



                                        Robert Gary, Esq.

Encl: **Formal Petition to the FAA** Dated 12 October 2001

**Robert Gary, Esq.**
**2211 Washington Avenue (#301)**
**Silver Spring, MD 20910-2620**
**(301) 587-7147**
**Robert.Gary@prodigy.net**

Lee Kreindler, Esq.                                October 15, 2001
Kreindler & Kreindler
100 Park Avenue
New York, NY 10178

Dear Mr. Kreindler,

I have filed a petition with the FAA to place security bars on
the cockpit doors of all commercial airliners by November 30,
2001. The benefit of this would be added security for travellers
during the Christmas/Hanukkah season this year.

My problem is that although I have 22 years of experience as an
attorney in the field of emergency management, I have never done
a filing with the FAA before. I need some help by some lawyer in
the Washington area who would be prepared to come forward on a
pro bono basis to make sure that my petition gets a fair hearing
and proper consideration. I just need some support in the area of
procedural rules and maybe a little help with briefing the issue.

The FAA has 60 attorneys and if I have to go to Federal Court for
an injunction or mandamus I have no doubt that they will all
appear in opposition. I've sued the government enough times to
know this, and I don't want to do it again. There may be no other
way, however, to protect and serve the American flying public.

The FAA is temporizing. They say they want to fortify the doors
within a year or so, and that there's no need to issue an
emergency rule because the airlines are all in the process of
doing it. The American Airlines flight over Chicago on October 8,
2001 (28 days after the World Trade Center attack) did not have a
fortified cockpit door. Does the plane with that tail number have
a fortified cockpit door today? I doubt it. I don't think the FAA
has a list of the planes it regulates. If they do have such a
list, I don't think they have any idea which planes have got
security bars or equivalent fortification on their cockpit doors
and which do not. I don't think they are monitoring the voluntary
compliance of the airlines from day to day, week to week, or
month to month. I think the FAA plans to look into this area once
or twice a year in the hope that something will get done in a
year or so. The FAA is being negligent in relationship to the
circumstances taken as a whole. I think a Federal Judge would
agree, and than an injunctive remedy would be an appropriate
remedy to this negligent nonfeasance by the FAA.

Several large lawfirms in Washington have already turned down my
urgent request for pro bono assistance. They say that the

airlines are their clients, and that it would be a conflict of interest for them to take up the cause I have petitioned for.

I think it is contrary to the airlines interest to lobby for and receive $15 billion in security improvement money and bailout money and then to use their captive agency the FAA as a basis for not making the most rudimentary and obvious changes that need to be made to ensure cockpit security. I think they are building a case against themselves by presenting a modus operandi of doing business that is always trying to get away without spending a penny on safety or security that hasn't been commanded absolutely by law. That's why an emergency order that says "no bars --- no fly after November 30, 2001" is imperative to protect all Americans, in the air, and on the ground, and all members of the airline industry in their livelihoods. I don't think the airline executives are fully aware of the potential effects on their industry from another cockpit break-in, even if it is by a deranged man and not a terrorist as occurred on October 8, 2001. The next day -- October 9, 2001, Bin Laden's most senior military lieutenant said on Al Jazeera TV that "planes would rain from the sky all over the U.S." Apparently it didn't take long for the Al Queda cells in the U.S. to get word back to Bin Laden that cockpit doors were no more secure on October 8, 2001 than they had been four weeks earlier. One more incident involving a cockpit break-in and I think the industry will be irreparably damaged and may never come back to its former level of activity.

Security bars are very cheap. They are U shaped very thick steel. They are mounted on pivots to the left of the door. After the door closes they are brought down into catches on the right side of the door. There is a high bar and a low bar. It takes about three hours to install a set of security bars in a cockpit, using a team of two experienced craftsmen. The total cost has got to be well under $5,000 per plane -- so with a mere Billion dollars they could backfit a lot of planes - probably every plane that flies commercially. It would be money well spent. It should be spent right away. The economic benefit to the airlines would far exceed the cost of very rapid adoption of this obviously essential security measure, which is no panacea -- not the comprehensive solution, not the perfect engineering design, but which would foil most break-in attempts.

I expect the FAA can use their processes and procedures to wear down my initiative and force me to face them in Court or desist from proceeding. I would prefer to win at the petition level. That's why I'm asking for your help. Can you help me in any way, perhaps by joining in the petition, or taking it over as the attorney of record, or perhaps by referring me to a lawyer in Washington.

Very truly yours,

Robert Gary, Esq.

Encl: Petition 12 Oct 01

# Fax to : Jay Blackman  202-362-2009

From: Robert Gary

Date: 16 Oct 2001  2130 hrs EST

Jay,

I look forward to speaking with you tomorrow afternoon and here's the gist of what I have to say.

There are four numbers that are relevant in the cockpit security.

First: How many commercial airplanes are now under FAA jurisdiction? (Let n be greater than zero less than infinity)

Second: What percentage of these commercial airplanes now have Charlie Bars or better for cockpit security? (Let n be greater than zero, less than or equal to 100)

Third: On November 30, 2001 how many operational commercial airplanes will be under the jurisdiction of the FAA, give your best estimate (Let n be greater than zero less than infinity and probably less than the response to question #1 above).

Fourth: On November 30, 2001 what percentage of these operational commercial airplanes under the jurisdiction of FAA will have Charlie Bars or better for cockpit security, give your best estimate (Let n be greater than zero, less than or equal to 100)

These four numbers tell the whole story. If they go like this 5604, 15, 4973, 95 then there will be no reason for me take any action in any Court. But if they go like this 7831, 16, 7192, 22 then I will take whatever actions are appropriate and possible for me to protect and serve the public interest. It will be clear that the FAA has given us a line of unreliable information, and that their voluntary compliance program is a nullity.

You see, Jay, from a managerial perspective, numbers count. They really are the only thing that counts. We call them "results" or "outcomes". Everything else is window dressing. If you have something real to put in the window, it can be dressed up, no problem. But if you have nothing to put in the window except nonfeasance and nothingness then no amount of window dressing is going to make a manager think you have performed, or delivered results. Managers look at numbers. Why? Because they tell the real story, stripped of the "spin". If you have a chance to ask Ms. Jane Garvey a question on 17 October 2001 at the National Press Club, why not get the numbers from her?

Very truly yours,

Encl Petition 2nd copy

17 OCT 01

Actual 7000, 50, 7000, 95

CASE IS PROBABLY NOT NEEDED

**DMS Web**
**Docket Management System**

DOT          TASC

U.S. Department of Transportation 400 7th St. S.W. PL-401 Washington, D.C. 1-800-647-5527

| Search | ES Submit | Reports | Help | Support |

| Document FAA-2001-10864-1 | Hide | New Se |

## Docket Information

| Category | Docket Status |
|---|---|
| Petitions | Pending |

| Subcat. | Old Docket Num. |
|---|---|
| Airworthiness Standards | |

Docket Subject
Exemption/Rulemaking

Docket Title
Exemption/Rulemaking - Robert Gary

| Data Entry Date | RIN # | Action Office | Action Sought |
|---|---|---|---|
| 17-OCT-01 | | ANM | |

| Docket Parties | Stat. Deadline | Comment Close |
|---|---|---|
| | Last Update | Close Date |
| | 22-JAN-02 | |

Statutory Citation

| Statutory Judicial Requirement | -- CFR Citation -- |
|---|---|
| | 14-CFR-25 |

| Docket Attributes | Docket Abstract |
|---|---|
| ☐ ALJ Hearing | |
| ☐ Archived | |

## Document Information

| Document Type | Data Entry Date |
|---|---|
| Petition(s) | 17-OCT-01 |

| Document Title | Next Due Date |
|---|---|
| Robert Gary - Exemption/Rulemaking | |

| Document Date | Filing Date | Answer Date | Reply Date | Next Due Item |
|---|---|---|---|---|
| 12-OCT-01 | 17-OCT-01 | | | |

| Federal Reg. Citation | F. R. Pub. Date |
|---|---|
| | |

**132**

| Submitter | Submitters Representative | Service Date |
|---|---|---|
| Robert Gary<br>2211 Washington<br>Avenue #301 | | Effective Date |
| Assigned Document Numbers | Related Reply to Doc #s | Pages<br>1 |

Document Abstract

Emergency petition of Robert Gary for rulemaking regarding the installation of security bars to block unauthorized cockpit access on all U.S. commercial air carriers by November 30, 2001.

To download a document, click on a one of the following document format choices:

Scanned Image (TIFF)    (65831 bytes)

Adobe PDF    (110231 bytes)

| Refresh | Last | Docket | Hide | New Search |

**Note**: Beware of long scanned image file downloads if you are not on a high-speed connection. For exar 10 page TIFF image can take up to 3 minutes to download with a 28.8 modem.

| Search | ES Submit | Reports | Help | Support |

DMS2000 28-JAN-99

Robert.Gary@prodigy.net | English | Go | mail2web

☒

<u>Reply</u> - <u>Reply All</u> - <u>Forward</u> - <u>View Source</u> - Previous - <u>Next</u> - Message: **2 / 2**

From: **"Forest Rawl" Forest.Rawls@faa.gov**
To: Robert.Gary@prodigy.net, robert.gary@prodigy.net
Subject: **Re[2]: petition for rulemaking**
Date: Mon, 22 Oct 2001 16:10:07 -0400

Mr. Gary,
I am out of the office until October 26, 2001. I would try to work with Susan
or Marisa.
Thanks,
Forest
_____________________Reply Separator_____________________
Subject:   Re: petition for rulemaking
Author: "Robert Gary"
Date:      10/19/01 8:03 PM
October 19, 2001
1807 EST
Mr. Rawls,
Thank you for your message. I will call Susan Boylon on Monday. I ordered a
new
and better computer for my office today and it ships on October 29, 2001.
Perhaps you could check the docket for me sometime next week, and just let me
know by e-mail if anyone has filed anything against my petition. Just a one
line
e-mail is all I need. Then I'll go to the Library at Bethesda, like you
suggested. In ten days the problem will be solved (by the new computer), but
in
the meantime, Please give me a heads up if someone files any document that
opposes my petition. Voicemail would also work (301) 587-7147 -- it's on all
the
time, except as today when I'm on the line.
Due to the kindness of Susan Kapler of FAA in Washington I now have a copy of
the SFAR signed by Administrator Jane Garvey on October 3, 2001. Examination
of
that document suggests to me that my petition falls under SFAR No. 92 to part
121 of Chapter I of 14 CFR, of to put it the other way round 14 CFR Chapter I,
part 121, SFAR No. 92. My petition calls for a shorter deadline, and for
mandatory rather than voluntary compliance, and for a specific  directive
standard to be given for cockpit door modification -- i.e. "security bars or
equivalent cockpit door reinforcement".  Those are the only three points on
which my petition differs from Administrator Garvey's SFAR, so those are the
only issues raised by my petition. I recognize that Ms. Garvey's SFAR was
published 5 days before the incident on October 8, 2001, and that my petition
was made four days after that incident. I also recognize that DOT Secretary
Mineta has shortened the compliance time for the SFAR to 60 days instead of 90
days, thereby removing one of the three issues raised by my petition, leaving
only the other two. It comes down to a question of the criterion of adequacy
of
the modification and the manditoriness of the action to be taken. I want a
specific standard of door reinforcement to be met or the planes don't fly
after

November 30, 2001.
As mentioned to you by phone 50% of the fleet is now in compliance with my
standard (Charlie Bars or better) and by November 30, 2001 it is expected that
95% of the fleet will be in compliance. If the rate of installation of
adequate
door strengtheners continues as it is now, I expect to voluntarily withdraw my
petition on or about November 15, 2001. There will be no further need for a
docket process in this case, once it is clear that the facts meet or will very
shortly meet the requirements of my petition. Had the SFAR been written 6 days
later than it was, it might have been identical in substance to my petition.

      Very truly yours,
      /s/
      Robert Gary

----------

> Mr. Gary,
>
> I attempted to call you but the line was busy.  So, before I forget, Susan
> Boylon's telephone number is 425-227-1152.  Based on my assessment of the
> request, she (or someone in her office) will be handling this project.
> However,
> she may determine that you need to speak with Marisa Mullen (assignment of
the
> project is based on the issue involved – security of cockpit doors).
>
> Thanks,
> Forest Rawls
>

**Robert Gary, Esq.**
**2211 Washington Avenue (#301)**
**Silver Spring, MD 20910-2620**
**Tele: (301) 587-7147**

```
October 23, 2001                        FAX 202-267-5304

To: John McGraw                         Sent 23 Oct 01 22:58 EST
Asst Mangr Aircraft Engineering Div.
Federal Aviation Administration
Aircraft Certification Service
800 Independence Avenue, SW
(Attn: AIR-100)
Washington, DC 20591
```

Subj: FAA-2001-10864, 17-OCT-2001, Exemption/Rulemaking - Robert Gary (Emergency Petition for Cockpit Security Bars -- document date 12 October 2001, under 14 CFR, Chapter 1, part 121, SFAR No. 92.

1. Petition FAA-2001-10864 is hereby withdrawn.

2. It is no longer necessary, thus no longer appropriate

3. As of 23 October 2001 70% of fleet is in compliance, and best estimates indicate that as of 30 November 2001 99% of fleet will be in compliance.

4. Further procedures pursuant to abovementioned petition would serve no public interest, even though 1% of the fleet will not be in compliance by 30 November 2001 because the remoteness of the probability that terror organizations could effectively target non-compliers.

5. The requirements of the petition, having been substantially complied with, the petition is moot, and should be dismissed,on a voluntary basis,and without predjudice.

```
                              Signed,


                              Robert Gary
                              Petitioner
```

R O B E R T   G A R Y

Mr. John McGraw (Personal)                    November 13, 2001
AIR-100
Federal Aviation Administration
800 Independence Avenue, SW
Washington, DC 20591

Dear Mr. McGraw,

It was a pleasure to speak with you today by phone about my
process of withdrawing:

FAA-2001-10864, 17-OCT-2001, Exemption/Rulemaking - Robert Gary
(Emergency Petition for Cockpit Security Bars -- document date 12
October 2001, under 14 CFR, Chapter 1, part 121, SFAR No. 92)

As I said in our phonecall today, our prior correspondence on
this matter has apparently not gotten through for some reason --
unexplained.

Enclosed is a third copy that I'm sending out today with the hope
that one of the three copies will be filed by you with the
appropriate official person within the FAA/DOT system. Please
file this paper for me! I thought I had filed it by sending it to
you on October 23, 2001, but apparently that did not occur. The
paper somehow did not get through and into your hands. I plan to
send this out every day for the next three days with the idea
that one of the copies will arrive successfully on your desk. I
realize how hard the mail system is right now, so I've also sent
two copies by FAX.

If any of these copies or FAXES are ever actually received, it
would be very helpful to me if you could acknowledge that fact by
calling Robert Gary (301) 587-7147, or by letter to Robert Gary
(#301), 2211 Washington Avenue, Silver Spring MD 20910-2620, or
to Robert.Gary@prodigy.net By sending me some acknowledgement
that my withdrawal has been received, you would save me the
trouble of sending many copies of the same set of documents, the
content of which we already know, because of our conversations on
or about 23 Oct 2001 and again today 13 Nov 2001.

Thank you for your attention, **on a priority basis**, to this
matter.

                              Very truly yours,

Robert Gary (#301)
2211 Washington Ave.
Silver Spring, MD 20910

20 November 2000

Senator Richard Lugar
U.S. Senate
Washington DC 20510

Dear Senator Lugar,

Enclosed is the response received from CNO's office about my proposed transponder based proximity control system for situations like the USS Cole.

Based on a careful reading of this letter I feel it will take 30 Senators and 200 Members of the House to actively cause the navy to implement the system I propose. My own Representative happens to be on the Science and Technology Subcommittee in the House, which is quite helpful given the high tech nature of my proposal.

You are probably the single person on Capitol Hill with the greatest awareness of anti-terrorism safeguards, and so I'm hoping you will take an interest in this matter. Given a reasonable opportunity -- i.e. 15 minutes in the Secretary of the Navy's office for a face to face meeting -- I strongly feel that I could have a demonstration project up and running on three Navy ships by the Fall of 2001.

The Navy has proceeded to broaden the security issue more and more since the USS Cole terrorist strike, and to look into deeper and deeper historical issues. Several years from now, probably by the end of the next Administration, there will, no doubt, be a formidable 10 foot high stack of reports. I could have actual hardware up and running in 12 months, given 15 minutes of SECNAV's time. Could you arrange it?

Sincerely,

Robert Gary

(301) 587-7147

Robert.Gary@prodigy.net

Encl: Ltr from CNO's Asst Mr. Cavileer of 16 Nov 2000
      Robert Gary's answering letter of 20 Nov 2000

OFFICE OF THE VICE PRESIDENT

WASHINGTON

November 27, 2001

Dear Mr. Gary:

Thank you for contacting Vice President Cheney about homeland security issues.  I am responding on his behalf.

Your correspondence has been forwarded to the Office of Homeland Security for review. You will hear back directly from that office.

The Vice President appreciates hearing from you.  Thank you for taking the time to write.

Sincerely,

*Cecelia Boyer*

Cecelia Boyer
Special Assistant to the Vice President
for Correspondence

Mr. Robert Gary
2211 Washington Ave. #301
Silver Spring, Maryland  20910-2620

U.S. Department
of Transportation

**Federal Aviation
Administration**

800 Independence Ave., S.W.
Washington, DC 20591

DEC 1 4 2001

Robert Gary, USN
LT, JAGC, Retired
2211 Washington Ave (#301)
Silver Spring, MD 20910-2620

Dear Lieutenant Gary:

Thank you for your recent letter offering your thoughts and suggestions for increasing aviation security.

In the aftermath of the events of September 11, the Federal Aviation Administration (FAA) immediately implemented enhanced security measures to provide for the safety and security of the traveling public. Subsequently, the FAA began a process to identify, collect and evaluate suggestions that might offer improvements to aviation security. Your suggestion is included in that process.

Please accept our appreciation for your taking the time to share your thoughts and suggestions with us. Your help and support is an important contribution to ensuring the safety and security of the Nation's aviation system.

Sincerely,

Kenneth W. Peppard
Director
Tell FAA Task Force

2211 Washington Avenue (#301)
Silver Spring, MD 20910-2620
Tele: (301) 587-7147


Michael Jackson Deputy Secretary DOT          July 16, 2002
Attn: Ashley Connati
U.S. Department of Transportation          FAX 202 366 3937
400  7<sup>th</sup> Street SW
Washington DC 20590

**<u>Subj: Matter Referred to TSA by Ms. Connati Today</u>**

Dear Secretary Jackson and Ms. Connati,

Thank you for your responsiveness to my telephone call today. I understand that someone at the Transportation Security Administration will review my letter dated June 6, 2002 and addressed FAA to Administrator Jane Garvey.


For clarification of some of the points raised in my conversation with Ms. Connati I would like to offer the following remarks. My position is that all of the international terrorists that have made war on the U.S. since and including September 11, 2001 have in fact been Muslims, and this includes the shoe bomber and John Walker Lindh. My proposed rule is beyond any question a form of profiling of Muslims <u>who are foreign visitors</u> to the U.S. It would in no way affect any U.S. citizens, (such as Mr. Lindh), whether they are Muslims or non-Muslims.


I hold this view as a matter of ordinary common sense and I believe that in 30 minutes I could convince any open-minded American that this view is sensible. If foreign Muslim visitors to the U.S. were selectively disprivileged from any participation in general aviation <u>a few hundred foreign visitors a year</u> would be disappointed or slightly inconvenienced. Weigh this against a possible <u>10 trillion dollars worth of damage</u> and deliberate in a rational way about the balance of hardships and the tradeoff is fairly clear.


It is true that I am a lawyer – a public interest lawyer with 25 years experience much of which centers around national security and public health issues and none of which involves any action that has ever been anti-Muslim in any way. It is also true that my proposed rule could well be called the "Protection of Muslims and Others in America Rule" since the event that I'm seeking would save dozens perhaps hundreds of Muslims along with 2 or 3 hundred thousand others in the USA.


As a member of the Bar of the U.S. Supreme Court I am of course very sensitive to the Constitutional implications of my proposed rule. I suggest today that it be made a condition of issuance of new visas to Muslims. They agree as a condition of getting their visa that they will not participate in  any way in general aviation while in the USA. Why

1

not do the same for Norwegians or Shinto people or Eskimos? Well, that would be obvious to about half of us and a deep question to the other half. That's why rational open minded deliberation is so vital in this case.

Here's another reason. I believe this case in non-justiciable. Had I thought it was justiciable I would have filed a petition for a rulemaking, as I did in the matter of the security bars for the cockpit doors (FAA-2001-10864-1). In this particular matter the FAA and DOT would not be violating any of their own rules or any statute or clause of the Constitution if they granted my request or if they denied my request. It is a matter entirely of **Executive discretion** to be exercised entirely in the **Executive Branch** of our government (including the Agencies and the White House, but not including the Congress or the Courts). The only cure for mis-exercise of executive discretion is impeachment, there is no legislative or judicial cure.

Why is this true? Because this matter deals with foreigners and with national security and Courts have consistently ruled in matter of this kind that the Executive branch is uniquely qualified to address regulation in these areas. Cases of this sort are deem non-justiciable or they are called political questions. Therefore bringing my request before an ALJ, a U.S. District Court Judge or even the Supreme Court would be a waste of time. Beyond that it would diminish the efficacy of the rule by suggesting that such a rule could appropriately be revolked by our Courts. Since I think the Courts would and should stay clear of the rule, it would be inconsistent for me to place the matter before an ALJ or any Court, and I won't do it.

Is it appropriate for the DOT, FAA, and TSA to hear me out on this matter? I think it is. Since my request is non-justiciable and I have special qualifications in the area of nuclear hazards and national security and all I want to do is be heard and considered in a deliberative open-minded way, yes I think it's alright for an Agency to listen to a citizen under those conditions as does Senator Sarbanes and Congressperson Connie Morella who have both written letters on my behalf (in spite of the fact that there senior staff feel very strongly that my proposal is a non-starter).

Being reasonable is no crime. Failure to bar foreign Muslim visitors to the US from participation in general aviation at this time is, from my humble perspective, a crime against reason and good sense in light of the fact that **all of the attackers on September 11, 2001 and since then have been Muslims** and the fact that no one in this world can reliably tell the difference in advance between the 99% of Muslims who are peaceful and the 1% who wish to do us harm. On the very first day that someone can reliably make this distinction I will be the first one to say only foreign Muslims who are terrorists should be barred from general aviation and that the rest should be allowed to fly. On the very day that we are attacked by Eskimos or Shintoes or Taoists or Norwegians I will say that the class of foreigners barred from general aviation in the US should be broadened. Being reasonable is no crime, and <u>for an Agency and a citizen to reason together is a good thing not a bad thing.</u>

Now you ask "What about hazardous materials trucks and 100 other things?" Good question. Here's my answer. Those things are covered in my letter to Attorney General John Ashcroft of 12 July 2002 on the subject of the Homeland Security Observers Program – which by the way is remarkably similar to the TIPS Program announced by the Attorney General today. If I didn't think that general aviation was a special case, I wouldn't come with a letter to the FAA (which they say should have gone to the TSA, but I'm not sure the TSA has the authority to grant my request and issue an emergency rule barring all foreign Muslim visitors to the US from any participation in general aviation). There is no vector like a general aviation plane to deliver an explosive charge to a spent fuel storage pool, and I think the NRC would bear me out on that. Commercial airliners are tracked too carefully, trucks would be stopped at the facility perimeter, individuals could not carry adequate weight of explosives. Keep in mind that there is no rule that bars a foreign visitor to the US from buying explosives, or from buying a Learjet, or from putting his explosives in his Learjet, or from flying from point A to point B in the US such that part of that track might come within 100 miles of a nuclear power plant with an onsite spent fuel storage pool. If he departs from his 100% lawful track at 450 miles per hour and makes a beeline for the spent fuel storage pool, humanity has <u>12 minutes to save itself</u> – not enough time in my humble opinion – considering that a Cessna flew almost directly over the White House on June 19 2002 and wasn't even detected until it was out of restricted airspace.

**<u>If we are to save ourselves it has to be before the Muslim foreign visitor gets into that plane and takes off</u>**. That's my case in a nutshell. That's why I want to argue for profiling in this matter. That and the fact that there's not a scintilla of evidence to suggest even to the most Pollyannaish optimist that we can at this time reliably tell (i.e. by "security screening") which Muslims are law abiding peace lovers and which are secret Jihad warriors. One does not become popular by proposing such politically incorrect profiling. Sometimes what is security correct is not politically correct. My idea has been widely scorned and ridiculed on Capitol Hill by staffers. Serving the public interest is not always fun. But I'm hoping that this officer of the Court can be heard within the Executive branch Departments and Agencies who are sworn to protect the Constitution and the people of the US from all enemies foreign and domestic. I have no legal case. If DOT/FAA/TSA decides to listen to me it's got to be because you are dutiful public servants who want to deliberate reasonably even about ideas that at first hearing sound "unacceptable". Reasonable deliberation means taking in a diversity of opinions and examining them on their merits, and on the facts and circumstances as they really exist in the US right now. By taking my views into serious consideration the country would be well served even if ultimately you decline to issue the emergency rule as it has been proposed in my letter of June 6, 2002 to Administrator Jane Garvey.

Very truly yours,


Robert Gary, Esq.

# Part C

# Preventing Airborne Attacks on Nuclear Power Plants in USA

## (5 Aug 2002 - 13 Jan 2004)

2211 Washington Ave (#301)
Silver Spring, MD 20910-2620
Tele: (301) 587-7147

Roy P. Zimmerman                                        August 5, 2002
Director Office of Nuclear Security and Incident Response
U.S. Nuclear Regulatory Commission                     FAX: 301-415-2234
Washington DC 20852

Subj: Our Telephone Conversation this date

Dear Director Zimmerman,

Enclosed are the tech specs on the Tactical High Energy Laser which was mentioned in our telephone conversation today. As you know, I want you to be my ambassador to Chairman Meserve on the subject of approaching FAA/TSA/DOT about barring foreigners who are Muslims and visitor to the U.S. from any participation in general aviation. The reasons are very plain from my letter to Administrator Jane Garvey of two months ago (see enclosed letter dated 6 June 2002).

The first question the Chairman will ask if you approach him about this matter is "Well, did Robert do everything that he could possibly do to get a response from FAA/TSA/DOT? That would be the moment for you to say "Well, here's letter from Senator Sarbanes asking FAA to respond to Robert, and here's a letter from Congresswoman Morella asking for the same thing – so it looks like he did everything he could possibly do."

My hope is that Chairman Meserve will see that my concerns are his concerns and that the issues I raise actually do fall within his province. And so he will say "I want to get behind this initiative, I want to support it, let's draft a letter to Admiral Loy, and to Administrator Garvey and to Secretary Mineta. Let's get on record our support for the provident and circumspect suggestions made by Robert. The Committee for Environment and Public Works will see that the NRC is in the business of Imagineering, we are ahead of the curve, we are not waiting to react to a bad thing happening – we are going to stop it from happening – that's our basic approach, and that's why we are ready to send a letter to FAA/TSA/DOT and and suggest that at least they acknowledge receipt of the many letters and faxes that Robert has sent to them.

There it is. It's a lot to ask, but I'm asking it. I need help dealing with these Agencies otherwise they just lose my mail, mislay my faxes, forget my phonecalls – it's like they are not there. $1.3 Trillion is probably not enough for the American People to pay every year to have a government in place. If it were $130 Trillion, they probably could answer their mail, and deliberate about the critical issues at the core of their missions. Things being as they are, however, it takes a lot of extra effort for a citizen to have any "input" into the content of policy.

1

On the subject of the Tactical High Energy Laser,  I can't hope to get action unless I have a chance to make a brief presentation and then overcome the objections of junior and senior people at NRC. I have to make them see that it works, it's cheap, it's timely, and that it would be good for NRC go forward with this initiative. It might be the one thing that would help prevent the emergence of an Energy Security Agency, which would clearly be a very bad idea, a total kludge – spaghetti like table of organization – completely inconsistent with the fact that the potential harm from nuclear power plants under attack is orders of magnitude different from any other imaginable threat the U.S. might face.  If hitting a dam, or a P-3 lab, or a chemical plant would cause $1 Trillion worth of damage, then hitting an aux building at a nuke would cause $10 Trillion worth of damage which is an order of magnitude greater.

I acknowledge that 25 years ago my main concern about a nuclear power plant disaster was long-term genetic damage and latent cancers – but that is not my concern now. I was a kid then. Public health was my main concern. I worried about mutations, especially after Three Mile Island and Chernobyl. Those are secondary issues for me at this point. I now feel that the impact of  $10 Trillion worth of damage would destabilize all parts of the U.S. economy. The government at every level would be unable to maintain control. We would revert to chaos and pandemonium – and no "consequence management" people and "homeland security" people would make the smallest particle of difference. If this were Norway of New Zealand I probably would not say that, but this country is a powder keg in about six ways and any major disruption would, in my opinion, trigger a national collapse into violence and poverty. Keep in mind that in 1973, when we had a gasoline shortage, people were shooting each other at gas stations because one cut ahead of the other in line. This happened several times, not just once. We are not ready for a Rassmusen Report WASH-1400 scenario. So my concern is not genetic damage or latent cancers, it's saving the land of my birth, the greatest democratic republic the world has ever seen, or is likely to see.

Without help or a chance to be heard there is no possibility that what I have to say can have a meaningful effect. But if you help me, and give me chance to make my case, there is some possibility that the FAA/TSA/DOT might come around and do the obviously smart thing, and there's an excellent chance that NRC will take a strong interest in laser cannons, that they will get the nuclear power plant operators to install them, and that the airspace around nuclear power plants will be protected in ways that talking on walkie talkies and looking at computer screens cannot possibly do. You have a twelve minute window. The choice is between doing something and doing nothing. A laser cannon gives you the chance to do something and in a way that is totally consistent with taking advantage of the strengths of a nuclear power plant. Always use your situation – if you are a nuke, you have certain self-defensive possibilities that nobody else has – so use them. All I am saying is --- give 10 megawatts a chance.

I look forward to knowing your thoughts, and hopefully to meeting with you.

Very truly yours

**NRC Presentation**

**by**

**Robert Gary**

Let's start with the broad policy issues and then work down into the technical details.

Should the NRC get into the combat business, and if so why?

Yes, it should for two reasons. First if it doesn't the Congress will probably create an Energy Security Agency to safeguard nuclear plants, dams, refineries, coal-fired plants, and nuclear materials in transit. Such an agency would have a diffuse responsibility, it would pre-empt and interfere with the NRC's routine work, it would appropriate part of the NRC's traditional responsibility and authority, and possibly part of its budget as well. In my estimation it would do a poor job at safeguarding nuclear power plants compared to the job that the NRC could do if it decided to get into the combat business.

Second, because it's better to be self-reliant than to rely on "the system" where the system means someone else, like the Air National Guard, the Airforce, the Army or some other organization performing combat duty on the NRC's behalf. Nukes are spread out all over the country. Some are in locations that are not close to available combat assistance. The cost of  a high level of risk mitigation using the system, which means someone else, and the need to coordinate with them, which means the need to maintain the capacity to coordinate with and get them in place to do the job within the 12 minute window – that cost would be extremely high in comparison to the cost of a self-reliant system that can be run from the control room directly with no need to coordinate with anyone else and no delay in taking necessary action against an incoming attacker.

To summarize why the answer is "yes" the 2 reasons again are to avoid dilution of authority and to avoid wasted expense.

Next issue: Could the NRC get into the combat business cheaply and on a small scale? Answer: Yes it could. It could do a demonstration project at Peach Bottom or Calvert Cliffs, or at any convenient nuke. I would take the High Energy laser used by the Israelis, developed by the U.S. and thoroughly tested out at White Sands. I would just use the actual laser cannon and the target acquisition/fire control radar. You don't need to buy the mobile power source because you are going to plug the laser cannon right into your nuke. So about half the cost is saved right there. You do need to wire up a panel in the control room, but you don't need to re-invent the panel. Just use the one the Israelis use in their mobile vehicle as modified for application to a fixed point laser cannon with a continuously available virtually unlimited power source. The

Israelis somehow were able to afford several mobile systems, we should be able to pay for part of one of them at least.

So to summarize, it is possible to try out the idea on a demonstration project basis because the technology is literally off-the-shelf, modular, turnkey, and affordable. Training up one senior man per shift to use the panel in an emergency, which would be a TAD sort of function, not a full-time job, could entail some orientation and training costs but again, these would be quite containable. Once a demonstration project is up and running NRC can do some tests and see if it likes the idea of laser cannon combat to protect nukes. You can see if it works. If it does, you can show others that it works, and they can see how cheap and how good it is. Policymakers can then make policy based on real information. Appropriators can spend money based on solid cost/benefit analysis. Galileo was perhaps the first one to come up with this idea of experimenting to find out how things are, the idea has caught on until today even management professors talk about the excellent business leaders who try things out on a small scale, and then if they work, they get scaled up. You try, you see, you decide, and then you do. Tom Peters perhaps put this concept in its most radical form when he said, "Ready, Fire! Aim" Norbert Weiner the founder of modern cybernetics points out that all well managed systems are based on the feedback concept – essentially the idea of experimenting and integrating information into future action.

How dangerous would this be? Not as dangerous as letting a small plane crash through the roof of an auxiliary building. But to answer the question directly it has pluses and minuses in terms of danger. If the off-track plane is initially spotted by an an alert air traffic controller, and if it is more than 100 miles out when it goes off track, there may be time, and it may be possible to go through a traditional chain of command fire control authorizing process through the

National Command Authority which I understand for these matters is pre-delegated to the Secretary of Defense or his designated deputy. If the possible attacker is not picked up by an air controller but is picked up for the first time by the nuke's own sky surveillance radar then it is up to the senior officer of the watch at the nuke to exercise pre-delegated authority to make the fire control decision. Basically if you are within the 12 minute time frame the nuke has to defend itself, and make its own decisions. If you are way outside the final 12 minutes then there's time for a more elevated authorizing person to be in the loop.  The panel has to include some capacity to do something other than fire the laser cannon. Obviously you want to be able to establish radio contact with the pilot to warn him off. I would be very comfortable with something like a Bofers cannon set up right next to the laser cannon and load up with flashbang anti-aircraft shells. These would be made of cellulose and designed to make bright flashes and loud bangs but to avoid any harm to the plane. You also want a spotlight you can put on the plane. You have a radio warning going out on many frequencies, you have your spotlight, you have your flashbang anti-aircraft fire. The idea is that only a genuine combatant or a total fool would continue to fly a course fraught with such warnings. If the plane keeps coming, you fire up the laser and lase the cockpit enough to blind or stun the pilot, if that doesn't work you cut off some parts (like the tail), and if the plane is still on course for your aux building you blow it up into a fireball in the sky. So those are the minuses. There are dangers to being combat ready. Probably some fools are going to get themselves killed by flying in real fast planes, when the air traffic controllers are tired or on a break, and veering suddenly into restricted airspace over a combat ready nuke with all their cockpit radios turned off and with their ears plugged and without looking out the cockpit window. Such a person could get shot down even if he was not a terrorist, and his family would be understandably irate when they write to their Congressman about it, and when they present of tearful tale of their victimhood. To deny such risks would be incorrect. It's better to be explicit about them, weigh them, and accept them as concomitant risks that are unavoidable if this plan is adopted.

But what are the promised plusses (apart from averting a $10 Trillion terrorist attack from which the U.S. would never recover)?

Here's one: The laser cannon equipped nukes might be able to do more for the country than just protect themselves. If you think it would be glorious for the NRC to shoot down a terrorist attacking a nuke, that is certainly correct, but the glory would be even more visible if a laser cannon equipped nuke shot down a terrorist heading for Washington DC where the politicians live and conduct their deliberations in the Capitol and the White House and the Pentagon. When a plane veers off course and heads for Washington (or any other big city, or a military base, or a refinery, or a chemical plant, or a

P-3 lab) it's possible that the terrorist at the stick may not know or care that he's flying over or near a combat ready nuke. But if the nuke were alerted and asked for assistance they could perhaps do what the airforce could not do. The nuke could down that plane and save Washington. If you had laser cannons at nukes at many compass points around Washington, or any other target city, they could serve the way picket ships do defending a carrier in the Navy. Carriers don't rely entirely on their ability to scramble planes off their own decks to defend themselves – they rely on outlying ships called picket ships to detect and kill incoming attackers --- especially kamikazes which are a very close analog to our present day airborne terrorists.

So the bottom line is that the NRC could cover itself with glory and receive the undying support of politicians if it saved Washington DC from a terror attack by using a laser cannon to bring down a terror plane en route. Such a scenario is not highly likely but it will be more likely if we go to war in Iraq and stimulate the enmity of many Muslims on a worldwide basis. They come to the U.S. Some want to do us harm. Some can afford to buy or rent a general aviation plane, which is presently not illegal for them to do. Some can afford to buy thousands of pound of explosives, which is amazingly also not illegal for foreign Muslim visitors to do in the U.S. at a time of war. It's not illegal for them to put their property in their plane. Since there's no crimes here there's no basis for warrant based searches or wiretaps. The FBI and CIA have no specific knowledge to alert them, and no legal basis to acquire knowledge by search, surveillance or wiretap. The first time anybody knows anything is when then plane goes off its track, maybe with a 90 degree change of course from a track that is tangent to a 100 mile radius around a nuke. If it's a Gulfstream moving at 450 miles per hour, loaded up with 15,000 pounds of Semtex, and one unflinchingly suicidal pilot humanity has 12 minutes to save itself. It either does or it doesn't – there's no such thing as "trying" in this situation.

That aux building has a much better chance of keeping its roof if the NRC doesn't have to call anybody to save it. If the nuke in combat ready, self-reliant, technically equipped, properly alert and correctly trained the happy ending is possible. Without these  providential measures a very sad ending is likely.

That's why the NRC should get into the combat business.


But why is the laser cannon the weapon of choice?


Because it doesn't put any ordnance up in the air. What doesn't go up, cannot come down and when you are working in a populated area where the population is comprised of your own fellow citizens this is an important consideration. You don't want to let off missiles or machine gun bullets to try to knock down a wayward plane, when those projectiles have a substantial chance of coming down on innocent Americans.

With a laser cannon you either hit the target or you hit nothing. So this particular weapon is well suited to use on an anti-aircraft basis in highly populated areas, which is probably why the Israelis chose it, bought it and deployed it. It cost them about $3,000 per shot to fire their mobile laser cannons. It would cost a nuke about 10% of that to fire a fixed-point stationary laser cannon powered by the nuke itself.

Lasers being as precise as they are, radar being as good as it is, especially against non-stealthy non-jamming, non-chaff equipped planes, it may be possible to surgically disassemble an attacking plane in the air – allowing for a semi-controlled landing, far from the nuke, but possibly without killing the pilot or others on the plane. Galileo would say you have to conduct the experiment if you want this data. I agree. I don't know what's possible, but a demonstration project would show what's possible. If you did it at Peach Bottom you could have a gallery of policymakers and appropriators there to be appropriately amazed (or not, depending on how the experiment goes).

So combat is a righteous and necessary addition to NRC mission, given our current conditions, lasers are a cost effective, highly precise, and relatively low risk weapon that takes full advantage of the strengths that are particular to a nuclear power plant (lots of power, trained vigilant operators, and good communications). The idea is feasible at least at the demonstration project stage, and after that you will have a database from which to decide if it's worth scaling up, or if you just want to close it down, write it up and put it in the archives. You have the liberty of informed decisionmaking that is the fruit of having the courage to do the experiment. I think it will take some courage in Washington even to propose the experiment. But I think the NRC is on a riskier course if it makes no proposals, has no initiatives, presents no bold suggestions because someone else will and the policy driver who does have a plan always seems to erode the authority of

organizations that don't have a plan, who have no innovative

ideas, who seek no demonstration projects, who don't want

breakthrough data from fresh experiments. I don't want NRC

to be pre-empted by some sort of  Energy Security Agency,

which I am convinced would be a kludge and an organizational

Rube Goldberg machine like every other all-inclusive new

agency the government tries to build to coordinate everything.

The NRC is not perfect, but it does a pretty good job keeping

man and radioactivity separate from each other. Growth is

always disruptive, it's usually resisted, it's rarely easy. The

NRC needs to grow into its combat role and I have every

confidence that it will choose to do so and that it will be

successful in doing so.

**ROBERT GARY**
2211 Washington Avenue (Apt. 301)
Silver Spring, MD 20910-2620

Director Roy Zimmerman                         November 13, 2002
Nuclear Regulatory Commission
Washington DC

Dear Director Zimmerman,

Since my transmission to you of the 14 page FAX on October 9, 2002 we have had a good conversation about it, but I don't know that anything has actually been done. So, I would like to offer some additional considerations in support of my proposal at this time.

Going ahead with a demonstration project to defend a nuclear power plant with a laser cannon would be a way for the NRC to participate in our national Homeland Defense effort. I'm asking the NRC to get involved in this national effort in spite of the fact that the particulars of my suggestion are something that you have not in fact done before. The NRC would have to initiate a new program to get this demonstration project up and running. The suggestion comes from outside the Agency, and I realize how difficult it is to work something like this in to your ongoing plans and operations. There has to be a strong reason for it or it will simply be brushed aside by organizational inertia.

So here's a reason that I didn't mention before. When the facts change the security threat changes, and the facts have changed,  and thereby greatly elevating the security threat faced by our nuclear power plants. In the absence of any indication of new countermeasures designed to offset that greatly elevated threat, it seems to me that the Price-Anderson Act should be re-examined to determine if it is still reasonably related to the well being of this country. To an outsider it might appear that the industry is so reluctant to spend additional funds on new countermeasures that it causes its captive regulatory Agency to disregard the kind of suggestion that is contained in my FAX. This, if true, would constitute heedless and reckless conduct which might take the industry outside of the insurance protection currently afforded to it by the Price-Anderson Act. When the facts change, good faith risk mitigation requires that the countermeasures have to change to keep up with the threat profile.

Probably the most powerful weapon that Muslim terrorists have in their arsenal is their ability to operate in the United States without being singled out as Muslims. This anonymity provides them with cover, and using that cover they can take a plan 99% of the way toward completion before we detect it or have the ability to begin formulating a response. That's why nuclear power plants have to start thinking about defending themselves in a tactical real-time situation.

As you know, I made very vigorous efforts at the Federal Aviation Administration (FAA) to get foreign Muslim visitors to the United States, who are not citizens barred completely from any participation in general aviation. In almost any country in the world,

1

throughout all of history, under similar circumstances, this would be considered a completely reasonable thing to do. During the Battle of Britain, German foreign visitors to Britain were not permitted to rent general aviation planes in Britain and fly around in British skies. When we were at War with Japan, we didn't let Japanese foreign visitors to the United States, who were not U.S. citizens rent general aviation planes and fly around in American skies. Due to an unfortunate combination of personnel selection for leadership positions at DOT/FAA/TSA, and heavy influence by the State Department, whose mission it is to be diplomatic and not offend anyone, and a heavy influence by junior staff people on Capitol Hill and at the White House who want to "feel good about themselves" and be politically correct at all times in every action they take, what we have here is a situation of logical impairment which has led to a security gap.

As a result of this security gap which is continuing and growing the nuclear industry as a whole is now imposing and externalizing greater risks and greater potential costs on the entire remainder of our society and this is exacerbated by the refusal, so far, of the industry or the NRC to implement new security countermeasures to meet the new security threat. I asked Chairman Meserve to help me approach the FAA with my proposal to get foreign Muslims barred from general aviation. It didn't happen. The head of TSA was fired and replaced, but it still didn't happen, and it hasn't happened as this letter is being written. So expect skies in the U.S.A. to contain foreign Muslim visitors to this country who are not citizens. Expect that maybe some of them would have a bad attitude toward this country and a desire to injure this country and kill Americans. Expect that among these there might be some who could afford to buy a Gulfstream and pack it with 15,000 pounds of Semtex or C-4. Expect that all the people who try this will be 100% anonymous and invisible to law enforcement and security agencies until they are about 12 minutes out from a nuclear power plant moving at around 450 miles per hour, headed for that Aux Building and for Paradise. With this expectation in mind ask yourself, "Is it reasonable that we disregard a suggestion which if implemented could greatly mitigate this threat?" I think, based on our excellent conversations on the phone, that you will come to the view that my suggestion should not be disregarded.

It is far better of the nuclear industry to protect itself, nuke by nuke, on a real time basis than for this protection to be afforded any other way. It is much more cost effective and much more likely to succeed. It is technically possible, and laser cannon equipped nukes would create collateral benefits for other parts of our society – possible partial protection of cities, like Washington D.C. for example. If the nukes have to be brought under some umbrella of protection organized by someone other than the NRC it will be a poor and clumsy and costly arrangement which in the critical moment may well turn out to be dysfunctional, as many things are both in and outside of government.

Inaction and unresponsiveness by the NRC is imposing costs on businesses. When the risk goes up, their insurance goes up, if they can even get it. As a practical matter businesses are moving away from, or deciding not to locate to, areas around nuclear plants. These decisions create economic dislocations because they are not essentially market-based but rather they are based on an uncontrolled exogenous variable to which business has to adapt. These dislocations are invisible except to an economist but they are real, they are costing people jobs, they are reducing our Gross Domestic Product, they are cutting into the productivity and efficiency that might be there if businesses were free of the worry about being close to nukes. The cost of going ahead with my proposed demonstration project is so miniscule compared to the economic value of these business dislocations that it would seem very reasonable for the NRC to take my proposal seriously, hear me out fully on its content and workability, and then go ahead and write it up as a program to be presented for consideration by the newly constituted Environment and Public Works Committee that will be seated in the Senate in January of 2003. These are going to be very serious people, with a very serious Chairman. The first question they are going to ask the NRC is "What have you got that's new to show us?" Perhaps my little demonstration project could be part of the package that you provide in response to this question.

So, I look forward to working more actively with you. I would still like to come to your offices and make a presentation or have a discussion with you and your staff. I do not sell laser cannons. I am not connected with any group, and specifically with any environmentalist group, or activist group, I am not a member of any political party or religious organization. I have absolutely no agenda or motivation except to do what is reasonable to protect the lives, health, and property of the American people. My record of action along these lines is easily researched. It goes back for 25 years, it's in every law library and case research database. I'm hoping that this is enough to get me in the door of your office. My sense is that you are a person of goodwill, intelligence, and integrity who earnestly wants to do what is best. So let's reason together and see what is possible.


Respectfully yours,

Robert Gary

**ROBERT GARY**
2211 Washington Avenue (Apt 301)
Silver Spring, MD 20910-2620

President George W. Bush                                              18 December 2002
The White House
1600 Pennsylvania Ave., NW
Washington DC 20500

Dear President Bush,

I have written to the Nuclear Regulatory Commission (NRC) and spoken briefly with one of the Directors there about my idea of defending nuclear power plants from airborne attacks by the use of tactical high energy lasers. I sent a fairly complete technical paper to the NRC describing the use by the Israelis of high energy tactical laser cannons on mobile units to knock down incoming SCUD missiles. My materials, I think, may have gotten lost in the shuffle at NRC. I sent them a 14 page FAX with a complete presentation and asked for their response. They have not sent me back any comment on my presentation, nor have they agreed to meet with me. I asked for a 15 minute meeting or a 1 page letter responding to my FAX, but so far, it hasn't happened. I would be very grateful if you or your staff could communicate with NRC and encourage them to meet with me for 15 minutes or send me a one page letter at least acknowledging that my FAX was received and perhaps offering some comment on its contents.

Apart from that issue, I have two brief remarks to offer on the possible future military engagement in Iraq. I don't think that Hans Blix is going to find anything. I think his "work" is an impediment to the progress of reason and to the interests of the U.S. At the same time I think that a general war and an invasion of all of Iraq without absolute proof positive of the Iraqi weapons of mass destruction program would be exceedingly costly in terms of risk to our soldiers and possible destabilization of the region. I also think the C.I.A. has definitive information about precisely where to look and how to find Saddam's WMD arsenal. So, I would propose a military raid on a specific site for the specific purpose of seizing the evidence that would prove to all persons the fact that Saddam has lied, that he is flouting the U.N. and that he is preparing to wreck havoc on those he opposes using chemical, biological and nuclear weapons.

The ideal place to make this raid would have three characteristics. First, it must be a place where we are absolutely certain that we will be able to seize evidence that is so compelling that no one anywhere in the world can reasonably deny its meaning. Second, the place must be some considerable distance from Baghdad. Third, the place should be fairly isolated so that it is surrounded not by dense civilian populations but rather by large flat empty areas extending out several tens of miles all around. I don't know if such an ideal site for such a military raid to seize evidence can be identified, but if it can, I would propose going in with airborne assault forces. Conquering the site with total force. Imprisoning all Iraqis found at the site and not killed in the assault. Setting up a helicopter landing zone for re-supply, and an intensive combat air patrol for perimeter

1

defense, and then bringing in our experts and technicians to take the site apart brick by brick if necessary until we find the evidence we seek.

There are several advantages to this approach. First, it does not preclude going into full-scale, country-wide war mode at a later point – it leaves that option open. Second, it is parsimonious in terms of risk to American life. It's an unexpected lighting strike on a fairly remote site that couldn't possibly be heavily enough defended to cause large American casualties in overwhelming that remote site. Third, once the site is taken, and the on site Iraqis are imprisoned we get to fight on the defense in a fairly remote, flat, and isolated area. Defending a firebase (like Camp Rhino) is far less hazardous than patrolling through the streets of Baghdad or Tikrite in search of Saddam. If the Republican Guard comes out of their barracks and into the field they can and should be killed en masse, and if they bring armor or artillery, it can be destroyed once and for all. We would be in an air-war mode but not in a jungle country (like Vietnam was) but in a flat desert country where we can see every part of the battlespace and we can kill everything we see.

The fourth advantage of this tactical approach is that if it doesn't pan out we can retreat from it with very little harm done, and **relatively** little risk incurred. There would be no massive civilian casualties, or massive civilian suffering. The world already knows we want to look for weapons in Iraq, there would be no surprise in that. Much of the Moslem world already hates the U.S. It is unlikely that this would be substantially increased by the evidence-seeking raid I propose. But an all-out invasion causing significant collateral damage (as Saddam would make sure it would), could trigger a global struggle of all Moslems against the U.S. If the raid does pan out, and we do come up with indisputable evidence, we can bring people from all countries in the look at it right where we found it. The French and the Russians could be satisfied completely, as could the U.N.

That's the point at which we would be in the position we would like to be in now. We would have a unified world, including the perennial dissenters in the U.S. who are very vocal and very critical and who, as we learned from Vietnam, can bring enormous pressure to bear to end a U.S. military engagement.

That is the point at which we tell Saddam he has a choice between total disarmament and death. We also tell him that if we are compelled by him to invade his whole country to disarm him, then on the morning that we **begin** doing that there is no longer any such thing as Iraqi Oil. Every drop of oil in Iraq becomes legitimate spoils of war (fully authorized under international law and custom for a treaty-breaker and for a truce-breaker and for a terrorist promoting and preparing for unconventional warfare contrary to the Geneva Conventions, and to universally recognized international norms). What formerly had been Iraqi oil becomes at that **moment** a part of the U.S petroleum reserves which we happen to be storing in the ground under Iraq and which we will remove when it is convenient for us to do so.

If are going to wage full-scale country-wide war in Iraq, we should make it a paying proposition, so that it is taxpayer friendly for U.S. taxpayers. Doing a good deed for all mankind is a wonderful thing (like shooting a rabid dog in the street), but it would get even better and fuller support from the American People if it were a paying proposition as well. If it meant that we no longer have to be deferential and polite to the Saudis when deference and diplomatic courtesy is not justified by their actions as they affect us, then I think the war would get better support. If it meant that Americans would have 50 cent a gallon gasoline for the next 50 years, if they wanted it, then the war would get better support. If it meant a reconstruction project to rebuild Iraq that provided very good jobs for a quarter of a million Americans over a period of 20 years at no cost to the U.S. Treasury, the war would get better support. I offer these comments not as a retired military lawyer, (although I am), and not as an MBA, (although I am), but simply as a practical realist in the assessment of the military and political situation that we face. I do not think the State Department would find my suggestions either legal or reasonable, but history, the actual law, and the precedents set by our Departments of Defense and Justice, bear me out fully. Prizes of war are o.k. They are not mandatory but they are also not prohibited. If the war is justified and the prizes taken are reasonably proportionate to the costs of waging the war, and do not impose undue suffering on the civilian population of the losing side, it is o.k. to just take Iraq's oil as a prize of war.

This is what Saddam needs to understand. First he will be dead. Then after he is dead everyone will see that we have taken all his assets and all his weapons. He will have no successor. The memory of Saddam will be the memory of a man who lost everything his country had, and no one will think back fondly on him, not in Iraq, not in any other part of the Moslem world, or any part of the rest of the world. He will get death right away and infamy forever, or if wants he can open his files to us and reveal every weapon, every lab, every site of interest to us, and every person of interest to us. In exchange for that he can live in Guantanamo Bay for the rest of his life in a nice house with decent amenities not including contact with anyone outside of Guantanamo Bay. It would be sort of like what Napoleon got on the island of Elba. Also in exchange for his total capitulation we would refrain from destroying his country. We would not kill his subordinates, his troops, or his civilians. We would not take his country's oil as a prize of war. He would die, perhaps after a long life, with the possibility of being well thought of among some people in Iraq and maybe in other places as well.

Stark choices don't always convince madmen. Ultimatums work on some and don't work on others. We should make the ultimatum to Saddam public in almost every detail so that all of mankind can hear it, and know the choice that is offered. If we are rebuffed, we should carry out on our threat with speed and totality. Kill Saddam, kill any soldiers that try to assist him, take his oil, occupy his country, liberate his people, use the place as a base from which to reform the Arab world in toto.

The cost is never small when such a military action is done, and it won't be small this time. We might lose several thousand men and women, more perhaps than died on that fateful day September 11, 2001. The historical **outcome** of a war is the only thing that can possibly "justify" it and I'm not sure anything can completely justify it to a grieving parent or sibling. Gallant men and women fight our wars, they always have, they always will. If we do it this time it should be based on incontrovertible evidence that is so compelling and abundant, and for every doubting Thomas to come and visit and touch with his own finger, that there can be no doubt of the justice of our cause. That having been established, beyond any sensible cavil, we then make clear to the world that Saddam, in the face of our reasonable offer, compels us to engage in total war against his whole country. And if he does, we take him out, do what we have to do to prevent any future Saddam (probably a military governorship for 20 years, as we did in Japan), and defray **all** the costs of the entire venture by taking the prize oil for our own use and selling it to the Europeans. Consider me a volunteer for such an effort. I would serve on the front lines or anywhere else where I could be of value. No one should counsel war who cannot with a sincere heart make such an offer. Based on the right foundation, the cause would be worth dying for.

Very Respectfully,

Robert Gary

**Robert Gary**
2211 Washington Ave (#301)
Silver Spring, MD 20910-2620
(301) 587-7147

Senator Paul Sarbanes                                          January 24, 2003
309 Hart Senate Office Building
Washington DC 20510

Dear Senator Sarbanes,

Thank you for your letter of January 2, 2003 and the enclosed letter from Admiral Loy at the Transportation Security Administration.

The weakness of his position might best be illustrated by the following analogy. Imagine that there has been a rash of biting incidents where children have been bitten in schoolyards by pitbull dogs. No other kind of dogs have been involved. The schoolyards where the incidents have happened are all over the world, but particularly in the U.S. In one schoolyard there was a massive mauling and killing incident in which hundreds of children were mauled or killed by a pack of pitbulls.

Now a citizen comes forth with the following suggestion "Why don't we make a rule keeping pitbulls out of schoolyards?" And the high government officials give the following answer: "Because there could be other kinds of dogs that also might bite children, and cats too, and raccoons as well, plus the fact that not all pitbulls are vicious. Some pitbulls might be in the schoolyards and not bite children. So we are not going to profile pitbulls."

The logic is clearly deficient. I've talked to dozens of people in Maryland about my suggestion and no one disagrees with me. Barring foreign visitors to the U.S. who are Muslims from any participation in general aviation is an obviously reasonable thing to do at this time and under these circumstances. The only person in the U.S. that doesn't agree is Secretary Norm Mineta (Admiral Loy's boss) and this may be attributable to some regrettable occurrences that happen during Mr. Mineta's youth and that have affected his views in this area. I think this individual is well meaning and honestly wants to do the right thing as he sees it, but I think his vision is drastically skewed and totally unreasonable and needs to simply be set aside by wiser and more circumspect leaders.

Once it was clear to me that TSA was not going to cooperate with my suggestion, I went to the Nuclear Regulatory Commission with a suggestion that nuclear power plants be defended with laser cannons. I gave them a full set of plans and technical details on the Tactical High Energy Laser (THEL) which was tested at White Sands in the 1980's and is now deployed and active in the Israeli Army where it is mounted on a Bradley Vehicle and used to shoot down incoming SCUDS.

What the highly placed officials don't seem to grasp are the following facts. One, if you don't bar foreign Muslim visitors to the U.S. from general aviation planes, then that means that they are going to be in those planes flying around in our skies. Two, a

Gulfstream moves at 450 miles per hour and can be packed with 15,000 pounds of explosives. Three, such a plane crashing down through the roof of an auxiliary building at the nuclear power plant (not the main containment dome, but the thinly roof auxiliary building where the spent fuel rods are stored in pools) would create a $10 Trillion disaster, killing 200,000 Americans and making an area the size of Pennsylvania uninhabitable for at least 100 years. Four, a plane going 450 miles per hour on a legal and filed flightplan that departs from that flightplan 100 miles away from a nuclear power plant can close the distance in 12 minutes. Five, knowing that a bad thing is about to happen does not stop it from happening. Six, scrambling military jets to intercept is not an option within a 12 minute timeframe.

If Admiral Loy understood these six points he would see right away that the notice that he sent to the airmen will not do the job of stopping such an attack. It would be found crumpled up in the pocket of the suicide bomber along with a message probably in Arabic. Knowing that a plane has gone off coarse and that it is being flown by a person who is probably not a law abiding pilot will not do the job of stopping such an attack. It's one thing to know you are being attacked and it's another thing to be able to do something about it (within a 12 minute window of opportunity). Preventing foreign nationals from flightschool training for planes above 12,500 pounds only affects foreign nationals that are not already fully qualified pilots. Fully qualified foreign nationals who are suicide pilots and who don't need to be trained in the U.S. would be unaffected by this countermeasure. This countermeasure only applies in cases where a more or less exact repetition of the 911 scenario is contemplated. Terrorists seem to have more imagination that highly placed government officials in some cases. Maybe next time they will send a pilot. Turning now to the ID card countermeasure mentioned by Admiral Loy at the end of his letter, this would have some slight level of effectiveness if there were someone there at every fixed based operator and commercial airport to check ID cards before a pilot went out to the flightline and took off a small plane. But even if we assure such ID checkers are in place on every flightline, the countermeasure is still ineffective because we lack the necessary overseas intelligence to connect ID information in a reliable way to the potential that the identified individual is a terrorist. If I thought we could reliably separate terrorist from non-terrorist Muslim foreigners I would never have suggested to TSA that all Muslim foreign visitors be barred from any participation in General Aviation. Knowing someone's name and knowing what they are likely to do are very different things, and we are dealing with terrorists who are clever enough to be 100% law abiding and socially respectable right up until the hour of their suicide attack. So when Mr. Muhammad Ali Akbar Jihad (a fictional name) shows his pilot ID card on the way to his rented Gulfstream (packed with 15,000 pounds of C-4) there is absolutely no reason to stop him that would be known to a fixed based operator on a small strip in Western Pennsylvania. Again, Admiral Loy's ideas are wholly ineffective because they don't stop the plane from hitting the nuclear power plant.

The laser cannon would do the job. It would be cheap to install. The power source is right there. It would be relatively safe to fire because it doesn't put any ordnance into the sky (which could be dangerous in populated areas). It provides some flexibility in its tactical use. It's remotely possible that  a plane could be forced to land in a non-lethal way by the use of the laser cannon (either disabling the plane or the pilot).

So the suggestion I made to the Nuclear Regulatory Commission, over a period of six months with many letters and phonecalls, was a reasonable one, and in fact a much more reasonable suggestion than what NRC and TSA are currently doing, which amounts to nothing, or more precisely, nothing that would be effective in mitigating the threat. The NRC has been largely unresponsive – they don't want to get into the air combat business. Apparently they feel that the air national guard and the military are adequate defenses for nuclear power plants facing airborne suicide pilots. Maybe those planes could somehow be scrambled and do the intercept within 12 minutes, but in any case the NRC doesn't want discuss the issue, doesn't want to do anything any differently than they have in the past.

The combination of my experience with the TSA and the NRC has caused me to retire as a public interest lawyer (specializing in nuclear safety, security and public health matters) after 25 years in practice. My sense is that the government has no interest whatsoever is Homeland Security regardless of the presentation it makes to the general public. A veil of secrecy hides what they do, but more importantly what they do not do. My overall impression is that, with the notable and commendable exception of the Attorney General, the government is inept, inert, and braindead. I have made some significant breakthroughs in the area of mathematics and I feel that my time is more productively spent getting those papers written up and published than fussing with government agencies who I now believe are not sincere, who apparently do not think clearly, and who have no evident desire to act in effective ways.

However, I would like you to feel free to take up the cause that I have thus far advanced. You may use this letter in any way that seems appropriate, including quotation or publication in whole or in part. It's not impossible that the public business could be productively conducted, I just no longer see a way to personally participate in that, although, as a citizen, I certainly hope it all goes well. I understand that on the House side Rep Nancy Pelosi has some interest in security matters, and I know that several members of the Senate, including yourself, have a strong and abiding dedication in this area.

So, again, I thank you most sincerely for your letter, and conclude with what all of us must hope -- may God bless America.

Respectfully Yours,

Robert Gary, Esq.

**ROBERT GARY**
2211 Washington Avenue (#301)
Silver Spring, MD 20910-2620
(301) 587-7147

Senator Barbara Mikulski                                    Jan 27, 2003
Senator Hillary Clinton
Rep. Nancy Pelosi
Rep. Dennis Hastert

Dear Senator Mikulski and Others,

Enclosed is a letter dealing with Homeland Security/National Security recently sent to Sen. Sarbanes which I hope you will read carefully and handle with the discretion that is appropriate for sensitive material.

After 25 years as a public interest attorney at the Federal level, dealing with nuclear security, nuclear safety, and public health issues, I am retiring and the letter to Sen Sarbanes contains my final statement to try to help the U.S. National Security.

There are six questions that involve mathematics at the first grade level which might be posed to Admiral Loy (TSA), Secretary Tom Ridge (Homeland Security), and Chairman Meserve (Nuclear Regulatory Commission). Simple "yes or no" answers is all that is required to answer these first grade math questions. If the answers were actually given, the complete vacuity of the Administration's position on nuclear reactor security would be 100% obvious and plain to every English speaking adult of normal capacity.

Question 1.

If there's no rule that bars foreign visitors to the U.S. who are Muslims from renting and flying a general aviation plane, is it possible that a Muslim foreign visitor to the U.S., who was a qualified pilot, could, without breaking any rules, rent and fly a general aviation plane.

Question 2.

Could a Gulfstream or a Learjet be packed with several thousand pounds of C-4 explosives?

Question 3.

Could a Gulfstream or a Learjet fly at speeds in excess of 400 miles per hour?

Question 4.

Could a Gulfstream or a Learjet cover a distance of about 100 miles in about 12 minutes?

Question 5.

If a Gulfstream or a Learjet departed from its legal flightplan 100 miles away from a nuclear power plant, and made a new and illegal course directly toward the nuclear power plant, would there be enough time to scramble military jets to intercept and interdict the incoming jet plane?

Question 6.

Is the roof of the Auxiliary Building at most nuclear power plants in the U.S. thick enough to withstand a planeload of C-4 arriving in a vertical dive and detonating on impact.

These are questions that can be answered with simple "yes or no" answers. The people at TSA know all about airplanes, and the people at NRC know all about nuclear power plants so there's no need for extensive delay to research these questions. They could be answered accurately in 30 days time with no great effort or cost.

If these six simple questions were answered then the Congress may wish to know why my suggestions have been disregarded and disrespected by TSA and NRC. I believe that there are people in Congress who are thoughtful and who want to foster better Homeland Security and National Security. As I mentioned, I am retiring from my public interest legal practice so I'm in no position to carry the matter any further. My general desire as a citizen to see the country on a more secure footing regarding a possible airborne suicide terror attack on a nuclear power plant abides, but I must tell you that I am deeply distraught and discouraged by the treatment I have received from an Administration that claims publicly to have such a strong and sincere interest in the National Security and in Homeland Security.

So, I leave the matter in your capable hands, with my best hopes and wishes that all goes well and that Providence guides your inquiries and your actions toward the fruitful and productive results that have eluded me.

Faithfully yours,

Robert Gary, Esquire

Enclosure: Ltr to Sen Sarbanes dated 24 January 2003

## ROBERT GARY
2211 Washington Ave (#301)
Silver Spring, MD 20910-2620
(301) 587-7147

Hon. Christopher Shays                                                    March 10, 2003
Subcommittee for National Security
Veterans Affairs and International Relations
U.S. House of Representatives
Washington DC 20515

Dear Chairman Shays,

Your witness Mr. Slobodeen (spelling might not be right) from Entergy had a few things wrong today in his testimony, perhaps not intentionally.

It is correct that the Auxiliary Building where the spent fuel storage pools are located is generally located at the lowest point on site at a nuclear facility. It is correct that the pools themselves are often under ground level. It is correct that coming in through the roof by a general aviation aircraft would be difficult because of the defilade provided by adjacent buildings. But it is incorrect to suggest that such an attack is improbable or unlikely to succeed.

If it were not highly likely to succeed I would not have raised the issue with the Nuclear Regulatory Commission for the last six months. Suicide bombers don't care if they dive a plane straight down (which is what it would take) to take out an Auxiliary Building and cause 10 Trillion Dollars worth of damage to the U.S.A.

The details are very complex but trust me on this, the terrorist act is possible, easy, and likely. They will do the worst thing that can be done cheaply. This is it. My enclosed letter to Hon Mikulski, Hon Clinton, Hon Pelosi and Hon Hastert has a lot of the details right there for your consideration. If Mr. Slobodeen comes back I hope you will ask him questions based on this letter.

The bottom line is that if a plane is coming at a Nuke we either can do something, or we can do nothing. I respectfully suggest that with the present configuration we can do precisely nothing. I further suggest that all government agencies everywhere will say that the other ones were responsible for doing something. So we can do nothing, and we have absolutely no idea who, if anyone, should do something. You have 12 minutes. You get it done, or you don't get it done. It's not that big a deal. It's 10 Trillion dollars and 250,000 American lives – we can recover from this – in about 100 years. So I hope that if Mr Slobodeen comes back you will ask him some serious questions. I want you to call me or write to me if there's any possible additional information I can provide. I do have a lot of information in this area, and 25 years of experience.

2211 Washington Avenue (Apt. #301)
Silver Spring, MD 20910-2620
(301) 587-7147

Hon. Chris Van Hollen                                    March 12, 2003
U.S. House of Representatives
Washington DC 20515

Dear Representative Van Hollen,

I am a constituent of yours who writes to ask that you introduce a piece of legislation dealing with the physical security of nuclear power plants. I practiced public interest law for 25 years most of which was spent in the area of public safety, public health, and nuclear radiation cases.

A piece of legislation needs to be written and introduced that calls for some ability on the part of nuclear power plants to defend themselves against an attack by air. This would be a different idea than the concept of having nuclear power plants defended from airborne attack by the Department of Defense or the Air National Guard.

My apprehension is described in some detail in the enclosed letter dated January 27, 2003 and sent to Senator Mikulski, Senator Clinton, Leader Pelosi, and Speaker Hastert. I listened with great care to the hearings conducted by Chairman Christopher Shays in the Subcommittee for National Security of the Veterans' Affairs and International Relations Committee of the House which were conducted yesterday. These hearings raised some of the issues that I have been working on for the past six months but they did not focus on any solution.

My reason for wanting nuclear power plants to be able to defend themselves is really a matter of very simple arithmetic. A Learjet moves at 400+ mph and can cover a 100 mile distance in about 12 minutes. Such a plane loaded with C-4 or Semtex, piloted by someone who seeks their own "martyrdom" is capable of penetrating the roof of an Auxiliary Building at a nuclear power plant. This is a different idea than penetrating the containment dome, which such a plane could not do, and nor could a 747 fully loaded with fuel.

I have raised these points in writing and by phone with the NRC. I spoke on two occasions at some length with Director Roy Zimmerman (Reactor Safety Systems). I wrote to Chairman Meserve several times. Over the course of six months I requested a brief meeting at the offices of the NRC at least a dozen times, but they were apparently too busy to see me, even for a 15 minute opportunity to present my proposal.

I did send them a fairly detailed technical description of the Tactical High Energy Laser (THEL), which was tested at White Sands in the 1980's, works just fine, and has been bought by the Israeli Army to knock down SCUDS. They use a mobile power source and mount the laser cannon on a Bradley type vehicle. But if such a laser were used to enable a nuclear power plant to defend itself, the power from the nuclear power plant could be used to energize the laser, and there would be plenty of it, so a fairly long-range tactical high energy laser could be used (with an effective, radar-guided kill range of about 5 miles). Such an approach would avoid putting any ordnance in the sky which is a high risk idea is a high population area. The only thing that goes in the sky is the light beam. It puts a basketball sized hole or two in the approaching unauthorized aircraft, and thus brings it down before it can get into its final dive trajectory.

Auxiliary Buildings are where the spent fuel storage pools are. These pools usually contain several old cores, hundreds of millions of Curies of radiation, Uranium, Plutonium, Strontium, and Cesium mostly. These buildings are located at the lowest point on the site, and they are surrounded by much higher buildings and by electric lines, so they are in defilade. Hitting an Auxiliary Building means diving straight down vertically through its relatively thin roof. Such a hit with a concomitant explosion of about 15,000 pounds of C-4 or Semtex would create a massive fire and enormous dispersion of the spent fuel rods, pellets, and aerosolized particles therefrom. The damage would be the loss of about a quarter of a million American lives, and something like $10 Trillion in financial costs.

The problem is a serious one. The structure of the problem is based on the fact that once a high-performance executive jet goes off its legal flightplan and makes a run for a nuclear power plant at full throttle, a nation has 12 minutes to save itself – not enough time to call the Air Force, or even the Air National Guard. The nuclear power plant has to be able to defend itself. The alternative is that it is undefended. Having undefended nuclear power plants is a bad idea in time of war against a vast constellation of enemies that have a lot of money, a lot of planning ability, and a lot of suicide bombers. The cost of the Tactical High Energy Laser is extremely modest in relation to the problem it mitigates.

The Agencies have failed the American People on this issue. They spend so much time organizing themselves and coordinating themselves that they never actually do anything concrete about security. The NRC, I fear, does not want to do anything because putting in the kind of system I suggest would be bad Public Relations for the nuclear power industry. It would draw attention right back to the old public concerns about whether nuclear power is a good idea or not. That is not my intent. My public interest law career is over. I am neither pro nor anti nuclear. But I firmly believe that public safety has to come before public relations. It's not clear to me that making nuclear power plants safer from terrorist attack would be a public relations disaster for them. People might be more comfortable with nuclear power if the plants were harder to attack successfully.

So I come to my reason for writing to you (and I will take the liberty of sending a copy of this letter to Senator Mikulski, Senator Sarbanes, Senator Clinton, Leader Pelosi, Speaker Hastert, and Chairman Shays). I think legislation would be helpful. It would cut through the clutter -- the bureaucratic haze of wondering who really has the responsibility to do something, rather than nothing – the inclination to delay, study it some more, study it forever, have an interagency task force, then a blue ribbon commission, then a thick printed document to collect dust on the shelves of the Archives. No – I say the country would be better off just passing a law.

Here's what it should say. By January 1, 2005 three commercial nuclear power plants in the U.S. **shall** have tactical high energy lasers installed, tested, operational, and ready to shoot down unauthorized, prospectively harmful, approaching aircraft. This includes buying the laser cannons, bolting them in place, hooking them up to the busbar power source, installing the fire control radar, training at least one control room operator on each shift to activate the radar, lock on an incoming target, and fire the laser cannon. It's not necessary for the nuclear power plant to monitor the airspace continuously. That can be done by air traffic controllers, and military assets, both ground based and airborne. The idea of this Bill is to make three nuclear power plants able to defend themselves, after being notified of an incoming illegal aircraft. The idea is to get the tactical high energy lasers deployed in the field and demonstrate whether or not they are a good idea. The cost estimate for this proposed legislation is very small in relation to the problem that it addresses in a fairly meaningful way. GAO could, no doubt score this with some precision. I won't try to suggest legislative wording – you probably have legislative draftsmen that can do that quite well and in a very few simple words. But the idea of making a law that will cause smart and good action to occur in the Federal government is the recourse that I'm petitioning you for after six months of very painful failure to make any progress with the NRC, or any other part of the Executive Branch.

Difficult challenges cannot be met by milquetoast solutions. Big strong solutions are required to countervail against big strong problems – like terrorist suicide bombers in Learjets headed for nuclear power plants. It is a terrible thing to contemplate the need to take the life a another human being, but we live in a terrible world, and we try to resist the growth of terror, not by praying that it will go away, but by shooting it down. It is better to stop the suicide bomber than to have a quarter of a million innocent Americans die. Many of us are in denial about the fact that such a choice must sometimes be made. Many of us are in an ethical quandary about which way to choose, we just can't tell, it's too hard to decide, we wring our hands, we are wistful, we cringe at the very idea of thinking about such unthinkable things. That's why we have Representative Government rather than a Direct Democracy. The Founders hoped that our Representatives in Congress Assembled would be more courageous more provident and more prepared to assure the survival of this best Democratic Republic the world has ever seen. Surely, I don't mean to put any larger burden on your shoulders than you have taken on yourself. I earnestly hope that, after careful consideration, and consultation with experts, you will decide to go forward and introduce the piece of legislation that I hereby very respectfully request.

Sincerely,

/s/

Robert Gary

cc: Sarbanes, Mikulski, Hastert, Pelosi, Clinton, Shays

**THE WHITE HOUSE**

WASHINGTON

April 14, 2003

Mr. Robert Gary
Apartment 301
2211 Washington Avenue
Silver Spring, Maryland  20910

Dear Mr. Gary:

Thank you for your letter about the war in Iraq.  American and coalition forces are engaged in efforts to disarm Iraq of weapons of mass destruction, to end Saddam Hussein's support for terrorism, and to free the Iraqi people.  More than 40 countries are bearing the duty and sharing the honor of serving in our common defense.

Coalition forces will make every effort to spare innocent civilians from harm.  We come to Iraq with respect for its citizens, civilization, and religious faiths.  We have no ambition in Iraq, except to remove a threat and restore control of that country to its own people.  Along with other coalition leaders, I am strongly committed to delivering humanitarian aid to the Iraqi people throughout the conflict.  We also recognize our solemn obligation to help the people of Iraq build a new country that is united, stable, and free.

During this time of great consequence, we look to our Nation's Armed Forces, with the support of our coalition partners, to advance peace in a troubled world.  By answering the call of duty, these brave men and women serve as examples of courage, dedication, and sacrifice.  Laura and I join our military families and countless others in praying that all who serve return home safely and soon.

Thank you again for writing.  Best wishes.

Sincerely,

George W. Bush

BARBARA A. MIKULSKI
MARYLAND

SUITE 709
HART SENATE OFFICE BUILDING
WASHINGTON, DC 20510–2003

(202) 224–4654
TDD: (202) 224–5223

# United States Senate

WASHINGTON, DC 20510–2003

April 16, 2003

Mr. Robert Gary, Esq.
Principal Investigator
Gary Research
2211 Washington Avenue
Apartment 301
Silver Spring, Maryland  20910

Dear Mr. Gary:

Thank you for forwarding me a copy of your letter to Senators Warner and McCain regarding the Air Force Academy.

This is obviously a matter of great concern to you and I wanted to let you know that I appreciate your efforts to keep me informed of your views and actions regarding this matter.

Again, thanks for keeping in touch with me.  Please let me know if I may be of assistance to you in the future.

Sincerely,

Barbara A. Mikulski
United States Senator

BAM:aj

BARBARA A. MIKULSKI
MARYLAND

SUITE 709
HART SENATE OFFICE BUILDING
WASHINGTON, DC 20510–2003

(202) 224–4654
TDD: (202) 224–5223

# United States Senate

WASHINGTON, DC 20510–2003

April 25, 2003

Mr. Robert Gary, Esq.
Principal Investigator
Gary Research
2211 Washington Avenue
Apartment 301
Silver Spring, Maryland  20910

Dear Mr. Gary:

Thank you for getting in touch with me to express your views about nuclear power.

Your comments were helpful.  I believe the best ideas come from the people, and they guide our actions here in Washington. I also want to be responsive to the needs of Marylanders, and information from people like you is essential if I'm to reach that goal.

If I can be of assistance in the future, or if there is any other federal issue on which you would like to comment, please feel free to let me know.

Sincerely,

Barbara A. Mikulski
United States Senator

BAM:as

PAUL S. SARBANES
MARYLAND

309 HART SENATE OFFICE BL
WASHINGTON, DC 20510
202–224–4524

# United States Senate
WASHINGTON, DC 20510–2002

May 14, 2003

Lieutenant Robert Gary, (Ret).
2211 Washington Avenue, #301
Silver Spring, Maryland  20910

Dear Lieutenant Gary:

Thank you for contacting me to express your concerns regarding the United States Air Force Academy (USAFA).  I share your concerns and appreciate having the benefit of your views.

As you know, cadets and administrators at USAFA are currently the subjects of an investigation regarding allegations of sexual harassment and assault.  In the wake of these serious offenses, the Air Force has reassigned several administrators at USAFA.  Additionally, I want to be certain you are aware that during consideration of legislation providing supplemental appropriations for FY 2003, the Senate adopted an amendment that would establish an external panel to determine the effectiveness of policy and actions taken at USAFA in response to these problems.  This measure passed both the House and Senate and was signed by the President on April 16, 2003.

Again, I appreciate hearing from you on this important matter.  Please do not hesitate to contact me about other issues of concern to you in the future.

With best regards,

Sincerely,

Paul Sarbanes
United States Senator

PSS/jwg

BARBARA A. MIKULSKI
MARYLAND

SUITE 709
HART SENATE OFFICE BUILDING
WASHINGTON, DC 20510–2003

(202) 224–4654
TDD: (202) 224–5223

# United States Senate
WASHINGTON, DC 20510–2003

June 5, 2003

Mr. Robert Gary
2211 Washington Avenue
Silver Spring, Maryland  20910-2620

Dear Mr. Gary:

Thank you for contacting me.  It's nice to hear from you. I apologize for the delay in responding, and I hope this has not inconvenienced you in any way.  I take the views of Marylanders very seriously, and I would like to address your concerns.

I also appreciate you contacting me regarding your questions about federal aviation regulations and homeland security.  In response to your concern, I have been in touch with the Department of Homeland Security.

I have requested that the Department of Homeland Security respond to you directly, providing me with a copy.  Please feel free to contact me in the meantime should you have any questions or further comments.

Sincerely,

Barbara A. Mikulski
United States Senator

BAM:mh

ROBERT GARY
2211 Washington Avenue (Apt 301)
Silver Spring, MD 20910-2620
Tele: (301) 587-7147

Hon Condoleeza Rice                                    31 June 2003
National Security Advisor
The White House
1600 Pennsylvania Ave
Washington DC  20500

Dear Dr. Rice,

I write to you as an ordinary citizen with two ideas that I honestly feel would be quite valuable for the pursuit of our efforts in Iraq, and for Homeland Security.

My first idea is to equip all our personnel in Iraq with GPS locator bracelets. These are used in the United States to prevent kidnap of small children. If a child goes missing it is possible to interrogate the bracelet using a satellite signal, and the bracelet transponds back its GPS location. When the location is then converted to map coordinates, help can then be vectored in the recover the child. These bracelets cost a few hundred dollars apiece, but if the military bought them en masse, they could no doubt get a much better price. I do know the name of a company that offers this locator service and sells the bracelets but in the interest of avoiding any appearance of a commercial plug for one particular company I will refrain from mentioning it, but I know that DOD could find the company with a 5 second internet search.

My second idea is to publish on the internet, and if requested on printouts at airports the names on the passenger manifests of all commercial airlines flights in the U.S. This would be done without any comment whatsoever and on a real time basis, good to within say 1 minute. My premise for this is that the government can provide a service to the American People by being an honest and transparent information broker. There are several firms in the U.S. that would have an opportunity to get into the business of risk assessment and their positions, based on their own analysis, could be available in real time almost to persons who might be considering taking seats on that flight.

In this land of liberty we want to give people some liberty, or more precisely some choice, and there is no such thing as choice in the absence of information. Each person should exercise their own choice in relation to their own judgment about what's good for their own security. This means the government simply gives a list of names – there's no issue of profiling or discrimination or anything like that.

Companies that analyze these real-time passenger manifests could call or e-mail their clients and provide their "Seal of Approval" or "Notice of Caution" or "Alert of Very Serious Risk". They might do this based on many possible factors, the names themselves being one factor, and the ticket status of the persons with specific names being another factor, and their ages, and how many of them there are, and what sex they are, and where they were born, and many other factors could be taken into account by various competing analysis firms all seeking to rationally assess the risk and given the most accurate feedback possible to their clients.

It could be that on a flight from LAX to Dulles when a dozen young men with Arabic sounding names are added to the manifest a substantial number of the people seated in the cabin would get up, take their carry on bags, and get off the plane. They are not stealing anybody else's civil rights by doing that, they are merely exercising their constitutionally protected personal liberty as they see fit for their own protection. There could be dozens of other people in the cabin having access to and actually getting the exact same information whose personal judgment is that they would rather not profile anybody and if that means that a bad thing happens to them – so be it. It's like the smoking decision in some respects – we make our choices and we live (or not) with the outcomes.

This idea puts the government in the role that I think it can do best – be an honest and transparent information broker. A person buying an airline ticket has no reasonable expectation of privacy. They are going into a public place – a seat on a common carrier – and the passenger manifest is already a semi-public document available to all kinds of civilians and persons who are not affiliated with government agencies. I'm just saying make it a fully public document by putting it on the internet in real time. Let people have the freedom to protect themselves as they see fit.

Two quick notes: first this is really just an extension of the CAPS program into potentially more competent and capable hands and for the benefit of the public rather than just the security officials. Many people have no confidence whatsoever in TSA (especially now that it is clear they can't even do background checks on their own employees several of whom, according to the Newspapers, have been pilfering from baggage, and actually picking people pockets and stealing their money while searching them). This private industry free enterprise solution might be very suitable for people who do not have a lot of confidence in the government to perform air travel security in a competent manner. Second, my argument is based on freedom of choice (and thus information) and not on freedom of association. These are all First Amendment related rights, but they are not precisely the same. I would emphasize the liberty aspect and not the association aspect because I don't think people sitting together in a plane or train or bus are in "association" in the Constitutional sense and this is particularly true when the plane, train, or bus is a common carrier.

So, I hope these ideas are helpful to you and perhaps the Ambassador Paul Bremer, and to Admiral Loy at TSA with whom I hope you will share them, among others if you think others might be interested. I can be reached at the above number if I could be of any help in filling in missing details or points of interest.

Very truly yours,

Robert Gary, Esq.

## Robert Gary

**2211 Washington Avenue (Apt 301)**
**Silver Spring, MD 20910-2620**
**(301) 587-7147**
Robert.Gary@prodigy.net

Hon. Chris VanHollen                                                    July 3, 2003
U.S. House of Representatives
Longworth LHOB (Room 1419)
Washington, DC 20515

**Subj: In Re Nathaniel Travis Heatwole**

Dear Congressman VanHollen,

**Heatwole, the fellow who committed civil disobedience by taking clay and bleach and boxcutters aboard Southwest Airlines planes was sending a message that TSA and FBI do not want to hear. They find that it is within their power to punish him, and they are doing it, by bringing a massive criminal complaint against him.**

Has a piece of clay ever brought an airliner down? I think not. How about a bottle of bleach? Again, no. Boxcutters in the hands of terrorists have been instruments to take over airplanes, but since when do terrorists get on planes with everything they need to commit their acts of terror except a boxcutter, hoping that maybe they will find one in the lavatory behind some panels? No one is suggesting that Heatwole himself had any intent to commit any act of terror. They accuse him of bringing a boxcutter aboard and having access to it during flight. But **only by doing that could he clearly and convincingly send the message he wanted to send** – TSA is completely incompetent.

We actually pay people (called Red Teams) to do this kind of work for us in the nuclear power plant security business. People working for the Congress undercover have taken weapons aboard airplanes to show that TSA is completely incompetent, but they can't be punished – they don't leave notes with their names and addresses – they have badges and TSA and FBI know that it would be futile and foolish to try the punish these official security testers.

**American values are forged from volunteerism and have been shaped by the honorable tradition of civil disobedience** – Thoreau, Gandhi, King. Now just as then, there are men, honorable men -- who take risks to send essential messages to people in power.

TSA and FBI through their amazingly foolish hard line prosecution of Heatwole will create a public relations disaster for their agencies which will hurt Homeland Security, will hurt the President's chances of being re-elected, and will hurt the credibility of the U.S. government as a whole. Accordingly, I offer the following modest alternative proposal. **Heatwole should get a medal, in the Rose Garden, with a citation that praises his courage, his patriotism, and his honorable sense of civic duty, and then**

**says he is enjoined in the strongest terms to cease and desist from any further message sending because TSA "gets it". His point has been made**. Going further would be detrimental, so he should stop now having done a service to his country. This would be a kind of American big-hearted, far-seeing, fair-minded generous-in-spirit approach. All it would take to make this happen would be good judgment. **This medal should be called "The Emperor is Not Wearing Any Clothes Medal" and it should be awarded to public-minded citizens whose show or reveal or describe true facts in a way that is not harmful to anyone and where the statement of the facts greatly advances the public good.** Jefferson would have loved the idea of such a medal and Franklin would have smiled at the thought.

.If you want to give a one-minute speech along these lines (to the usual empty chamber) I would be very proud of you for doing it. If you want to include this letter (or part of it) in the record, appended to your one minute speech, then go ahead and give it a chance to be disseminated. Others might join its sentiments, and maybe **TSA could be prevented from shooting itself in the foot by trying to "shoot the messenger" who brings news of it own total incompetence.**.

Know the truth – be free. Live in a land of liberty – **value the truth, and the truthsayers, and those whose innocent and civic-minded actions make the truth evident**. All facts are friendly when you're making decisions. Heatwole elegantly brought us some very useful and surprising facts, (sort of like the Pentagon Papers did 30 years ago). Would those facts have been known anyway? Maybe. But not as soon and possibly not as harmlessly. **Heatwole, at great personal risk, has given us the gift of self-knowledge, and the gift of time to make things better**.

Very Truly Yours,

Robert Gary, Esq.

cc: Sarbanes, Mikulski, Shays, Bush, Card, Rove, Ashcroft, Muller, Loy

**ROBERT GARY**
2211 Washington Avenue (Apt 301)
Silver Spring, MD 20910-2620
(301) 587-7147
Robert.Gary@prodigy.net

Hon. Chris VanHollen                                         July 3, 2003
U.S. House of Representatives
Longworth LHOB (Room 1419)
Washington, DC 20515

Dear Congressman VanHollen,

I spoke today with one of your office professionals who was very courteous and
suggested that I write you with my request.

My request is that you **transfer one or more of my homeland security related ideas
onto your letterhead** and send it directly to Secretary Tom Ridge at the Department of
Homeland Security and **ask him for a response directly to you.** You might choose to
include all the ideas or just whichever one(s) you think are good.

**So here is my list of ideas**:

**Idea #1**                         Biometrically enabled locks could be built in to shipping
containers which are locked and sealed overseas. These locks would not work unless the
fingerprints of three specific pre-identified people were placed on the touchpad at the
same time. If you know that these three people were present when the container was
packed, inspected, and sealed, then it is very unlikely that the container contains anything
harmful to the USA. These biometrically enabled locks transform a physical inspection
problem (we now inspect about 3% of incoming containers) into a personnel reliability
problem, which I think is much cheaper, faster, and better, and more likely to be solved.
Three people working in each other's presence but with different organizations and skills
would need to put their fingers on the touchpad to enable the lock. The lock would
remain enabled for 120 seconds to allow time for it to be clicked into the locked position.
The time of locking and all the biometric data could be forwarded via secure digital
transmission to the port of entry security office in the USA. We would have some rational
basis upon which to believe that a real inspection was done by people known to be honest
who were in each other's presence and thus trying to do their jobs well. Total cost to the
U.S. government = zero dollars – the shippers can pay for this system, and I think they
would be happy to because it will save them money too.

**Idea #2**        TSA should provide data on what percentage of commercial airliner
cockpit doors have actually been strengthened with Charlie Bars or better. Two years ago
the Airline lobbyists assured me that the refits were running 90% or better. Charlie Bars
are very inexpensive to install even on a jumbo jet. They are not 100% reliable, but they
are much much better than not having any effective reinforcement behind the cockpit

door. Getting a number written down on Department of Homeland Security letterhead would cost about a nickel. Congress has a right o know this number, and DHS has a duty to have the number at their fingertips – so no extensive research is needed to say what this number is. Let them take a piece of paper. Let them write it down. Let them send it back to you. I don't think they are going to want to knowingly give an incorrect number. If they give the correct number, then they will have provided a truthful answer to a Congressman, and that is part of the highest traditions of all government agencies and departments.

**<u>Idea #3</u>** The High Energy Laser (THEL) which was demonstrated at White Sands in the mid 1980's is the perfect unit for the defense of nuclear power plants from airborne attack by a suicide dive bomber in a Learjet loaded up with Semtex. The laser cannon puts no ordnance into the air, just a very powerful lightbeam that can bring down an aircraft at a range of about 5 miles. Nuclear plants have the energy source right there – they are after all nuclear power plants, so there's no shortage of electricity on site. The idea of scrambling fighter to intercept a Learjet that suddenly goes radically off course 100 miles away from a nuclear power plant is mathematically absurd. The jet moves at 600 miles per hour which means it can close the distance in 12 minutes. No jets anywhere of any kind can be scrambled, make intercept, and accomplish shootdown in 12 minutes. So nuclear power plants must be able to defend themselves against sudden high speed airborne attack. A laser cannon could be activated, acquire its target on tracking radar, and fire a shootdown burst in 1 minute. This means that after a plane 100 miles out goes suddenly off course and makes a beeline for the nuclear power plant, the high ranking persons and on-site authorities have 11 minutes to deliberate and formulate their response. This is much better than being utterly hapless and helpless.

**<u>Idea #4</u>** There is no valid reason to permit foreign Muslims to fly in general aviation planes in the USA. There's no law that requires that they be permitted to do so. There's no provision in the U.S. Constitution that gives them the right to do so. Sometimes the simplest solutions are the best. Barring foreign Muslim visitors to the USA from general aviation would be a very reasonable and very effective way to reduce the threat profile this country has to face every day. It would be a very very minor inconvenience to a very very small number of foreign visitors to the USA, most of whom have neither the desire, nor the funds, nor the occasion to have any reason to fly in general aviation planes. Were it possible to reliably separate in advance terrorist foreign Muslim visitors from non-terrorist foreign Muslim visitors then of course only the terrorist foreign Muslim visitors should be barred from general aviation. There is absolutely no indication that any agency or combination of agencies in the U.S. government can at this time make that separation in a reliable way. It is extremely expensive to try to provide security against airborne attack using a general aviation plane as a weapon of mass destruction in the absence of the proposed rule. The rule is valid because it reduces this expense and mitigates this grave risk.

**<u>Idea #5</u>**　　　　The CAPS program run out of TSA already screens names on all passenger manifests on commercial airliners in the US. But it does so in a way that is not clearly competent. A person reserving a seat on a commercial airliner has no reasonable expectation of privacy. He must disclose his (or her) name. He is booking a seat on a common carrier, which by definition is a public place. All kinds of civilians and non-officials already have access to that name booked in that seat on that flight. Why not put passenger manifests for commercial flights on the internet in real time? Doing so would revolutionize air transportation in a very good and very cost-effective way. Highly competent security screening firms in the private sector would be able to make detailed assessments based on their extensive databases of the terror risk on a particular flight. This information could be relayed in real time by pager or e-mail to persons considering whether or not to place themselves on that flight. There would be an opportunity for people to make informed choices just as they do when they read the label on a packet of cigarettes and decide whether or not to smoke them. This idea of informed choices is part of liberty, and it's part of the right to life and the pursuit of happiness as well. It would be completely legal and very much in the American tradition to allow the private sector to participate, in an advisory capacity, offering risk assessments to help air travelers take or decline to take whatever risk level they are comfortable with. Competing firms would soon get a reputation if they were too lax or too overcautious in their assessments. The public would gravitate toward the excellent providers of risk assessments. Each firm would have its own way of approaching the analysis, and its own channels of access to key information. Airlines could provide, on a voucher basis, access to some or all of these assessments. This was all passengers would be treated equally, there would be no digital divide or differential disadvantage based on poverty. Getting competent minds into the air transport security analysis process would be a good thing not a bad thing. Many of the people in the private sector who do this sort of work are brilliant by any standard – they work for security firms, insurance companies, prospective employee assessment firms, and personnel reliability assurance firms. Moreover they are not politicians. They are not running for office. They can focus on security rather than political correctness. They worry about losing lives, not losing votes. They don't have to pose for any constituency, or appease anyone in order to keep their jobs. There's only one standard that guides them – security, not diplomacy, not popularity, not ideology – just security. These people are competent far beyond many "official" persons in security positions, and they are focused in ways that public sector people cannot possibly be just by the rules of the political game here in Washington DC.

So, I ask you as your constituent, to please take one or more of these five ideas, word them any way that suits you, put whatever you decide is right on your own U.S. Congress letterhead and send it over to Secretary Tom Ridge. If you can get a genuine authentic substantive response to any of these ideas I will never forget the favor you will have done for me. I have asked the same things of Senator Barbara Mikulski and Senator Paul Sarbanes both of whom have been very active in helping me. They have known me for ten years. They trust me because they know that I am experienced and because I never ask for anything for myself. I'm not seeking a job or a consulting contract, and I have no products to sell the government. I am a decorated military veteran, a retired attorney whose practice was in the Federal Courts mostly dealing with security related issues.

Buck slips have not worked with DHS – they just send back very routine generic letters "We're always happy to hear from citizens about [x] … etc … and, again, thank you so much for writing to us." They fill in the stopcode [x] based on a 5 second glance at the incoming letter. This is work that could be done, (and probably is done) by a GS-3 or a GS-5. Buckslips get answers, but they are not substantive answers. I would like just one substantive answer, and that means the request for it should go out over your signature on your letterhead, although you could tell them that these are not your ideas, tell them they are my ideas if you want to, or if you wish, go the other way, and tell them that these are ideas that you have selected and adopted based on constituent correspondence.

Quite apart from the act of obtaining a substantive answer from DHS – (the value of the answer itself, which I think would be very high no matter which idea(s) you select), **you would be performing an enormous service to the American People if you could break through the wall of silence around DHS** which is the poster boy for unresponsive government and actually makes the whole government look bad. Never has an agency had such thick and impenetrable walls. Never has an agency isolated itself so completely from all incoming information (except for what comes to it from the West Wing). DHS relates to the citizens of this Country not at all. Marylanders are not accustomed to agencies like that. Poor Senator Warren Rudman got a rude shock when he sent DHS a deeply insightful report that he had prepared himself for 20 years to write and which he spend six months composing so that it would be useful to DHS. It took them about a day to send a letter back saying they are very happy with the way they are presently doing things. Senator Rudman, a true patriot, a rigorous thinker, a devoted seeker of the interests of this country was, I think, appalled by the treatment he got from this upstart Department headed by an arguably mediocre former Governor with no actual security experience whatsoever. The nation as a whole was dismayed when we observed this spectacle of disrespect and disregard. You can do something as a Congressman to help bring this newly formed DHS into a better and more effective shape. **My request to you can be the vehicle and opportunity for your action** and your contribution to an effort that has been well begun by Senator Mikulski, and which I earnestly hope that you support and will actively join.

Very truly yours,

Robert Gary

cc: Sen Barbara Mikulski, and Mr. Andrew Johnston in Sen Mikulski's office

ROBERT GARY
2211 Washington Avenue (Apt 301)
Silver Spring, MD 20910-2620
(301) 587-7147
Robert.Gary@prodigy.net

Hon. Barbara Mikulski                                    July 14, 2003
(Attn Andy Dentamaro)
Suite 709 Hart Office Building
U.S. Senate
Washington DC 20510-2003

Dear Senator Mikulski,

I spoke today with one of your office professionals who was very courteous and suggested that I write you with my request which is to get an appointment to see an official at the Department of Homeland Security.

**Here is my list of ideas**:

**Idea #1**          Biometrically enabled locks could be built in to shipping containers which are locked and sealed overseas. These locks would not work unless the fingerprints of three specific pre-identified people were placed on the touchpad at the same time. If you know that these three people were present when the container was packed, inspected, and sealed, then it is very unlikely that the container contains anything harmful to the USA. These biometrically enabled locks transform a physical inspection problem (we now inspect about 3% of incoming containers) into a personnel reliability problem, which I think is much cheaper, faster, and better, and more likely to be solved. Three people working in each other's presence but with different organizations and skills would need to put their fingers on the touchpad to enable the lock. The lock would remain enabled for 120 seconds to allow time for it to be clicked into the locked position. The time of locking and all the biometric data could be forwarded via secure digital transmission to the port of entry security office in the USA. We would have some rational basis upon which to believe that a real inspection was done by people known to be honest who were in each other's presence and thus trying to do their jobs well. Total cost to the U.S. government = zero dollars – the shippers can pay for this system, and I think they would be happy to because it will save them money too.

**Idea #2**      TSA should provide data on what percentage of commercial airliner cockpit doors have actually been strengthened with Charlie Bars or better. Two years ago the Airline lobbyists assured me that the refits were running 90% or better. Charlie Bars are very inexpensive to install even on a jumbo jet. They are not 100% reliable, but they are much much better than not having any effective reinforcement behind the cockpit door. Getting a number written down on Department of Homeland Security letterhead would cost about a nickel. Congress has a right o know this number, and DHS has a duty to have the number at their fingertips – so no extensive research is needed to say what this number is. Let them take a piece of paper. Let them write it down. Let them send it back to you. I don't think they are going to want to knowingly give an incorrect number. If they give the correct number, then they will have provided a truthful answer to a Congressman, and that is part of the highest traditions of all government agencies and departments.

**Idea #3**     The High Energy Laser (THEL) which was demonstrated at White Sands in the mid 1980's is the perfect unit for the defense of nuclear power plants from airborne attack by a suicide dive bomber in a Learjet loaded up with Semtex. The laser cannon puts no ordnance into the air, just a very powerful lightbeam that can bring down an aircraft at a range of about 5 miles. Nuclear plants have the energy source right there – they are after all nuclear power plants, so there's no shortage of electricity on site. The idea of scrambling fighter to intercept a Learjet that suddenly goes radically off course 100 miles away from a nuclear power plant is mathematically absurd. The jet moves at 600 miles per hour which means it can close the distance in 12 minutes. No jets anywhere of any kind can be scrambled, make intercept, and accomplish shootdown in 12 minutes. So nuclear power plants must be able to defend themselves against sudden high speed airborne attack. A laser cannon could be activated, acquire its target on tracking radar, and fire a shootdown burst in 1 minute. This means that after a plane 100 miles out goes suddenly off course and makes a beeline for the nuclear power plant, the high ranking persons and on-site authorities have 11 minutes to deliberate and formulate their response. This is much better than being utterly hapless and helpless.

**Idea #4**     There is no valid reason to permit foreign Muslims to fly in general aviation planes in the USA. There's no law that requires that they be permitted to do so. There's no provision in the U.S. Constitution that gives them the right to do so. Sometimes the simplest solutions are the best. Barring foreign Muslim visitors to the USA from general aviation would be a very reasonable and very effective way to reduce the threat profile this country has to face every day. It would be a very very minor inconvenience to a very very small number of foreign visitors to the USA, most of whom have neither the desire, nor the funds, nor the occasion to have any reason to fly in general aviation planes. Were it possible to reliably separate in advance terrorist foreign Muslim visitors from non-terrorist foreign Muslim visitors then of course only the terrorist foreign Muslim visitors should be barred from general aviation. There is absolutely no indication that any agency or combination of agencies in the U.S. government can at this time make that separation in a reliable way. It is extremely expensive to try to provide security against airborne attack using a general aviation plane as a weapon of mass destruction in the absence of the proposed rule. The rule is valid because it reduces this expense and mitigates this grave risk.

**Idea #5**        The CAPS program run out of TSA already screens names on all passenger manifests on commercial airliners in the US. But it does so in a way that is not clearly competent. A person reserving a seat on a commercial airliner has no reasonable expectation of privacy. He must disclose his (or her) name. He is booking a seat on a common carrier, which by definition is a public place. All kinds of civilians and non-officials already have access to that name booked in that seat on that flight. Why not put passenger manifests for commercial flights on the internet in real time? Doing so would revolutionize air transportation in a very good and very cost-effective way. Highly competent security screening firms in the private sector would be able to make detailed assessments based on their extensive databases of the terror risk on a particular flight. This information could be relayed in real time by pager or e-mail to persons considering whether or not to place themselves on that flight. There would be an opportunity for people to make informed choices just as they do when they read the label on a packet of cigarettes and decide whether or not to smoke them. This idea of informed choices is part of liberty, and it's part of the right to life and the pursuit of happiness as well. It would be completely legal and very much in the American tradition to allow the private sector to participate, in an advisory capacity, offering risk assessments to help air travelers take or decline to take whatever risk level they are comfortable with. Competing firms would soon get a reputation if they were too lax or too overcautious in their assessments. The public would gravitate toward the excellent providers of risk assessments. Each firm would have its own way of approaching the analysis, and its own channels of access to key information. Airlines could provide, on a voucher basis, access to some or all of these assessments. This was all passengers would be treated equally, there would be no digital divide or differential disadvantage based on poverty. Getting competent minds into the air transport security analysis process would be a good thing not a bad thing. Many of the people in the private sector who do this sort of work are brilliant by any standard – they work for security firms, insurance companies, prospective employee assessment firms, and personnel reliability assurance firms. Moreover they are not politicians. They are not running for office. They can focus on security rather than political correctness. They worry about losing lives, not losing votes. They don't have to pose for any constituency, or appease anyone in order to keep their jobs. There's only one standard that guides them – security, not diplomacy, not popularity, not ideology – just security. These people are competent far beyond many "official" persons in security positions, and they are focused in ways that public sector people cannot possibly be just by the rules of the political game here in Washington DC.

We have know each other for at least five or ten years and worked together during the recent problems at the U.S. Naval Academy where you serve as a member of the Board of Visitors and Governors. I had some issues about the academy admissions process and the fact that it didn't meet the Recruiting Manual standards. You were kind enough to put me in touch with Admiral Larson at that time. I still do public interest law in the national security area, I'm not looking for a job, and not selling any product. So I hope you will feel comfortable about helping me get heard at the Department of Homeland Security.

Sincerely,

**Transportation Security
Administration**

JUL 2 2 2003

Mr. Robert Gary
2211 Washington Avenue, #301
Silver Spring, MD  20910-2620

Dear Mr. Gary:

The Department of Homeland Security has asked me to respond to Senator Barbara A. Mikulski's letter, dated June 5, 2003, written on your behalf, regarding security at nuclear power plants to mitigate the threat of an attack from a general aviation aircraft.

After discussions within the Executive Branch, I have decided not to establish temporary flight restrictions above nuclear power plants at this time.  Security for these important facilities is an issue we will, of course, continue to assess routinely.  The Transportation Security Administration (TSA) and the Federal Aviation Administration (FAA) have been collaborating in an effort to secure potential targets on the ground from any aviation related threats.  One specific example is directly pertinent to your concerns.

A special Notice to Airmen (NOTAM) has been published advising pilots to avoid the airspace above, or in close proximity to, sites such as nuclear power plants, power plants, dams, refineries, industrial complexes, military facilities, and other similar facilities.  On February 26, 2003, FDC NOTAM 3/1655 was released to educate pilots more thoroughly on the sensitivity of airspace above these sites and to add language that more clearly defines the repercussions that violating pilots could face, including having their name entered into TSA's incident reporting system.  As you know, pilots are specifically admonished not to circle or loiter in the vicinity of such facilities.  By keeping the vast majority of conscientious, law-abiding pilots away from critical-sensitive infrastructure, it becomes much easier to identify others who might be approaching with malicious intent.

Please know that with regards to our ability to respond to a potential threat, the FAA air traffic controllers have the capability to track general aviation aircraft that enter into sensitive airspace.  When controllers become aware of general aviation aircraft loitering in the vicinity of sensitive airspace, they have the option of requesting military support or a follow-up visit to the pilot by an FAA flight standards inspector or by local law enforcement personnel.  Further, should TSA obtain any specific and credible threat information, I have the authority to restrict the airspace over vulnerable areas.

TSA and FAA have recently engaged in extensive collaboration with the intention of implementing changes to our security practices whenever the National Threat Advisory Level is raised to High Risk (ORANGE).

Thank you for your conscientious attention to the security of our Nation's nuclear power plants.  I hope this information addresses your concerns.

Sincerely yours,

J.M. Loy, ADM
Administrator

cc:  The Honorable Barbara A. Mikulski

# United States Senate

WASHINGTON, DC 20510–2003

July 23, 2003

Mr. Robert Gary
2211 Washington Avenue
Silver Spring, Maryland  20910-2620

Dear Mr. Gary:

Thank you for forwarding me a copy of your letter to Congressman VanHollen regarding homeland security.

This is obviously a matter of great concern to you and I wanted to let you know that I appreciate your efforts to keep me informed of your views and actions regarding this matter.

Again, thanks for keeping in touch with me.  Please let me know if I may be of assistance to you in the future.

Sincerely,

Barbara A. Mikulski
United States Senator

BAM:aj

**194**

R O B E R T   G A R Y

2211 Washington Avenue (Apt. #301)
Silver Spring, MD 20910-2620
Tele: (301) 587-7147

Admiral James M. Loy                                                July 24, 2003
Transportation Security Administration
601 South 12th Street
Arlington VA 22202-4220

Dear Administrator Loy,

Your letter to me of July 22, 2003 is non-responsive to my concerns and here's why.

You talk about calling in the military. My position as you know is that within the 12 minutes of available time you would have there is no military unit that could come to the defense of a nuclear power plant, acquire an airborne target, and accomplish shootdown.

It would be very easy for you to disprove me on this point. Just get some commissioned officer from any branch of the military, or the reserves, or the National Guard to come before the Congress and say that yes they do have the capability to get to a nuclear reactor under airborne attack and shootdown an aggressor within a 12 minute timeframe with no prior warning, anytime, anywhere. I don't think you could find any commissioned officer that would testify that way. In the absence of such testimony, you may want to consider that I could be right on this point.

But if I'm right about this, you see, then my argument that nuclear power plants need to be able to defend themselves takes on a certain cogency. We might have discussions about how that could be done. I have suggested the Tactical High Energy Laser (THEL) because it's got excellent range, it takes advantage of the available power source (the nuclear plant), and it puts no ordnance into the sky. I would be prepared to consider a phalanx gun or stinger missiles or other short range ground to air alternatives as ways that nuclear plants might defend themselves.

The measures that you suggest in your letter just don't make sense as ways to stop a suicidal pilot of a plane moving at about 600 mph loaded with 15,000 pounds of high explosive seeking to dive straight down through the roof of the aux building at a nuclear power plant. The pilot doesn't mind if you if you sent or did not send FDC NOTAM 3/1655. He doesn't mind if you plan the send local law enforcement people or even FBI people to his house after his flight. He will be dead after his flight. He knows it. He wants it. So memos and police visits don't mean a lot to him.

He also doesn't mind if you plan to call the military. He knows the military can't get there on time. During the 12 minutes of his beeline flight toward the nuclear power plant, starting from 100 miles out, you and he might talk together on the radio. You might say, "I'm calling the military now!" and he might say "Go ahead and call them it won't do you any good, my job will be done within 12 minutes, it doesn't make any difference how many military planes are flying around in the sky after that."

When you talk about getting a "specific and credible threat" as the trigger for your decision to restrict airspace over a nuclear power plant, I find the whole line of reasoning faulty. So the attacker gets a message on the radio that he's in airspace that has been restricted by Admiral Loy on South Street in Arlington. He would laugh – anyone would. If you don't stop the man before he gets into the plane your only way of stopping him is to shoot him down. I have suggested that Muslim foreign visitors to the U.S. not be permitted access to general aviation planes but you rejected this suggestion in a prior letter to me when you were working for Secretary Mineta.

The bottom line is that if a nuclear power plant is being attacked by a Learjet loaded with Semtex and the situation is on a 12 minute timeline the Homeland Security Process can either do something or it cannot do something. The only action that would count as something here would be shooting down the Learjet (or lasing it down). Every other imagined action would amount to doing nothing.

It may seem like a distraction to have to deal with answering these questions – I know you are **very busy** with Homeland Security matters, and these considerations may seem to be details. But they are not. Aux building roofs are very thin. Those buildings contain several spent nuclear cores, more every year, because Yucca Mountain has not opened up on time. There are billions of curies or radiation there in those spent cores. Now aux buildings are usually located at the lowest point on a nuclear site. They are in defilade from shallow attack because they are surrounded by much taller concrete buildings. There are also power lines running in many directions around aux buildings which provide some protection against anything but a direct vertical strike.

Let's assume Osama and Al Qaida and Hezbollah and Egyptian Jihad know that. They have shown themselves to be fairly careful and well informed planners. Let's further assume they get Landsat photos of the nuclear site, they identify the aux building, they place the image into a flight training simulator and they have their martyr pilot practice on the simulator every day for a year until diving vertically into the aux building is second nature to him.

If he succeeds the damage will amount to $10 Trillion. The death toll would be at least 100,000 Americans. An area the size of Pennsylvania would be uninhabitable for about 100 years (see NRC WASH-1400). So even though these issues may seem like a distraction and a detail in relation to the very **important** Homeland Security work you are doing, they actually are quite central, quite relevant, and dealing with these issues, by answering my letters in a serious way would be a good thing. So, please try again. You may want to talk to Chairman Meserve at the NRC in preparation for any future effort along these lines.

Very truly yours,

CHRIS VAN HOLLEN
8TH DISTRICT, MARYLAND

COMMITTEE ON
EDUCATION AND THE WORKFORCE

COMMITTEE ON GOVERNMENT REFORM

**Congress of the United States**
**House of Representatives**
**Washington, DC 20515**

1419 LONGWORTH HOUSE OFFICE BUILDI
WASHINGTON, DC 20515
(202) 225–5341

DISTRICT OFFICE:
51 MONROE STREET, #507
ROCKVILLE, MD 20850
(301) 424–3501

www.house.gov/vanhollen
chris.vanhollen@mail.house.gov

196

August 6, 2003

Mr. Robert Gary
2211 Washington Avenue Apt 301
Silver Spring, Maryland  20910-2620

Dear Mr. Gary:

Thank you for contacting the office of Representative Chris Van Hollen and for providing suggestions for improvements to the US Department of Homeland Security. Mr. Van Hollen has received your letter and asked that I respond. I am Ken Cummings, I handle homeland security issues for the congressman.

Your letter contained many interesting suggestions. On many occasions, I assist Mr. Van Hollen by sitting in on meetings on his behalf. In that capacity, I have attended meetings with the regional director for homeland security for the department and I have been assigned to be his staff assistant for the Maryland Homeland Security Office advisory board. I often have occasion to share my thoughts and make suggestions to the regional leadership regarding homeland security issues. The insights of constituents is especially helpful when considering the impact of security policy on the region's residents. I appreciate your suggestions and will bear them in mind when making policy or legislative recommendations to Mr. Van Hollen.

Again, thank you for contacting our office with your suggestions for the US Department of Homeland Security.

Sincerely yours,

Ken Cummings
Legislative Aide for Homeland Security

ROBERT GARY

2211 Washington Avenue (#301)
Silver Spring MD 20910-2620
Tele: (301) 587-7147

Hon. Asa Hutchinson                                    11 August 2003
Under Secretary for Border and Transportation Security
Department of Homeland Security
400 7<sup>th</sup> Street, S.W.
Washington DC 20590

Dear Under Secretary Hutchinson,

Enclosed is a letter from Admiral Loy dated July 22, 2003, which upon analysis appears to be a wholly inadequate response to my concerns which are best illustrated by the following two scenarios:

Scenario A

10:00 a.m. A Gulfstream aircraft departs from its filed flightplan by making a 90 degree turn and heading toward a nuclear power plant 100 miles away.

10:01 a.m. An alert air traffic controller notices this discrepancy and attempts to communicate by radio with the plane – no response.

10:02 a.m. The alert air traffic controller and his supervisor agree that a potential security situation is in progress. It is observed that the plane is moving at 470 miles per hour and is now 85 miles from the nuclear plant.

10:03 a.m. The Chief of the air traffic control center calls the Secretary of Defense and puts through an urgent notice that a security situation is in progress at nuclear plant X.

10:05 a.m. The Secretary of Defense comes to the phone and is briefed by the Chief Air Traffic Controller, the plane is now moving at 500 miles per hour and is 60 miles from the plant.

10:06 a.m. The Secretary of Defense acting with all deliberate speed is on the line to the Commanding Officer of an Air Force Base or Naval Air Station located 85 miles from nuclear plant X.

10:07 a.m. The authentication process for the emergency call from SECDEF has been completed, the uniformed Commanding Officer is preparing to scramble fighters into the air, he is calling his orders down to the ready planes on the flightline.

1

10:08 a.m. Two F-18's on the flightline are warming up their engines and going through emergency pre-flight checks. The Gulfstream is now moving at 520 miles per hour and is 38 miles from nuclear plant X.

10:09 a.m. The Control Room Officer in Charge at Nuclear Plant X gets word that there is a security situation in progress involving a non-responsive intruding aircraft coming toward the nuclear power plant at very high speed. This officer is completely trained and totally alert. He orders that the Phalanx Guns be manned up locked and loaded with their radars hot.

10:10 a.m. TSA discovers that the Gulfstream in question was rented by a visitor to the U.S. from Iraq. They discover, by piecing together a mosaic of intelligence information, that the plane contains a huge shaped charge composed of 8,000 pounds of Semtex which was observed by an informant to have been loaded into the plane the day before takeoff.

10:11 a.m. The Control Room Officer in charge takes a call from SECDEF informing him that help is on the way. As that call is being made the F-18's become airborne, weapons ready, aviators fully briefed for combat. The Gulfstream is now 19 miles from Nuclear Plant X.

10:13 a.m. The F-18's are approaching MACH 1 at full military power. They have been vectored in to the Gulfstream by relayed radar. They are programming their Sparrow missiles and preparing for the final target acquisition and fire control process. The Gulfstream is now four miles from the plant at 30,000 feet. It pitches over into a 45 degree dive.

10:14 a.m. The F-18's are now 25 miles away. They have acquired the target, their Sparrows are ready to launch as soon as they get within range. The Gulfstream is now in a 90 degree vertical dive headed for the roof of the Auxiliary Building. It is moving at 580 miles per hour. The Phalanx guns are radar hot and have acquired the target.

10:15 a.m. The Phalanx guns begin firing. They are firing almost directly upward to a target descending at 580 miles per hour which presents an extremely small cross section. The guns do not affect the trajectory of the incoming Gulfstream which strikes the roof of the Auxiliary Building. The shaped charged explodes. The building and its contents are turned into a huge fireball of burning dust and fragments. No other building at the site of Nuclear Plant X is damaged. The containment dome is not breached. The reactor vessel is completely unaffected. There are no broken coolant pipes. All the pumps keep working. The power stays on. Communications are not interrupted.

10:16 a.m. The President puts through a call to the CEO of the utility that owns Nuclear Plant X and asks "What kind of consequences do we have to manage here?" The CEO is a completely honest, candid, and forthright person so he tells the President "Well Sir there were fuel rods in that building from three spent cores. We were planning to ship them to Yucca Mountain but it never opened, so we had to store those spend fuel rods on site. Altogether they amount to about 15 Billion Curies of radiation. This amount of radiation depending on wind patterns and dispersion factors could make an area the size of Pennsylvania uninhabitable for 100 years, and could kill 100,000 Americans over the course of the next 15 years. So it looks like about $10 Trillion worth of damage, not counting pain and suffering, Sir."


Scenario B

10:00 a.m. A Gulfstream departs from its filed flightplan by making a 90 degree turn and heading toward a nuclear plant 100 miles away.

10:01 a.m. Air traffic Control realizes there is a potential security situation a progress because the plane does not respond to radio calls.

10:03 a.m. The Control Room Officer in Charge at the nuclear plant is notified of a potential airborne security threat. He orders his Tactical High Energy Laser (THEL) cannon to be made ready in all respects.

10:05 a.m. SECDEF has been notified and has begun conferring with the various parts of our National Security system, including TSA and HSD, and the White House.

10:11 a.m. SECDEF makes an executive decision that the Control Room Officer in Charge should be authorized to fire his Tactical High Energy Laser (THEL) as necessary to stop the airborne incursion. This decision is relayed to the Control Room. The Tactical High Energy Laser panel operator (a TAD task which one person in the control room always has to be able to do) activates the fire control radar on the THEL.

10:13 a.m. The THEL radar has locked on to the intruder at 5 mile range. The laser has got a full feed of power directly off the Nuclear plant BUSBAR. It is lasing at 100%. The Control Room Officer in Charge gives the order to the THEL panel operator to "FIRE!" About a tenth of a second later a fireball appears in the sky about 4.85 miles away from Nuclear Plant X. Very small pieces of Gulfstream plane rain down on country roads and cornfields over about a 3 mile stretch of land. One person is killed by a falling piece of debris, and ten more people are injured.

10:16 a.m. The President puts through a call to the CEO of the utility that owns nuclear plant X and asks "What kind of consequences do we have to manage here?" The honest CEO tells the President "Well we've got one person dead and 10 more injured, there's going to be compensation required for that. There's also the debris cleanup and the cost of the investigation, so I think $10 Million would probably cover all the consequences in this matter, not counting pain and suffering, Sir."

It's not necessary to go into an extended discussion of which is better Scenario A or Scenario B. In one case there is an impact from which the U.S. would probably never fully recover. In the other case there is a cost of doing business that is a minor bookkeeping entry that would have no material affect of the profits of the utility, but which would have a significant temporary psychological impact on the People of the U.S.

If Scenario A happened there would be a lot of Hearings to see if accountability could be fairly allocated between all the Agencies and Departments that had a sworn duty to prevent something like Scenario A from happening. Issues of foreseeability would be discussed for at least a decade, maybe longer.

If Scenario B happened there would be a period of sadness and shock as there is anytime an American life is lost or harm is done to this country. That period would last about two weeks. After that people would start talking about how professional and provident and competent the government had been in handling this most grave of threats. There would be visits to the White House. Some people would get gold medals. Homeland Security people would be revered as heros.

The cost of putting in the THEL at three nuclear power plants and a feasibility demonstration project is extremely small, particularly because a mobile power source does not need to be supplied. The system the Israelis have deployed on Bradley Vehicles to intercept incoming SCUDS is far more expensive because the mobile power source is based on a chemical reaction that requires very costly equipment.

The cost of meeting with me for about an hour to get a fuller and better brief on why this proposal would be feasible, reasonable, and cost-effective would be zero. I'm a volunteer, not a salesman, not a job seeker, not a lobbyist. No one is charged for my time. Your time is already a "sunk cost" (as accountants would say). The only issue is "Do you wish to meet with me?"

I have about 25 years of experience working in public health and nuclear issues, including security issues, as a public interest attorney at the national level. I'm a retired Navy JAG, personally decorated by SECNAV and have been a member of the Bar of the U.S. Supreme Court since 1985. I was born in the U.S.A. This is my country, and I would like to contribute as I can to its protection. I want you to accommodate my request for an opportunity to present my suggestion in a way that is consistent with its seriousness and content. This would mean some kind of dialogue with fairly senior people, for example, with you Asa Hutchinson.

Very truly yours,

Robert Gary, Esq.

CHRIS VAN HOLLEN
8TH DISTRICT, MARYLAND

COMMITTEE ON
EDUCATION AND THE WORKFORCE

COMMITTEE ON GOVERNMENT REFORM

1419 LONGWORTH HOUSE OFFICE BUILL **201**
WASHINGTON, DC 20515
(202) 225–5341

DISTRICT OFFICE:
51 MONROE STREET, #507
ROCKVILLE, MD 20850
(301) 424–3501

www.house.gov/vanhollen

# Congress of the United States
## House of Representatives
### Washington, DC 20515

August 15, 2003

Robert Gary
211 Washington Avenue, Apt. 301
Silver Spring, MD 20910-2620

Dear Mr. Gary:

Thank you for contacting me with recommendations for strengthening our homeland security. After reviewing your proposals with security specialists, I have forwarded those suggestions that appear most feasible to Secretary Ridge.

Again, I appreciate your taking the time to share your ideas on protecting the United States from terrorist threats. Your input is extremely valuable. I will contact you once I receive a response from Secretary Ridge.

Sincerely,

Chris Van Hollen
Member of Congress

Enclosure

CHRIS VAN HOLLEN
8TH DISTRICT, MARYLAND

COMMITTEE ON
EDUCATION AND THE WORKFORCE

COMMITTEE ON GOVERNMENT REFORM

# Congress of the United States
## House of Representatives
### Washington, DC 20515

1419 LONGWORTH HOUSE OFFICE ...NG
WASHINGTON, DC 20515
(202) 225–5341

DISTRICT OFFICE:
51 MONROE STREET, #507
ROCKVILLE, MD 20850
(301) 424–3501

www.house.gov/vanhollen

August 15, 2003

Secretary Tom Ridge
United States Department of Homeland Security
Washington, D.C. 20528

Dear Secretary Ridge:

I am writing to share with you suggestions from a constituent, Mr. Robert Gary, a veteran and retired attorney specializing in security related issues, on how to strengthen certain vulnerabilities in our homeland security.

One proposal recommends that containers coming into U.S. ports be sealed overseas before shipping with biometrically enabled locks to prevent harmful materials from entering the United States. Under this proposal, before a shipping container is sealed and shipped into the United States, three specific individuals would each have the responsibility for certifying the safety of the shipping container's contents.

Another suggestion recommends the use of high energy laser technology to defend American nuclear power plants due to their vulnerability to airborne attack. This technology does not fire any ordnance into the air; rather it emits a high power light beam that would be able to bring down an aircraft from as far as five miles away. As Mr. Gary suggests, if a terrorist aircraft flies toward a nuclear power plant, a military jet would not have enough time to intercept the hostile aircraft once identified. High energy laser technology as an onsite defense might be able to thwart such an attack.

I understand these proposals are not perfect and that serious questions of cost, implementation and rules of engagement would need to be addressed. However, I appreciate your taking the time to consider Mr. Gary's proposals and responding to me with feedback.

Sincerely,

Chris Van Hollen
Member of Congress

Enclosure

**Transportation Security
Administration**

SEP ⁃3 2003

Mr. Robert Gary
2211 Washington Avenue, Apt. #301
Silver Spring, MD  20910-2620

Dear Mr. Gary:

On behalf of Admiral Loy, thank you for your letter of July 24, 2003, regarding your continuing concerns about nuclear reactors and general aviation.

Notice to Airmen 3/1655 advises pilots to avoid the airspace above, or in close proximity to, power plants, nuclear power plants, dams, refineries, industrial complexes, military facilities, and other similar facilities.  This NOTAM is a result of a collaborative effort among the Transportation Security Administration (TSA), the Federal Aviation Administration (FAA), and the Nuclear Regulatory Commission (NRC), which is the agency responsible for the safety and security of nuclear power plants.  TSA will continue to collaborate with the FAA and the NRC to secure nuclear power plants from an aviation threat.

The NRC's scope of responsibility includes regulation of commercial nuclear power plants; research, test, and training reactors; fuel cycle facilities; medical, academic, and industrial uses of nuclear materials; and the transport, storage, and disposal of nuclear materials and wastes.  NRC also regulates the Nation's civilian use of byproduct, source, and special nuclear materials to ensure adequate protection of public health and safety, to promote the common defense and security, and to protect the environment.

In your letter, you discuss the installation and utilization of a Tactical High Energy Laser (THEL), short-range, ground-based air-defense laser system, as a possible defense tactic for nuclear power facilities.  I am not able to discuss specific security measures, current or proposed, for nuclear power facilities.

Additionally, your letter mentions NRC WASH-1400.  This was a Reactor Safety Study sponsored by the NRC in the 1970s and carried out by Professor Norman Rasmussen from the Massachusetts Institute of Technology.  This study represented the first application of probabilistic risk assessment techniques to quantify the risks of nuclear power plant operations.  According to a speech given by Chairman Richard Meserve of the NRC, these techniques have been refined over the ensuing years and incorporate the risk of internal and external events and the identification of accident sequences initiated by both.

2

Our primary goal has been and always will be ensuring the public's security from any and all aviation threats.  As we move forward, TSA will continue its trend of collaborating with and encouraging input from general aviation owners, operators, associations, and State and Federal Government agencies in an effort to strengthen and improve our security procedures while making them less disruptive to industry as a whole.

Thank you for your continuing attention and concern to the security of our Nation's nuclear power plants.  I hope this information addresses your concerns.

Sincerely yours,

Lee S. Longmire
Assistant Administrator for
Operations Policy

**ROBERT GARY**

2211 Washington Ave (Apt. #301)
Silver Spring, MD 20910-2620

George W. Bush                                           September 11, 2003
President of the United States
**(<u>Attn: Hon Andrew Card</u>)**
The White House
Washington, DC 20500

Dear President Bush,

I need to ask for your assistance in setting up a meeting with Secretary Ridge, Undersecretary Hutchinson, or Admiral Loy at the Department of Homeland Security. The meeting would be about the possible use of tactical high energy lasers to permit nuclear power plants to be effectively defended against sudden airborne attack.

You know that I have been a very strong supporter of yours, and now I need a little bit of help, so I'm hoping you will decide that it is appropriate to take my part in the matter of this request for a meeting. Your Homeland Security strategy, which includes taking the fight to the enemy overseas, can only be truly complete if it also includes cost-effective precautions here at home.

The day when we could imagine that our nuclear power plants could be effectively protected from sudden airborne attack by calling the military are past. Now we need a new approach, something that would work against a new kind of threat. I think I have ideas that would be useful in this regard. I want a chance to present them. I have taken every step possible before writing to you by contacting both of my U.S. Senators, my Congressman, Chairman Meserve, Admiral Loy, Undersecretary Hutchinson, and Secretary Ridge. So far, no luck. I look to you for leadership on this vital matter.

Very Respectfully,

Robert Gary

Encl: ltr dtd 11 Sept 03 to Lee S. Longmire (DHS)
     ltr dtd 11 Aug 03 to Hon Asa Hutchinson (DHS)

2211 Washington Avenue (Apt #301)
Silver Spring, MD 20910-2620

Lee S. Longmire
Assistant Administrator for
Operations Policy
Transportation Security Administration
U.S. Department of Homeland Security
601 South 12$^{th}$ Street
Arlington VA 22202-4220

September 11, 2003

VIA FEDEX OVERNIGHT

Dear Assistant Administrator Longmire

Thank you for your letter of September 3, 2003. In return I am enclosing two copies of a letter sent recently to Hon Asa Hutchinson. It mentions Admiral Loy, and thus I would be very grateful if you would pass along the second enclosed copy of the letter to him.

As to the substance of your letter, I would respectfully offer the following comments. It is true that NRC WASH-1400 has been refined since the 1970's, as Chairman Meserve says. But not nearly enough in my humble opinion. No major adjustments were made in the methodology or the assumptions to accommodate Three Mile Island or Chernobyl. The method of multiplying very small fractions to compute infinitesimal final risks is basically the same, and the fundamental axioms about individual component reliability have changed very little, as evidenced from the six volume study published by DOE in support of their Mixed Oxide Fuel program, on which I commented at some length.

More to the point for our present purposes the assumptions about consequences from an airborne attack on a nuclear plant have not changed nearly enough since WASH-1400. For one thing, the Rasmussen Report focused entirely on the possibility of a commercial airliner not loaded with high explosives impacting the containment dome which is six feet thick and reinforced with steel rebar. In 1979 I had clients in San Antonio that wanted me to put allegations about airliners crashing into containment domes when I was doing the South Texas Nuclear Project. I told them the NRC was right, and that airliners crashing into containment domes was not a serious threat. There would be a big ball of flaming fuel and small bits of duraluminum scattered far and wide, but almost no chance of any impact on the reactor vessel or any falling debris that might cause a major Loss of Coolant Accident (LOCA).

But <u>the auxiliary building is quite a different matter</u>. First of all, since WASH-1400 was written, auxiliary buildings have a lot more cores in them. Back in the 1970's we thought that Yucca Mountain would be opened up and ready for business at least by the mid 1980's. But it didn't happen. So those spent fuel rods have had no place to go for 35 years and they've been piling up in Auxiliary Buildings right next to 72 operating nuclear power plants. <u>They are the ultimate potential dirty bomb</u>, all they need is some high explosive to disperse the material.

Now we find that there are thousands of people who are ready to commit suicide in the course of attacks against the USA. We also find that they highly favor airborne attacks. The Department of Transportation has been unwilling to bar foreign Muslim visitors to the US from any participation in general aviation. We also find that the Saudis have hundreds of billions of dollars and

don't mind spending a lot of that money on terrorists to attack the USA. So
getting a Learjet or a Gulfstream rented or purchased would not be a problem for
them. Loading it up with high explosives would not be a problem. Training a
suicide pilot to fly it straight down into an Auxiliary building would be a
problem. The approach would have to be visual. It takes a lot of time in a very
high quality simulator to teach a Muslim terrorist how to precisely pitch an
executive jet into a vertical dive and hit a fairly small building surrounded by
much higher buildings and wires in the midst of a very complex architectural
site composed of 15 industrial buildings many of which look alike from the air.
The aim and angle of dive has to be perfect to within a quarter of a degree. But
such training is possible, it's fairly straightforward for people who know
precisely what they want to do and have plenty of LANDSAT photographs or other
overhead photos, which can be contracted for and bought by anybody who is
financially qualified, like the Saudis.

You are right -- WASH-1400 has been updated a little bit. But I'm also
right, it hasn't been updated enough, and if it were, <u>the dangers of the
scenario I'm trying to prevent would be even more glaring</u> than they already are.

I understand Admiral Loy's theory about using memos (NOTAM) to keep most
law abiding airmen away from nuclear power plants so that it's easier to
identify prospective malfeasors who are incoming. But I'm sure he knows that
memos won't deter suicide bombers, and they certainly won't stop executive jets
that have been turned into flying bombs. You can't shoot a jet down with NOTAMs.
<u>Admiral Loy apparently believes that the military could arrive in time to solve
the problem. I respectfully disagree.</u> That's what my letter to Hon Asa
Hutchinson (enclosed) is about. I want to present this information and if
possible discuss it with senior policy staff at DHS. Nuclear power plants have
to be able to defend themselves, or they will remain undefended. I've argued
that the Tactical High Energy Laser (THEL) as the logical way to go here, but I
would be open to any reasonable alternative that would get the job done.

So again thank you for your letter. In closing I would note that <u>DHS does
have policy discussions about this and similar matters with academics</u> who are
tapped for inclusion in the policy discussion process. I have thus far not been
chosen for such a conversation, but that does not mean it couldn't happen.
Discernment, as you know, is such a key quality for executives in the private
sector, and in the public sector. It's how we pick reliable employees, its how
we frame effective policies. I trust that you will discerningly respond to my
respectful and continuing request to be heard on this vital subject. I would
like to speak to Admiral Loy, Undersecretary Asa Hutchinson, or Secretary Ridge
with whatever staff they may wish to invite, at a time and place that fits well
into their busy schedules. <u>I would like you to assist in setting up this
meeting.</u>


                              Very truly yours,



                              Robert Gary

cc:    Card
       Sarbanes and Mikulski
       Van Hollen
       Ridge, Hutchinson, Meserve, and Loy

## Robert Gary

2211 Washington Avenue (#301)
Silver Spring, MD 20910-2620
Tele: (301) 587-7147

Chairman Richard A. Meserve                                    September 16, 2003
Nuclear Regulatory Commission
11555 Rockville Pike
Washington DC 20852

Dear Chairman Meserve,

Enclosed are two letters, one to Lee S. Longmire, and one to Hon Asa Hutchinson. I request that you circulate these letters to the other Commissioners at NRC.

The letters deal with two basic issues:

1. Is it reasonable to believe that the military could get to a nuclear power plant in time to defend it against an airborne attack?

2. If the military could not get there on time, is it reasonable to arrange for a nuclear power plant to be able to defend itself, and in this connection, would tactical high energy laser cannons be an ideal option?

It is possible that one or more of the Commissioners may feel that one or both of these issues is worthy of their attention, and some sort of process of inquiry, deliberation, and action. Security at nuclear power plants is within the purview of the Nuclear Regulatory Commission. Addressing the issues that I am seeking to raise would be a step that might lead to enhanced security.

Very truly yours,

Robert Gary

Encl: ltr to Longmire dtd 11 Sep 03 (2 copies)
        Ltr to Hutchinson dtd 11 Aug 03 (2 copies)

PAUL S. SARBANES
MARYLAND

309 HART SENATE OFFICE BL
WASHINGTON, DC 20510
202-224-4524

# United States Senate

WASHINGTON, DC 20510-2002

October 1, 2003

Lt. Robert Gary
2211 Washington Avenue, #301
Silver Spring, Maryland 20910

Dear Lieutenant Gary:

Thank you for getting in touch with me earlier about issues of concern to you. During the past year my office in the Hart Senate Office Building was renovated, requiring my Washington, D.C. staff to relocate to temporary office space before being able to return to the building in July. I regret that this dislocation disrupted normal operations and delayed my response to your inquiry.

I did, however, want to be sure you know that I received your communications regarding the physical security of nuclear power plants. I hope you will continue to contact me about issues of concern to you.

With best regards,

Sincerely,

Paul Sarbanes
United States Senator

PSS/kbk

R OBERT  G ARY

2211 Washington Ave (Apt. #301)
Silver Spring, MD 20910-2620
(301) 587-7147

George W. Bush                                                    October 1, 2003
President of the United States
**(Attn: Homeland Security Special Assistant)**
The White House
Washington, DC 20500

Subj: **Homeland Security at Nuclear Power Plants re Airborne Attack**

Dear President Bush,

   Enclosed are two letters related to my longstanding proposal to enhance security at nuclear power plants. The Letter to Lee Longmire is fairly general, the one to Asa Hutchinson is far more technical and detailed. They both argue that the military can't get there on time to save a nuclear power plant from airborne attack so nuclear power plants need to be able to defend themselves from such attacks, and I have suggested the Tactical High Energy Laser (THEL) as the ideal method for doing this job.

   .My only goal is to get NRC and DHS to address my issue and proposed solution in a serious and substantive way. So far they seem to have completely missed the point. So please forward my materials, hopefully with your own strong endorsement, and we'll see what happens. I remain willing to meet with them to provide any technical details that may be of interest.

Respectfully Yours,

Robert Gary, Esq.

Enclosures:  (1) Letter to Lee S. Longmire dated 9/11/2003
             (2) Letter to Hon Asa Hutchinson dated 8/11/2003

## ROBERT GARY

2211 Washington Avenue (Apt 301)
Silver Spring, MD 20910-2620
(301) 587-7147
Robert.Gary@prodigy.net

Hon. Barbara Mikulski                                          October 1, 2003
(Attn Andy Dentamaro)
Suite 709 Hart Office Building
U.S. Senate
Washington DC 20510-2003

Subj: Nuclear Power Plants, Defense Against Terrorists

Dear Senator Mikulski,

Enclosed are two letters related to my longstanding proposal to enhance security at nuclear power plants. The Letter to Lee Longmire is fairly general, the one to Asa Hutchinson is far more technical and detailed. They both argue that the military can't get there on time to save a nuclear power plant from airborne attack so nuclear power plants need to be able to defend themselves from such attacks, and I have suggested the Tactical High Energy Laser (THEL) as the ideal method for doing this job.

In two and a half years of working on this pro bono public interest legal effort there has been no progress. Your office and staff have been very supportive and I'm sure you have a thick file on this matter containing letters you have sent on my behalf.

This is I think the moment to move on to the next step which would be to take the matter to the staff of the Senate Environment and Public Works Committee, and to the Chairman, since they have direct oversight of the Nuclear Regulatory Commission in what it does or fails (unreasonably) to do. There is also a Senate Committee that has jurisdiction over the Department of Homeland Security. They need to be approached as well because my proposal calls for a joint effort by NRC and DHS.

My only goal at this point at this point is to get NRC and DHS to address my issue and proposed solution is a serious and substantive way. So far they seem to have completely missed the point. It is no longer important to me that either of these organizations answer me or respond in any way to me personally, although I do remain willing to meet with them, if they have a change of heart, a change or procedures, or a change of leadership. The fact that these organizations seem very closed, not to say closed-minded,  should not impair the process of communication if the communication arises from Chairmen of Committees that have direct oversight and funding authority. I need to be taken out of the loop and someone far more influential with NRC and DHS needs to be put in. So please forward my materials, hopefully with your own endorsement and we'll see what happens.

Respectfully Yours,

**212**

# United States Senate

WASHINGTON, DC 20510–2002

October 21, 2003

Lt. Robert Gary
2211 Washington Avenue, #301
Silver Spring, Maryland  20910

Dear Lieutenant Gary:

Thank you for contacting me again to bring to my attention your proposal to improve general aviation security in light of the tragic events of September 11, 2001.  In order to be of further assistance to you, I have taken the liberty of forwarding a copy of the information you have provided to Senator James M. Inhofe, Chairman of the Senate Committee on Environment and Public Works, and Senator Orrin G. Hatch, Chairman of the Senate Judiciary Committee, for review and to urge the appropriate consideration of your proposal.  As soon as I receive a response, I shall be certain to let you know.

Please do not hesitate to contact me if I can be of any further assistance.

With best regards,

Sincerely,

Paul Sarbanes
United States Senator

PSS/leb

PAUL S. SARBANES
MARYLAND

309 HART SENATE OFFIC **213** JG
WASHINGTON, DC 20...
202–224–4524

# United States Senate
### WASHINGTON, DC 20510–2002

November 5, 2003

Lt. Robert Gary
2211 Washington Avenue, #301
Silver Spring, Maryland  20910

Dear Lieutenant Gary:

Thank you for contacting me about security lapses on commercial aircraft.  I appreciate hearing from you about this important matter.

As you know, a student recently circumvented Transportation Security Administration (TSA) screening measures by planting box cutters and other prohibited items in aircraft lavatories.  This individual now faces charges of carrying a concealed dangerous weapon onto an airplane.  As a United States Senator, I am unable to intervene in pending judicial proceedings.  However, I share your view that TSA must continue to improve passenger screening and security measures.  The terrorist hijacking of passenger aircraft on September 11, 2001 was a catastrophic security failure that, in my view, warranted the creation of a Federal agency to oversee this process.  While I am not a member of the Senate Committee on Commerce, Science, and Transportation, you may be certain that I will continue to carefully monitor this situation, and I will keep your views in mind should the full Senate have the opportunity to consider relevant legislation.

I appreciate hearing from you about this important matter.  Please do not hesitate to contact me about other issues of concern to you in the future.

With best regards,

Sincerely,

Paul Sarbanes
United States Senator

PSS/jwg

**UNITED STATES**
**NUCLEAR REGULATORY COMMISSION**
WASHINGTON, D.C. 20555-0001

November 25, 2003

Mr. Robert Gary
2211 Washington Avenue
Unit No. 301
Silver Spring, MD  20910-2620

Dear Mr. Gary:

On behalf of the Nuclear Regulatory Commission (NRC), I am responding to your letter to previous Chairman, Richard A. Meserve, dated September 16, 2003.  For your information, following Chairman Meserve's leaving the NRC last spring, Commissioner Nils J. Diaz was appointed NRC Chairman.  In your letter, you ask two questions:

1.  Is it reasonable to believe that the military could get to a nuclear power plant in time to defend it against an airborne attack?

2.  If the military could not get there on time, is it reasonable to arrange for a nuclear power plant to be able to defend itself, and in this connection, would tactical high energy laser cannons be an ideal option?

First, let me acknowledge your letters of June 17, 2002, July 17, 2002, and August 5, 2002, to the NRC on a variety of issues related to nuclear power plant security, the last of which also dealt with the laser cannon concept.  The NRC continues to explore areas related to the vulnerability of our licensees and appropriate mitigating strategies in response to a possible terrorist attack.  We also continue to review potential consequences of events at nuclear power plants and NRC licensed activities to provide a more realistic assessment of vulnerabilities to those activities.  For example, I encourage you to review points 4-6 of the Point Paper on Current Homeland Security and Preparedness issues at the following WEB address, http://www.nrc.gov/what-we-do/point-paper.pdf .  You may find other areas of our WEB site on nuclear security informative as well.

In order to ensure that all reasonable action is taken by our licensees to protect nuclear power facilities against those potential attacks, the NRC has and will continue to ensure that robust security programs are developed and in place at those facilities.  We continue to work with our Federal partners including the Department of Homeland Security, Department of Energy, Department of Defense and others to address issues related to potential vulnerabilities to the Nation's infrastructure, including those related to aircraft attack and the ability of the military to respond in a timely fashion.

As I am sure you appreciate, any findings related to the analyses of these and other protection technologies and strategies may not be made available to the public due to concerns regarding the possible use of this information by potential terrorist organizations for malevolent purposes.

R. Gray                                    -2-

Thank you for your continued interest in the NRC and security at our nation's nuclear facilities.

Sincerely,

Roy P. Zimmerman, Director
Office of Nuclear Security and
Incident Response

cc:     Lee S. Longmire
        Assistant Administrator for
         Operations Policy
        Transportation Security Administration
        U.S. Department of Homeland Security
        601 South 12$^{th}$ Street
        Arlington VA 22202-4220.

        The Honorable Asa Hutchinson
        Under Secretary for Border and Transportation Security
        Department of Homeland Security
        400 7$^{th}$ Street S.W.
        Washington DC 20590

# U.S. Department of Homeland Security

JAN  6 2005

Mr. Robert Gary
2211 Washington Avenue
Silver Spring, Maryland 20910

Dear Mr. Gary:

Senator Barbara A. Mikulski has asked that we respond directly to your correspondence in which you presented several ideas to combat terrorism.  The U.S. Customs and Border Protection (CBP) has recently completed its review of the ideas that relate to its operations.  Please allow me to outline their findings.

The CBP is currently researching the concept of a secure (shipping) container. Integral to this concept is the development of a locking mechanism that will secure the container contents and identify intrusions.  A low cost but effective mechanism that will not overburden shippers with exorbitant costs or personnel requirements will be essential to the execution of this concept.  As hundreds of thousands of containers will require some type of security seal or lock mechanism, only the most cost effective and efficient mechanisms and procedures will be considered.

Since the events of September 11, 2001, and the consolidation of the various agencies into CBP, a concerted effort has been made to ensure that visitors and workers requesting admission to the United States are properly screened prior to and during the admission process.  Risk is assessed by the totality of information presented, not based on general religious affiliations.  The CBP will continue to address the terrorist threat utilizing established risk assessment mechanisms and make adjustments as threat levels dictate.

I appreciate your interest in the Department of Homeland Security and we look forward to working with you on future homeland security issues.  If we may be of further assistance, please contact the Office of Legislative Affairs at (202) 205-4412.

Sincerely,

Pamela J. Turner
Assistant Secretary for Legislative Affairs

cc:  Senator Barbara A. Mikulski

# United States Senate
WASHINGTON, DC 20510–2003

January 13, 2004

Mr. Robert Gary, Esq.
2211 Washington Avenue
Apartment 301
Silver Spring, Maryland   20910

Dear Mr. Gary:

Thank you for contacting me to share your views about Nathaniel Heatwole and his efforts to highlight security problems at our nation's airports.  I appreciate hearing from you.

I share your concerns about the vulnerabilities at our airports.  I believe that we need to do more to improve air safety.  This includes making sure that the Transportation Security Administration (TSA) is operating effectively, and preventing any prohibited items from being brought onto our nation's airlines.  Mr. Heatwole's attempts to breach security highlight that there are still weaknesses that need to be addressed immediately.  I will continue to support the Department of Homeland Security and the TSA's efforts to prevent further violations of airport security.

Thank you for contacting me to share you views about Mr. Heatwole and the security in our airports.  If I can be of any further assistance to you in the future, please feel free to get in touch with me.

Sincerely,

Barbara A. Mikulski
United States Senator

BAM:jrl

Zortman, J.M.          31, 32